Blank Canvas
My So=Called Artist's Journey

2

STORY &
ART

**Akiko
Higashimura**

Blank Canvas

My So-Called Artist's Journey

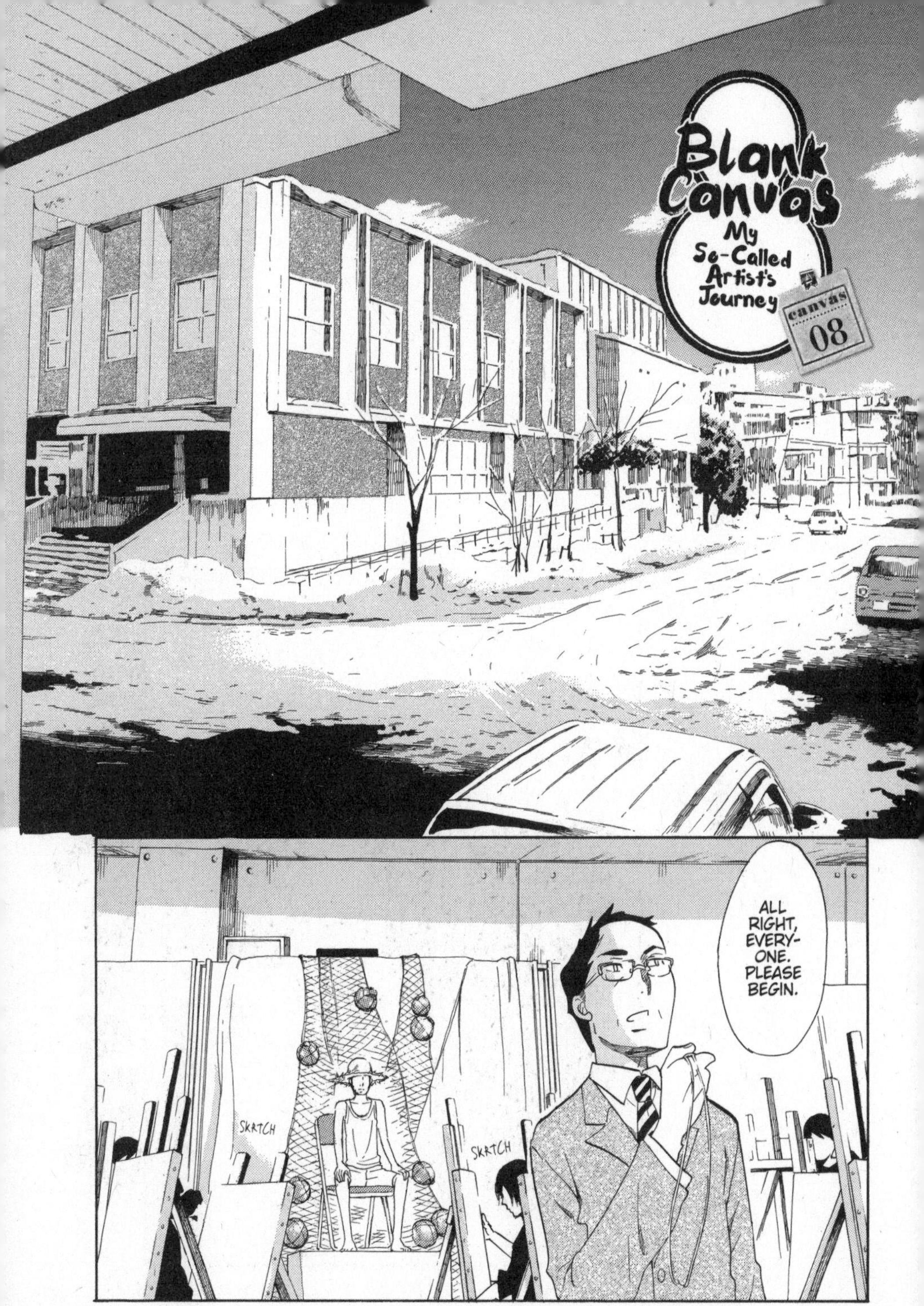
Blank Canvas
My So-Called Artist's Journey
canvas
08
ALL RIGHT, EVERY-ONE. PLEASE BEGIN.
SKRTCH
SKRTCH

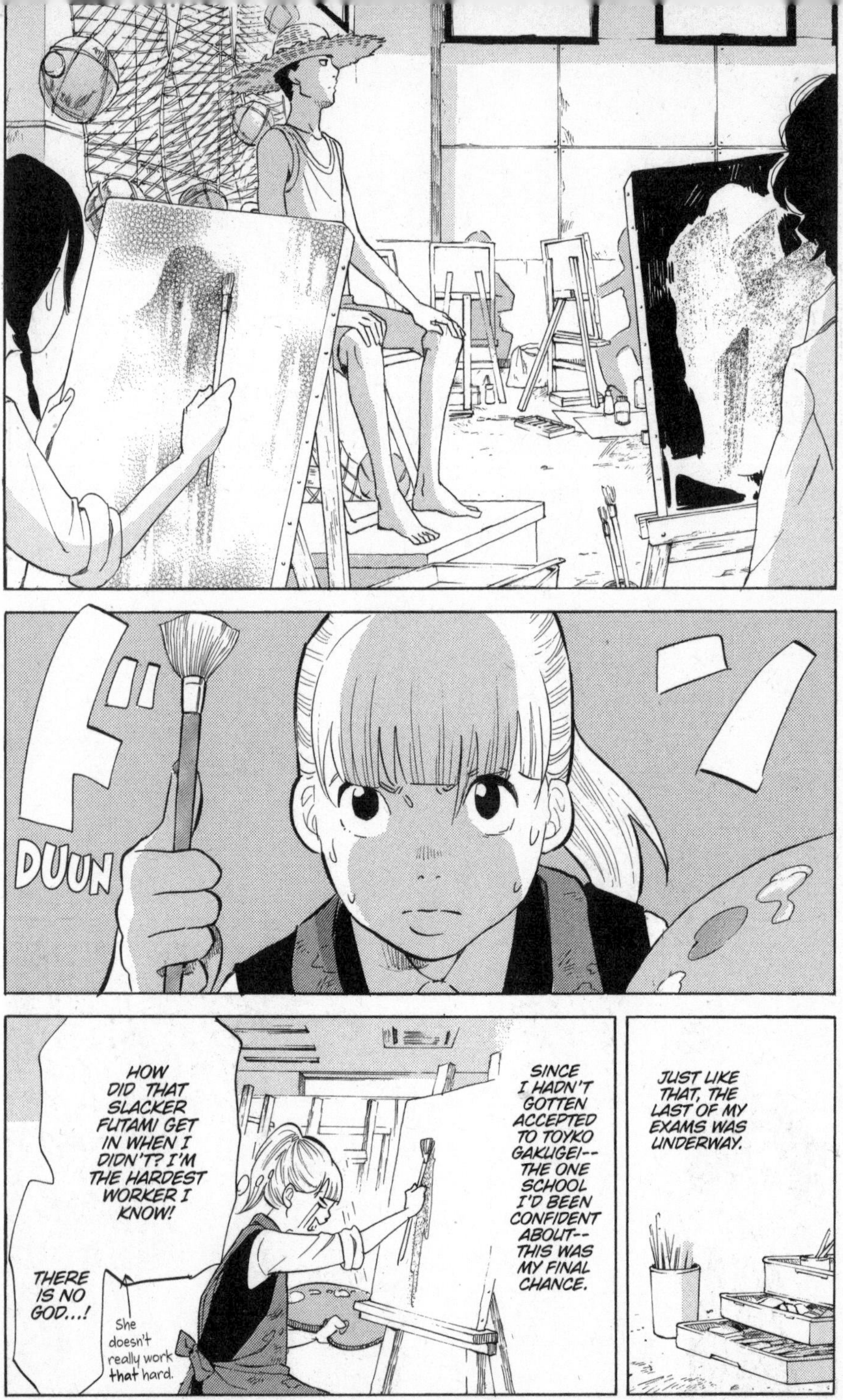
DUUN
JUST LIKE THAT, THE LAST OF MY EXAMS WAS UNDERWAY.
SINCE I HADN'T GOTTEN ACCEPTED TO TOYKO GAKUGEI-- THE ONE SCHOOL I'D BEEN CONFIDENT ABOUT-- THIS WAS MY FINAL CHANCE.
HOW DID THAT SLACKER FUTAMI GET IN WHEN I DIDN'T? I'M THE HARDEST WORKER I KNOW!
THERE IS NO GOD...!
She doesn't really work **that** hard.

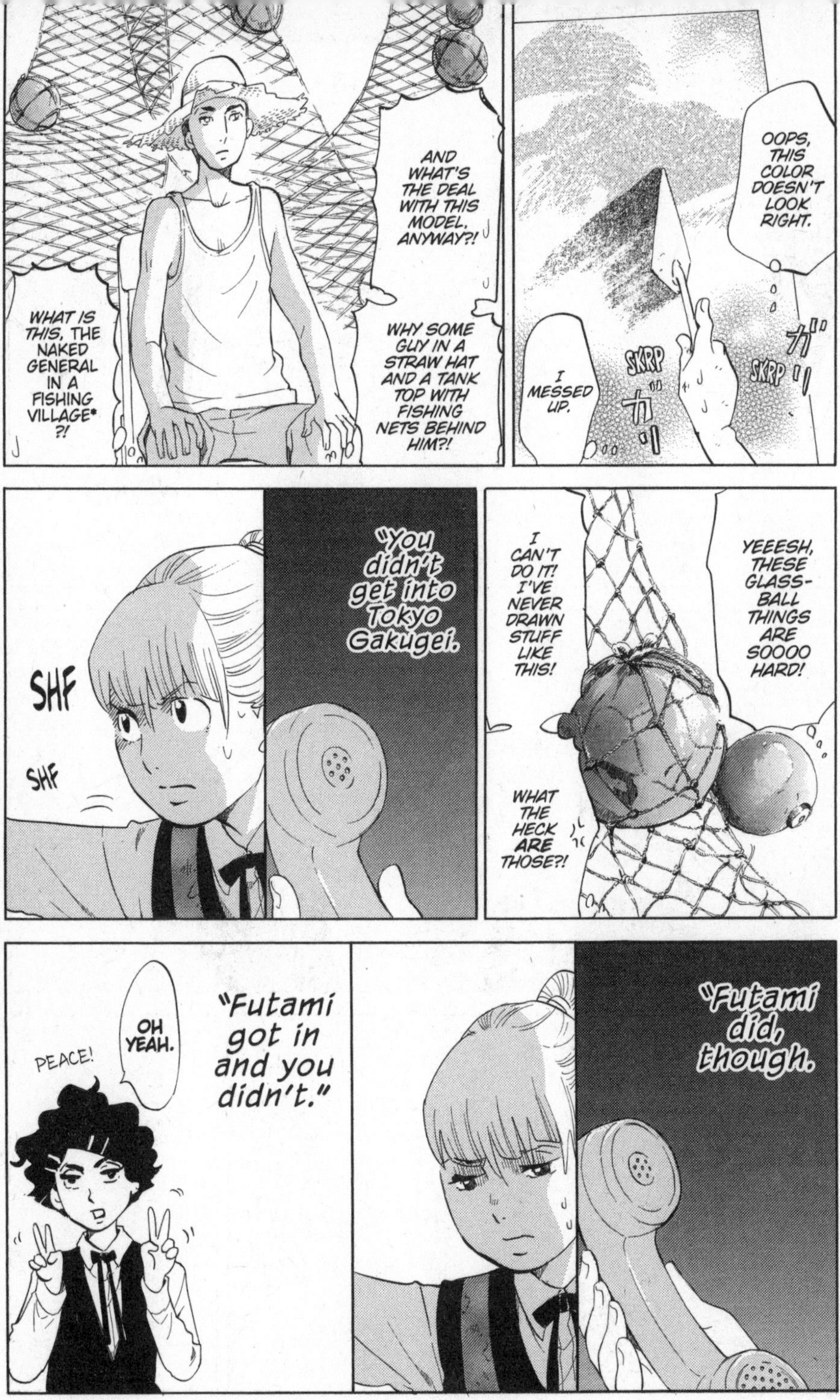
OOPS, THIS COLOR DOESN'T LOOK RIGHT.
ガリ
SKRP
SKRP
ガリ
I MESSED UP.
AND WHAT'S THE DEAL WITH THIS MODEL, ANYWAY?!
WHY SOME GUY IN A STRAW HAT AND A TANK TOP WITH FISHING NETS BEHIND HIM?!
WHAT IS THIS, THE NAKED GENERAL IN A FISHING VILLAGE* ?!
YEEESH, THESE GLASS-BALL THINGS ARE SOOOO HARD!
I CAN'T DO IT! I'VE NEVER DRAWN STUFF LIKE THIS!
WHAT THE HECK ARE THOSE?!
"You didn't get into Tokyo Gakugei.
SHF
SHF
"Futami did, though.
"Futami got in and you didn't."
OH YEAH.
PEACE!

*"The Naked General" was the nickname of Yamashita Kiyoshi, a Japanese painter famous for traveling in a tank top and shorts (and occasionally a straw hat).

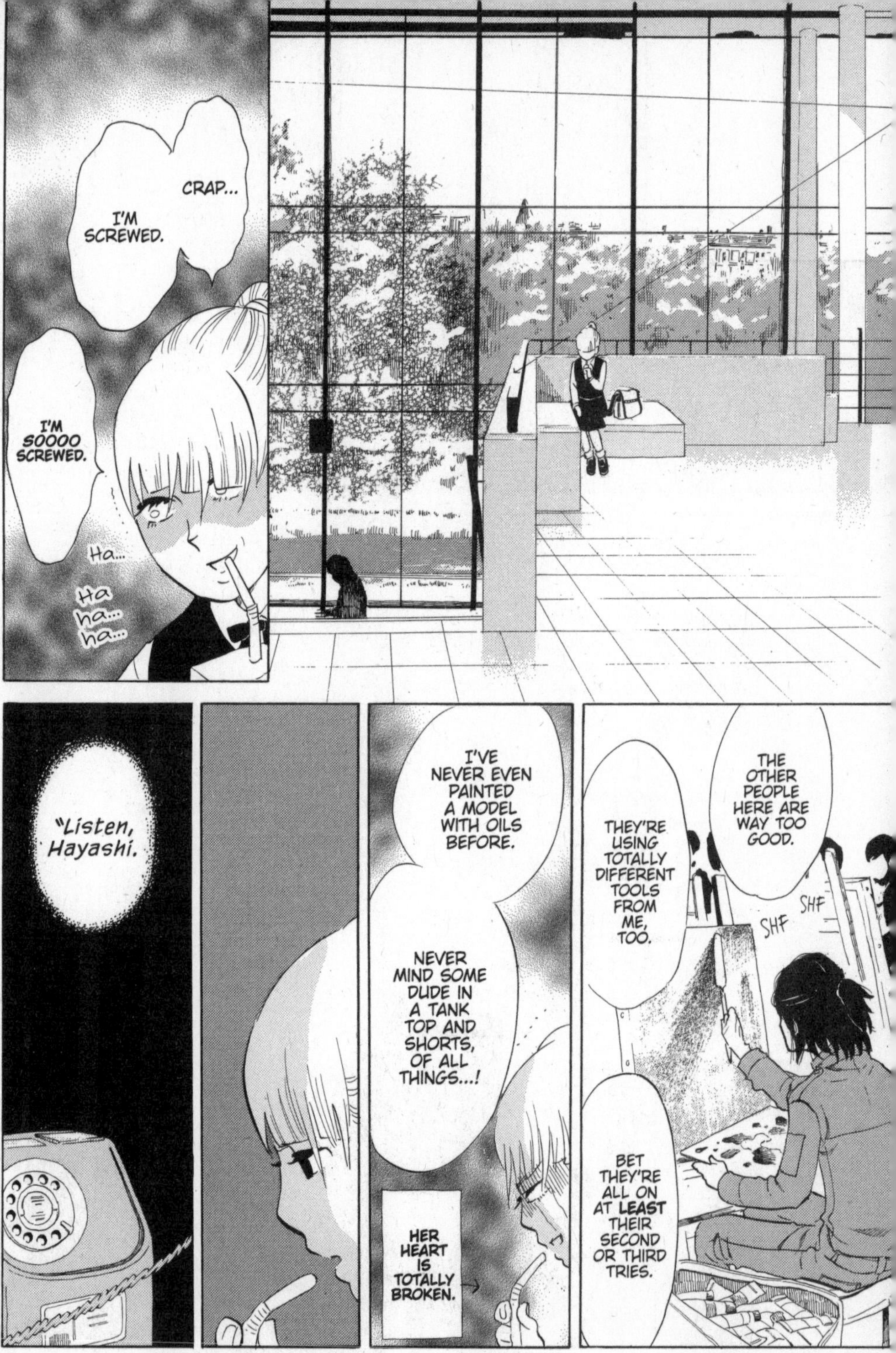
CRAP... I'M SCREWED.
I'M SOOOO SCREWED.
Ha...
Ha ha... ha...
THE OTHER PEOPLE HERE ARE WAY TOO GOOD.
THEY'RE USING TOTALLY DIFFERENT TOOLS FROM ME, TOO.
SHF
SHF
BET THEY'RE ALL ON AT **LEAST** THEIR SECOND OR THIRD TRIES.
I'VE NEVER EVEN PAINTED A MODEL WITH OILS BEFORE.
NEVER MIND SOME DUDE IN A TANK TOP AND SHORTS, OF ALL THINGS...!
HER HEART IS TOTALLY BROKEN.
"Listen, Hayashi.

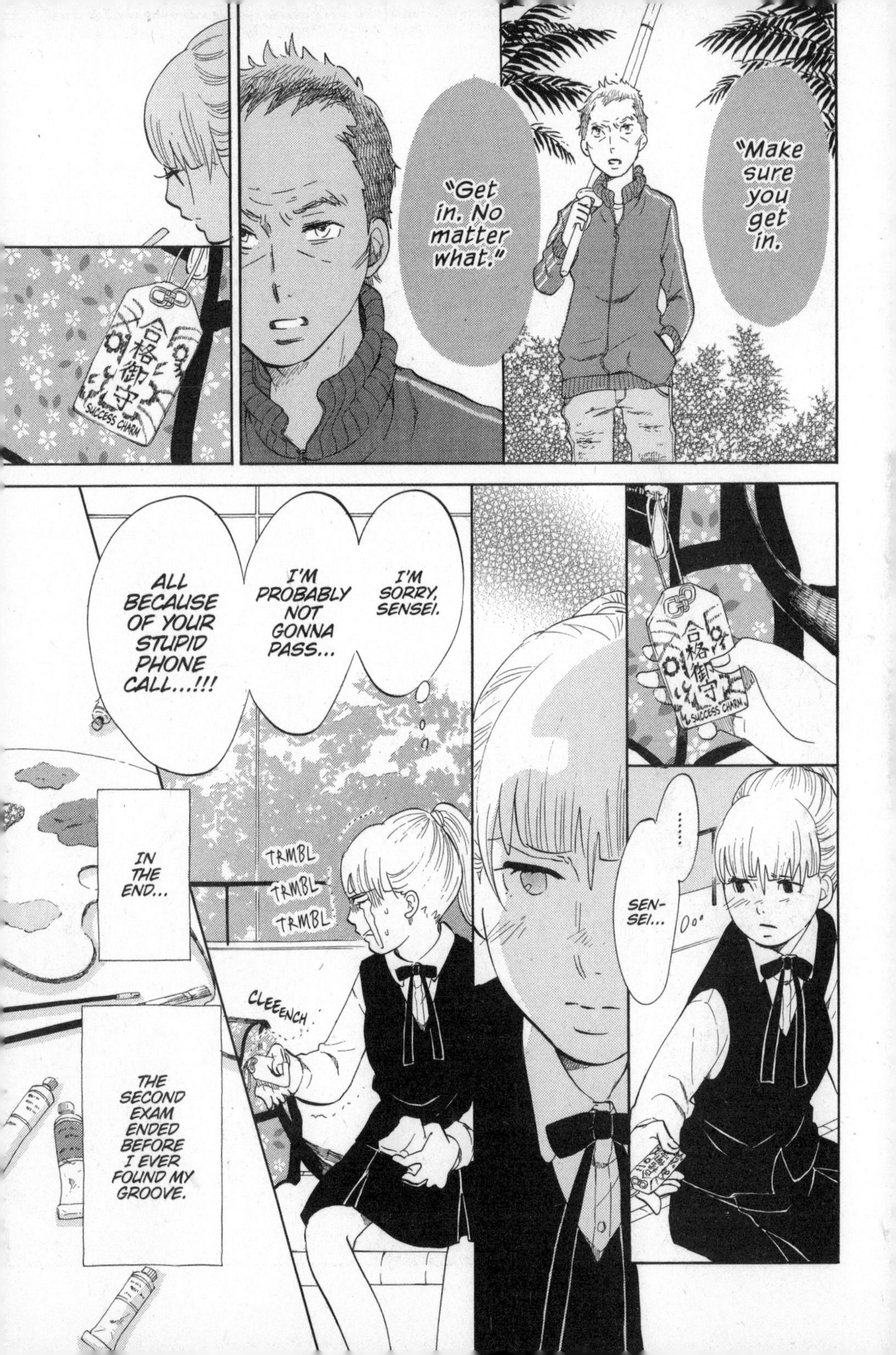
"Make sure you get in.
"Get in. No matter what."
合格御守
SUCCESS CHARM
合格御守
SUCCESS CHARM
......
SEN-SEI...
I'M SORRY, SENSEI.
I'M PROBABLY NOT GONNA PASS...
ALL BECAUSE OF YOUR STUPID PHONE CALL...!!!
TRMBL
TRMBL
TRMBL
CLEEENCH
IN THE END...
THE SECOND EXAM ENDED BEFORE I EVER FOUND MY GROOVE.

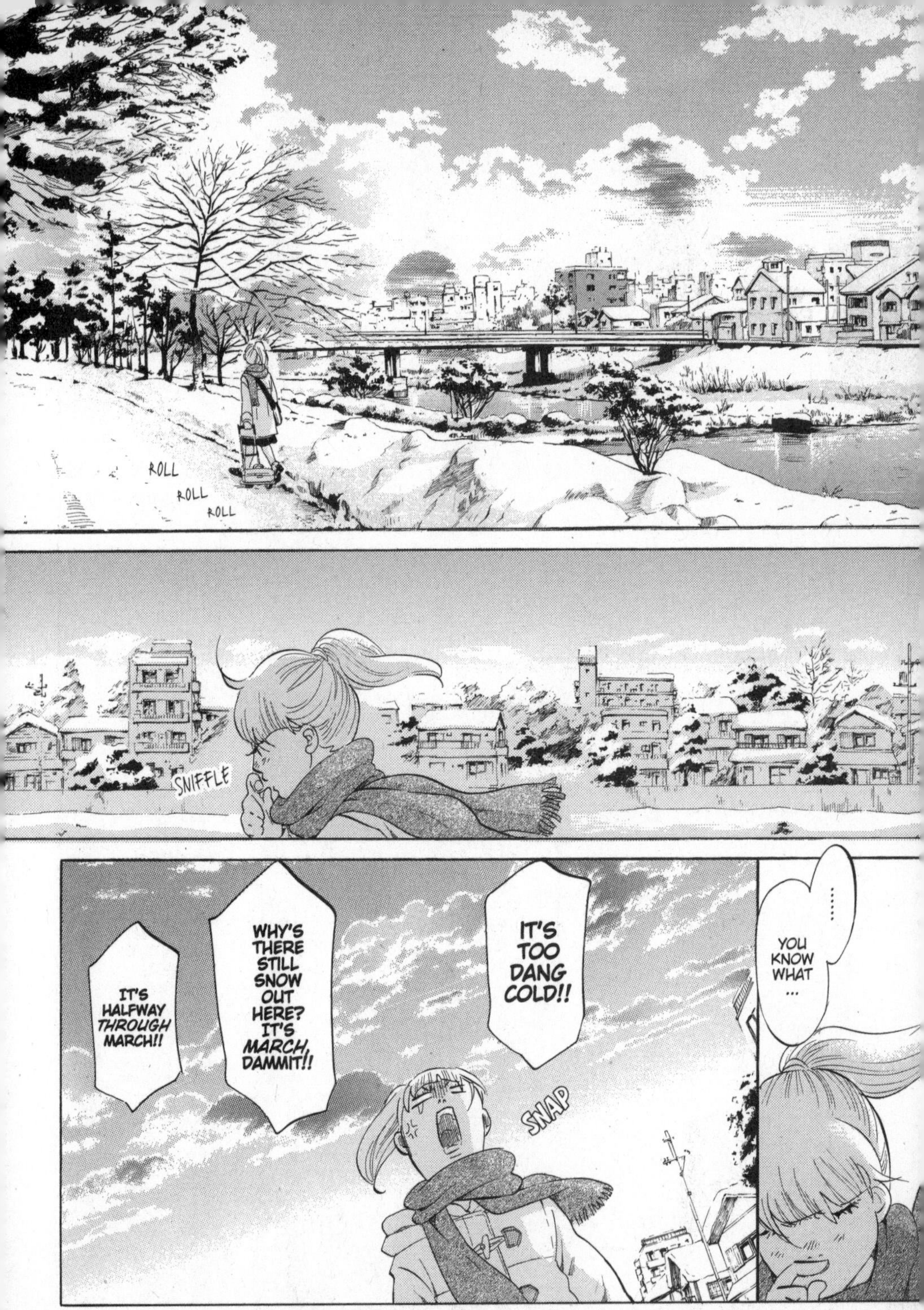
ROLL
ROLL
ROLL
SNIFFLE
.....
YOU KNOW WHAT ...
IT'S TOO DANG COLD!!
WHY'S THERE STILL SNOW OUT HERE? IT'S MARCH, DAMMIT!!
SNAP
IT'S HALFWAY THROUGH MARCH!!

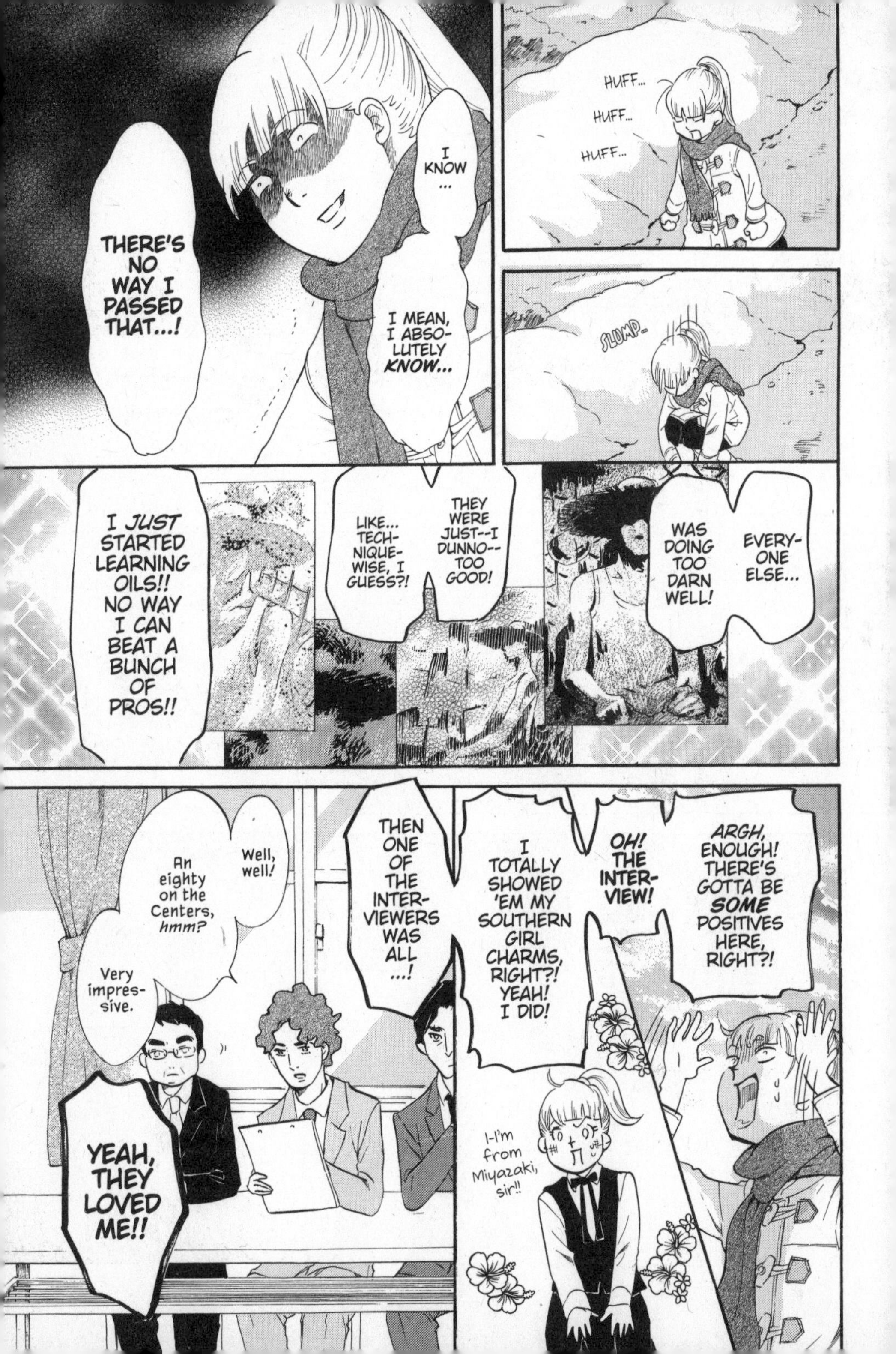
HUFF...
HUFF...
HUFF...
SLUMP...
I KNOW...
I MEAN, I ABSOLUTELY *KNOW*...
THERE'S NO WAY I PASSED THAT...!
EVERYONE ELSE...
WAS DOING TOO DARN WELL!
THEY WERE JUST--I DUNNO--TOO GOOD!
LIKE... TECHNIQUE-WISE, I GUESS?!
I *JUST* STARTED LEARNING OILS!! NO WAY I CAN BEAT A BUNCH OF PROS!!
ARGH, ENOUGH! THERE'S GOTTA BE ***SOME*** POSITIVES HERE, RIGHT?!
***OH!* THE INTERVIEW!**
I TOTALLY SHOWED 'EM MY SOUTHERN GIRL CHARMS, RIGHT?! YEAH! I DID!
I-I'm from Miyazaki, sir!!
THEN ONE OF THE INTERVIEWERS WAS ALL ...!
Well, well!
An eighty on the Centers, *hmm?*
Very impressive.
YEAH, THEY LOVED ME!!

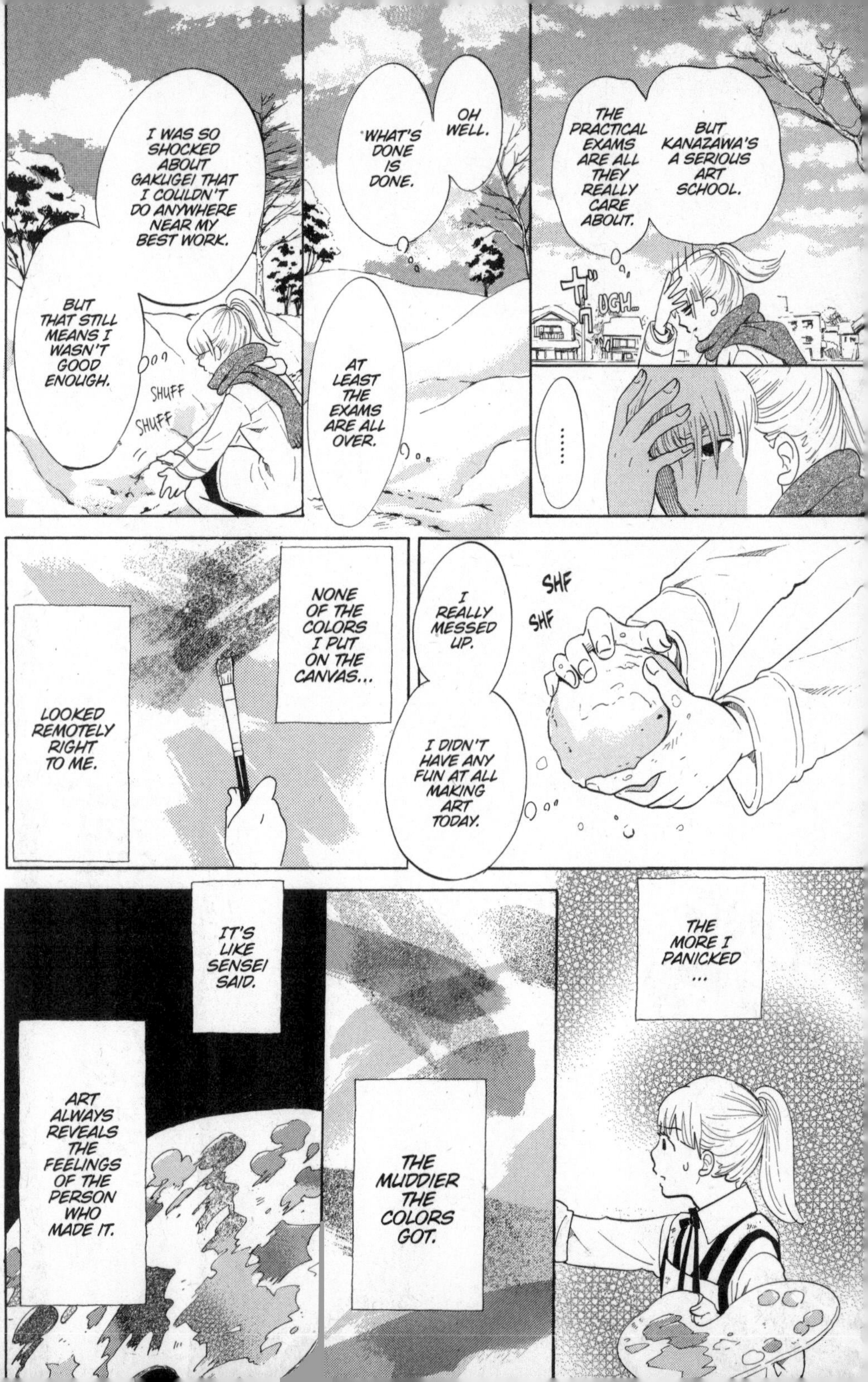
BUT KANAZAWA'S A SERIOUS ART SCHOOL.
THE PRACTICAL EXAMS ARE ALL THEY REALLY CARE ABOUT.
UGH...
......
OH WELL.
WHAT'S DONE IS DONE.
AT LEAST THE EXAMS ARE ALL OVER.
I WAS SO SHOCKED ABOUT GAKUGEI THAT I COULDN'T DO ANYWHERE NEAR MY BEST WORK.
SHUFF
SHUFF
BUT THAT STILL MEANS I WASN'T GOOD ENOUGH.
I REALLY MESSED UP.
SHF
SHF
I DIDN'T HAVE ANY FUN AT ALL MAKING ART TODAY.
NONE OF THE COLORS I PUT ON THE CANVAS...
LOOKED REMOTELY RIGHT TO ME.
THE MORE I PANICKED...
THE MUDDIER THE COLORS GOT.
IT'S LIKE SENSEI SAID.
ART ALWAYS REVEALS THE FEELINGS OF THE PERSON WHO MADE IT.

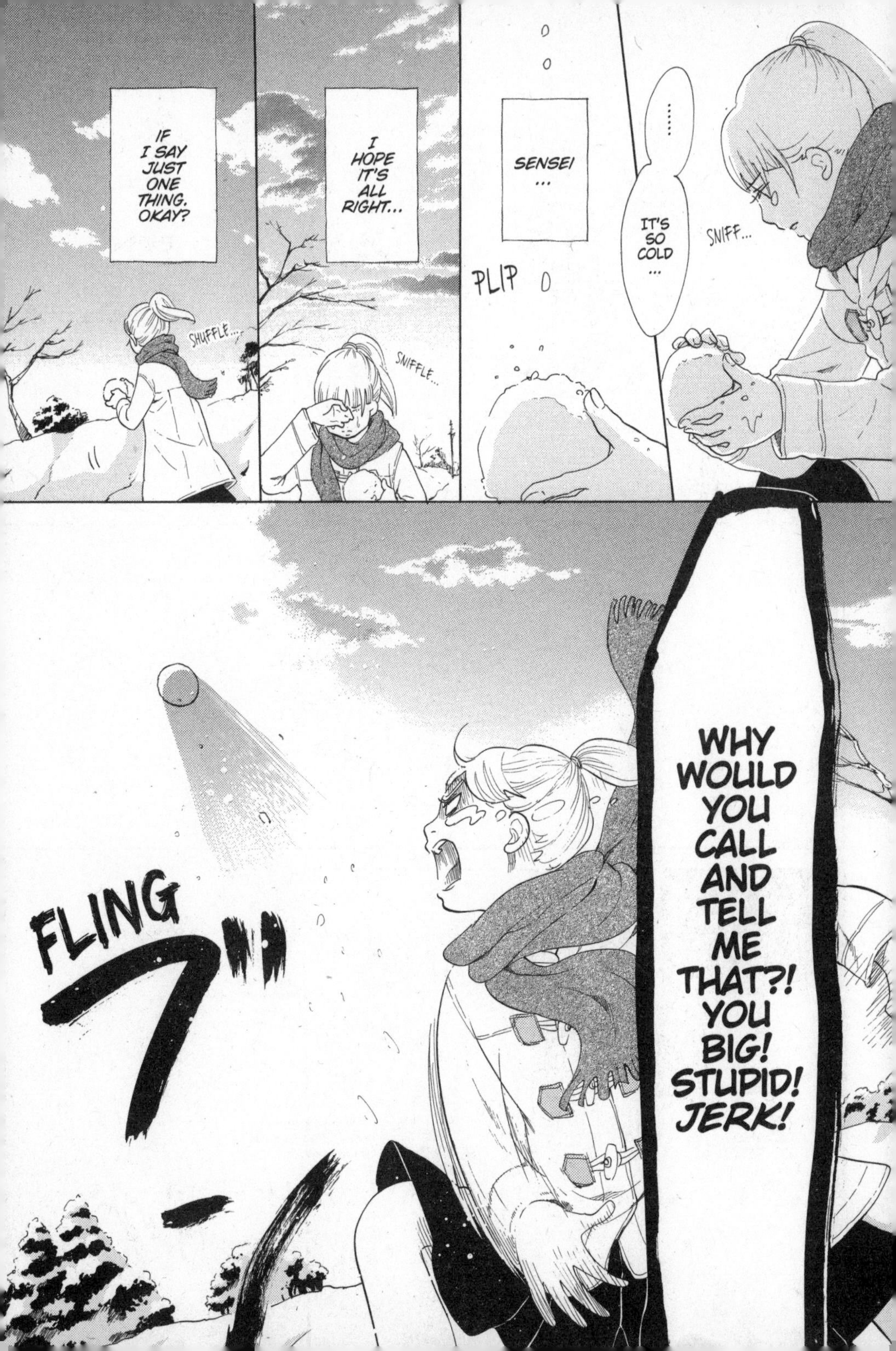
......
IT'S SO COLD ...
SNIFF...
SENSEI ...
PLIP
I HOPE IT'S ALL RIGHT...
SNIFFLE...
IF I SAY JUST ONE THING. OKAY?
SHUFFLE...
WHY WOULD YOU CALL AND TELL ME THAT?! YOU BIG! STUPID! JERK!
FLING

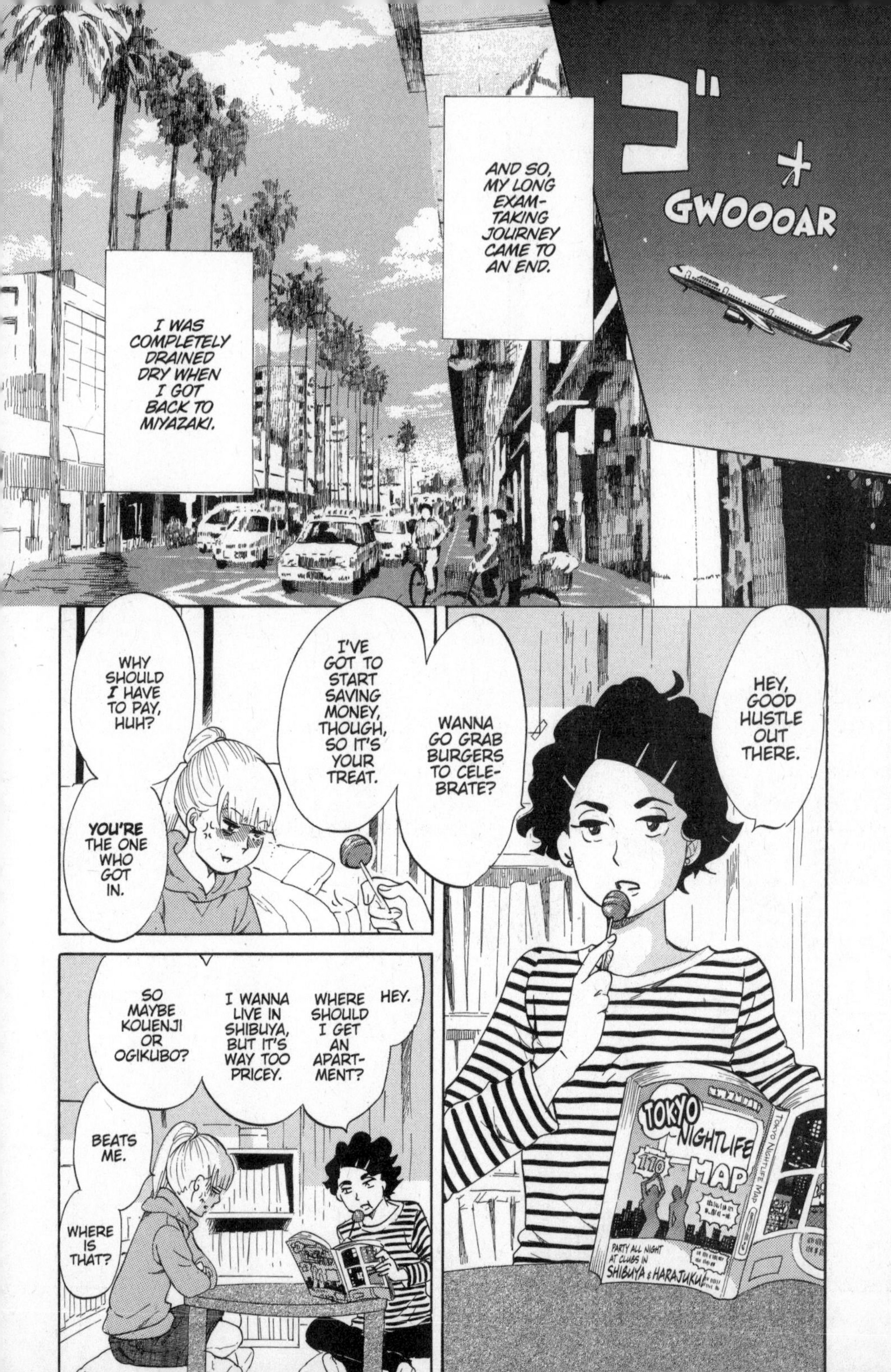
ゴ
GWOOOAR
AND SO, MY LONG EXAM-TAKING JOURNEY CAME TO AN END.
I WAS COMPLETELY DRAINED DRY WHEN I GOT BACK TO MIYAZAKI.
HEY, GOOD HUSTLE OUT THERE.
TOKYO NIGHTLIFE MAP
110
PARTY ALL NIGHT AT CLUBS IN SHIBUYA & HARAJUKU
TOKYO NIGHTLIFE MAP
WANNA GO GRAB BURGERS TO CELE-BRATE?
I'VE GOT TO START SAVING MONEY, THOUGH, SO IT'S YOUR TREAT.
WHY SHOULD I HAVE TO PAY, HUH?
YOU'RE THE ONE WHO GOT IN.
HEY.
WHERE SHOULD I GET AN APART-MENT?
I WANNA LIVE IN SHIBUYA, BUT IT'S WAY TOO PRICEY.
SO MAYBE KOUENJI OR OGIKUBO?
BEATS ME.
WHERE IS THAT?

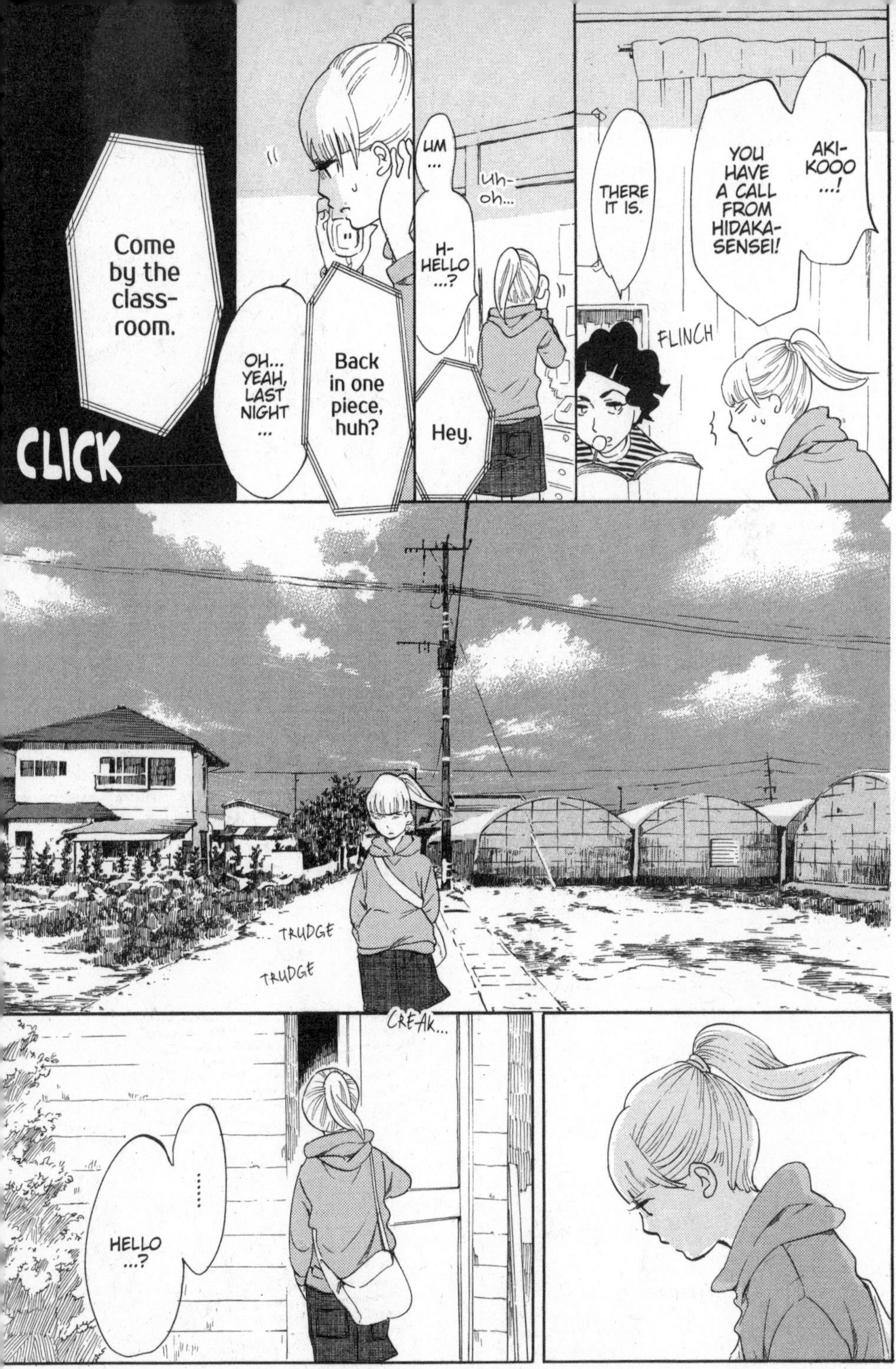
AKI-KOOO ...!
YOU HAVE A CALL FROM HIDAKA-SENSEI!
THERE IT IS.
FLINCH
Uh-oh...
UM ...
H-HELLO ...?
Hey.
Back in one piece, huh?
OH... YEAH, LAST NIGHT ...
Come by the class-room.
CLICK
TRUDGE
TRUDGE
CREAK...
......
HELLO ...?

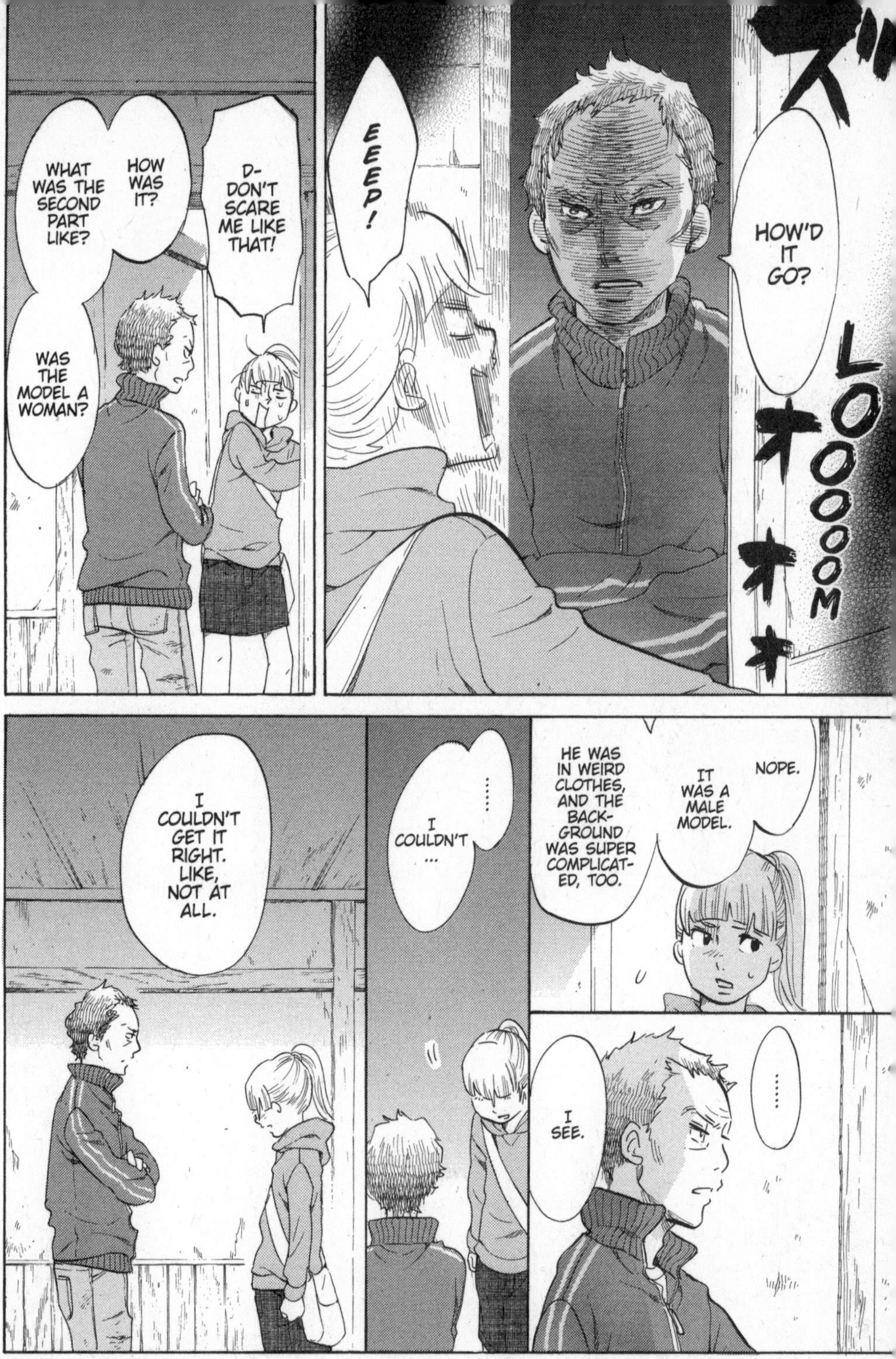
ズオオォ
HOW'D IT GO?
LOOOOOM
EEEP!
D-DON'T SCARE ME LIKE THAT!
HOW WAS IT?
WHAT WAS THE SECOND PART LIKE?
WAS THE MODEL A WOMAN?
NOPE.
IT WAS A MALE MODEL.
HE WAS IN WEIRD CLOTHES, AND THE BACK-GROUND WAS SUPER COMPLICAT-ED, TOO.
......
I SEE.
......
I COULDN'T ...
I COULDN'T GET IT RIGHT. LIKE, NOT AT ALL.

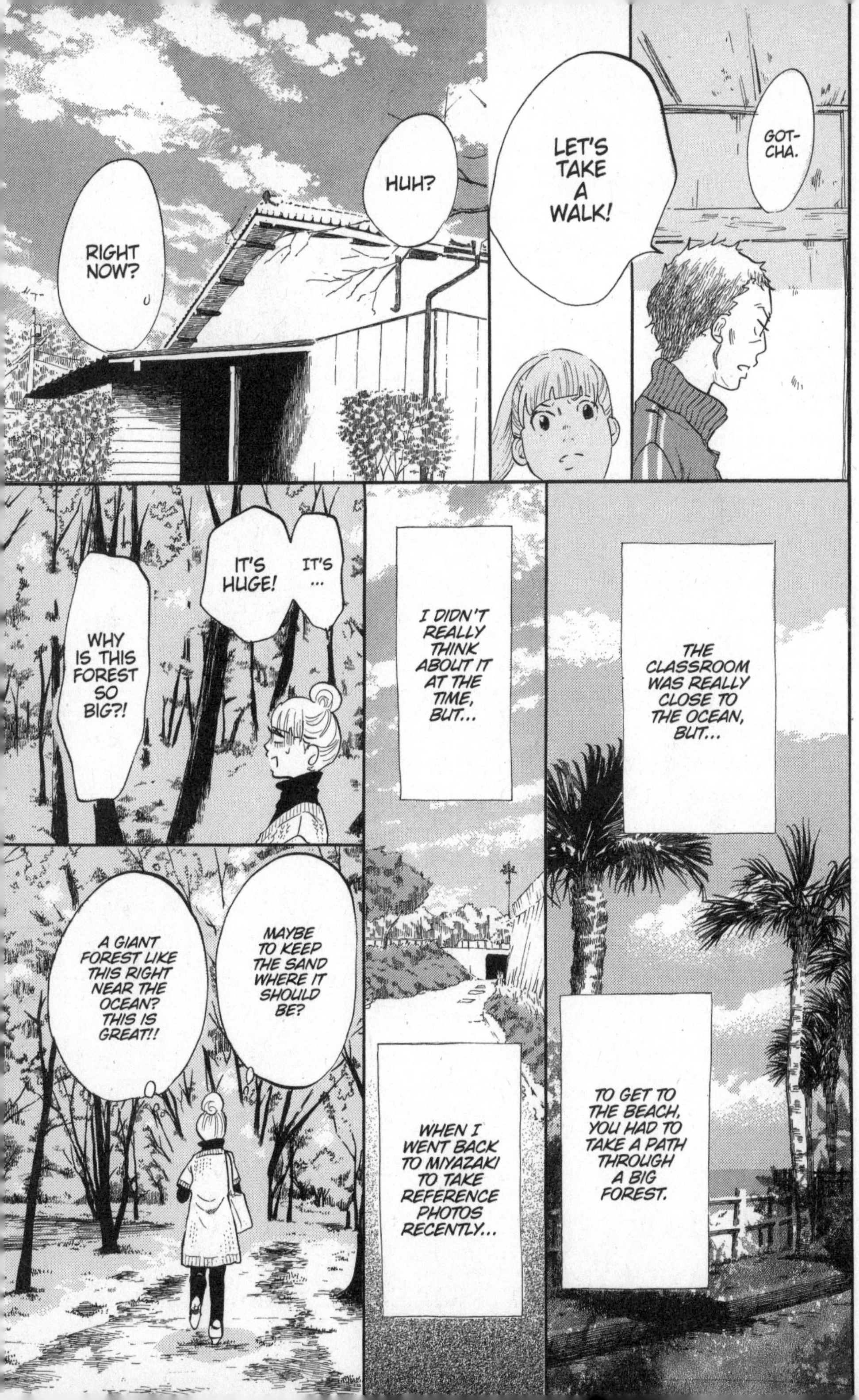

GOT-CHA.
LET'S TAKE A WALK!
HUH?
RIGHT NOW?
THE CLASSROOM WAS REALLY CLOSE TO THE OCEAN, BUT...
TO GET TO THE BEACH, YOU HAD TO TAKE A PATH THROUGH A BIG FOREST.
I DIDN'T REALLY THINK ABOUT IT AT THE TIME, BUT...
WHEN I WENT BACK TO MIYAZAKI TO TAKE REFERENCE PHOTOS RECENTLY...
IT'S ...
IT'S HUGE!
WHY IS THIS FOREST SO BIG?!
MAYBE TO KEEP THE SAND WHERE IT SHOULD BE?
A GIANT FOREST LIKE THIS RIGHT NEAR THE OCEAN? THIS IS GREAT!!

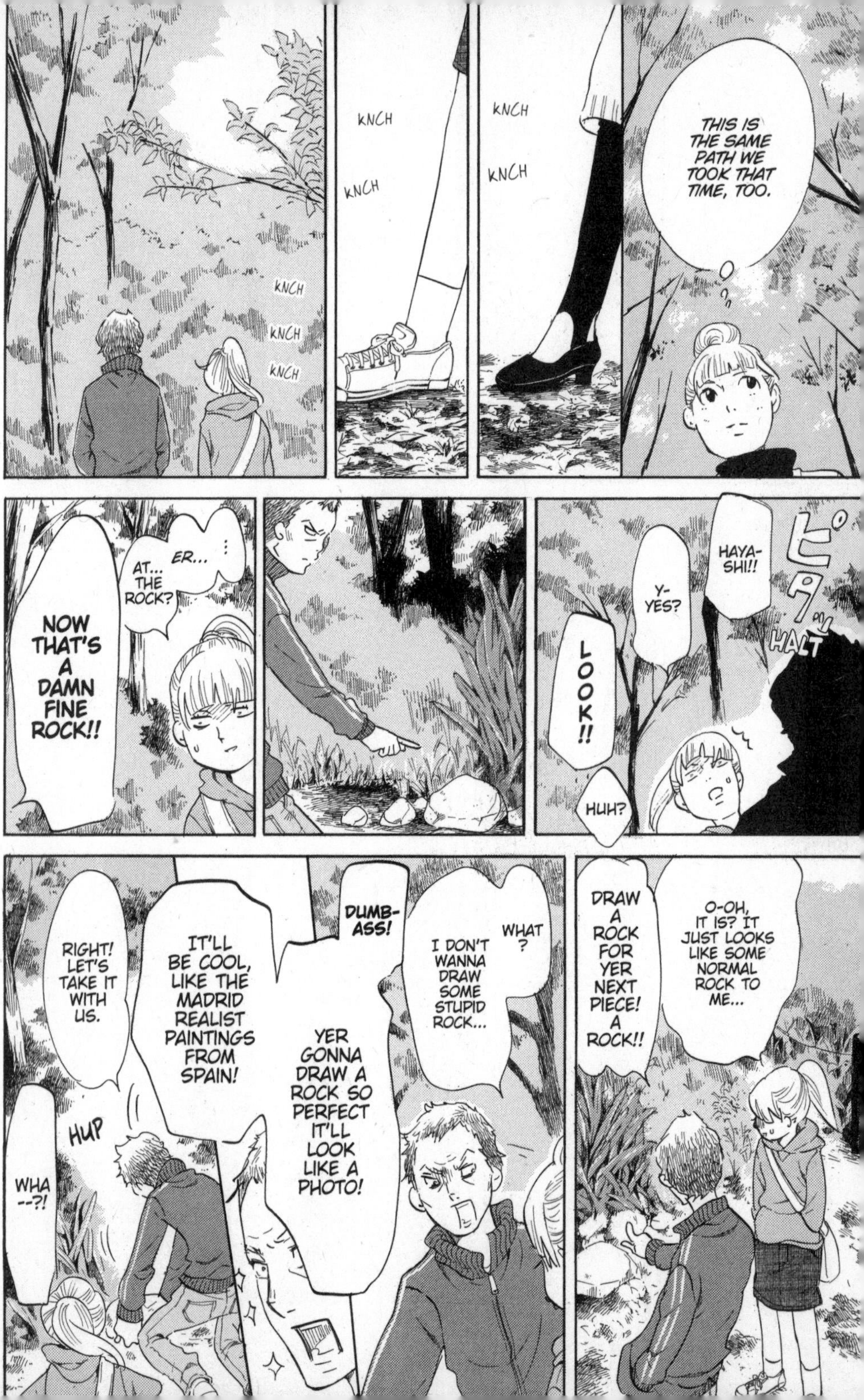
THIS IS THE SAME PATH WE TOOK THAT TIME, TOO.
KNCH
KNCH
KNCH
KNCH
KNCH
KNCH
KNCH
HAYA-SHI!!
ピタ
HALT
Y-YES?
LOOK!!
HUH?
...
ER...
AT... THE ROCK?
NOW THAT'S A DAMN FINE ROCK!!
O-OH, IT IS? IT JUST LOOKS LIKE SOME NORMAL ROCK TO ME...
DRAW A ROCK FOR YER NEXT PIECE! A ROCK!!
WHAT?
I DON'T WANNA DRAW SOME STUPID ROCK...
DUMB-ASS!
YER GONNA DRAW A ROCK SO PERFECT IT'LL LOOK LIKE A PHOTO!
IT'LL BE COOL, LIKE THE MADRID REALIST PAINTINGS FROM SPAIN!
RIGHT! LET'S TAKE IT WITH US.
HUP
WHA--?!

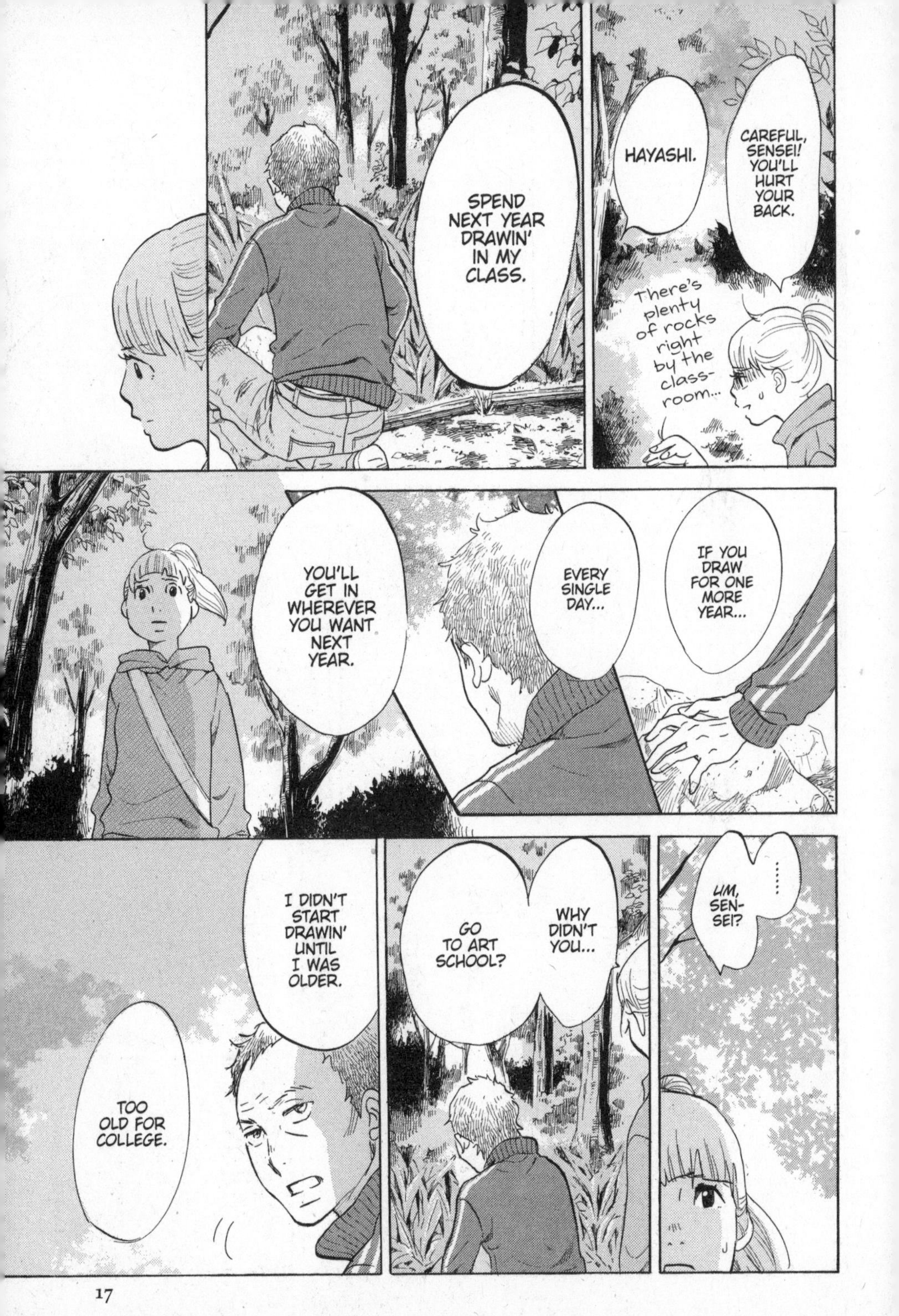

CAREFUL, SENSEI! YOU'LL HURT YOUR BACK.
HAYASHI.
There's plenty of rocks right by the classroom...
SPEND NEXT YEAR DRAWIN' IN MY CLASS.
IF YOU DRAW FOR ONE MORE YEAR...
EVERY SINGLE DAY...
YOU'LL GET IN WHEREVER YOU WANT NEXT YEAR.
......
UM, SENSEI?
WHY DIDN'T YOU...
GO TO ART SCHOOL?
I DIDN'T START DRAWIN' UNTIL I WAS OLDER.
TOO OLD FOR COLLEGE.

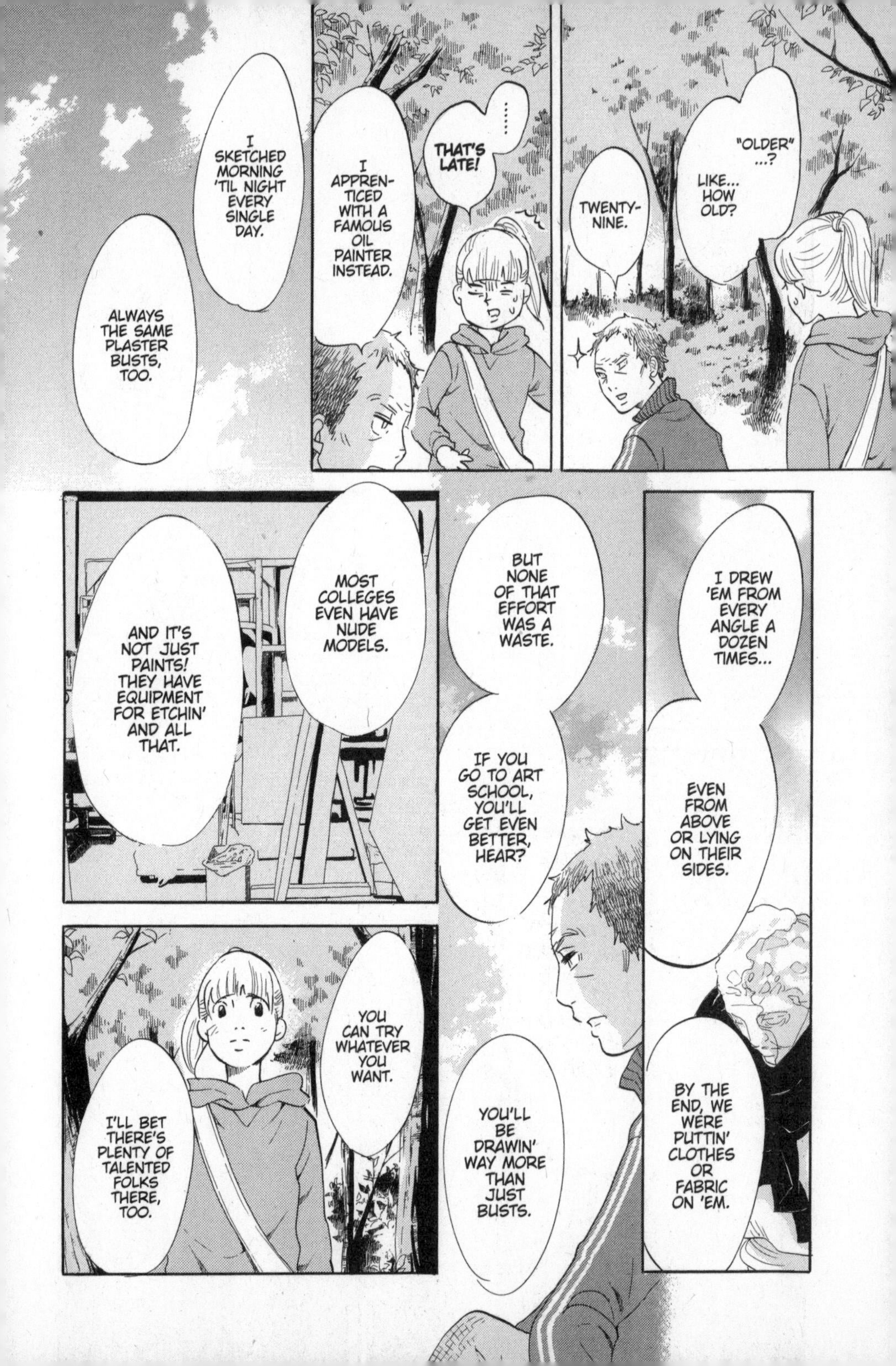
"OLDER" ...?
LIKE... HOW OLD?
TWENTY-NINE.
......
THAT'S LATE!
I APPRENTICED WITH A FAMOUS OIL PAINTER INSTEAD.
I SKETCHED MORNING 'TIL NIGHT EVERY SINGLE DAY.
ALWAYS THE SAME PLASTER BUSTS, TOO.
I DREW 'EM FROM EVERY ANGLE A DOZEN TIMES...
EVEN FROM ABOVE OR LYING ON THEIR SIDES.
BY THE END, WE WERE PUTTIN' CLOTHES OR FABRIC ON 'EM.
BUT NONE OF THAT EFFORT WAS A WASTE.
IF YOU GO TO ART SCHOOL, YOU'LL GET EVEN BETTER, HEAR?
YOU'LL BE DRAWIN' WAY MORE THAN JUST BUSTS.
MOST COLLEGES EVEN HAVE NUDE MODELS.
AND IT'S NOT JUST PAINTS! THEY HAVE EQUIPMENT FOR ETCHIN' AND ALL THAT.
YOU CAN TRY WHATEVER YOU WANT.
I'LL BET THERE'S PLENTY OF TALENTED FOLKS THERE, TOO.

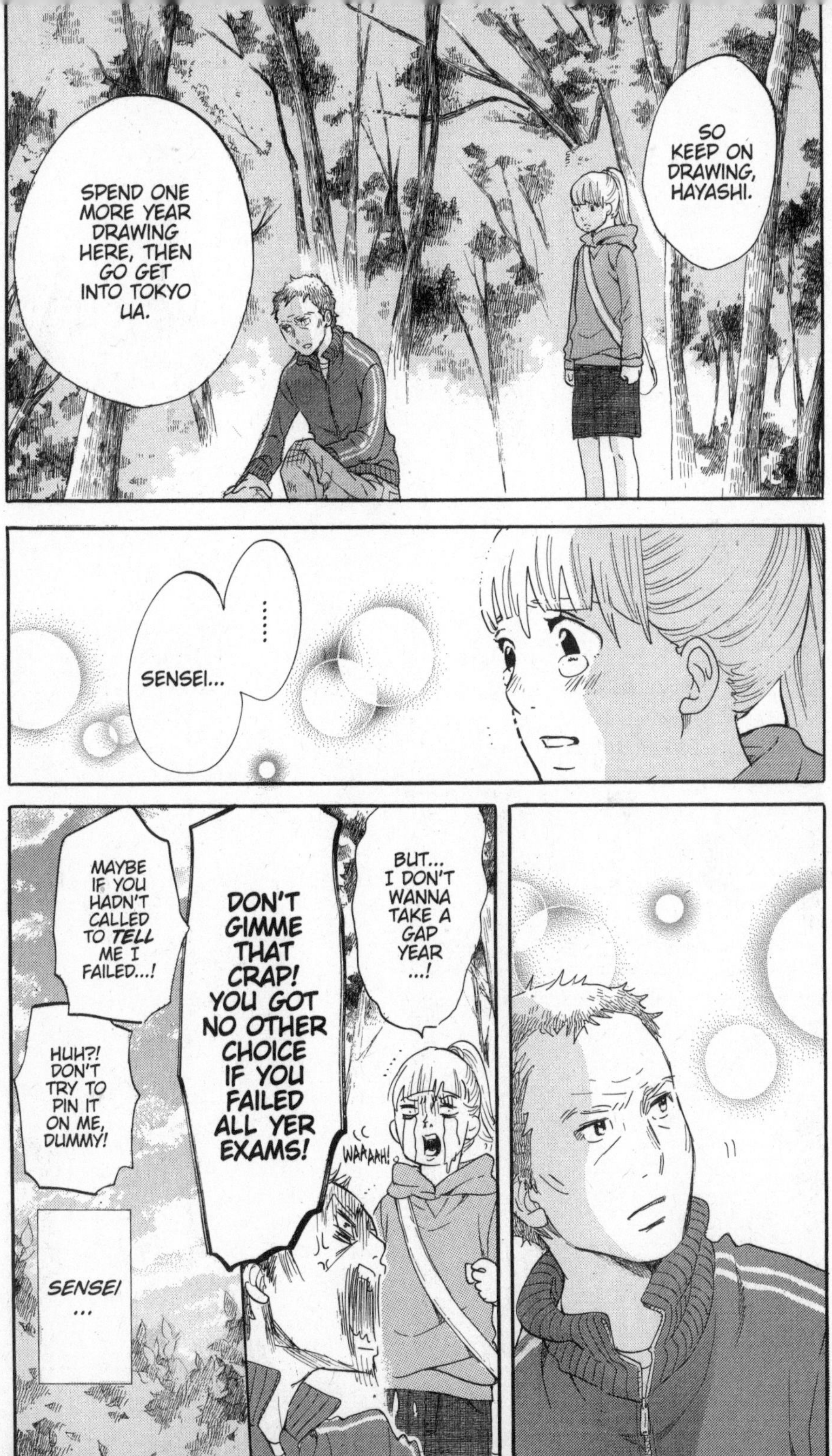
SO KEEP ON DRAWING, HAYASHI.
SPEND ONE MORE YEAR DRAWING HERE, THEN GO GET INTO TOKYO UA.
......
SENSEI...
BUT... I DON'T WANNA TAKE A GAP YEAR ...!
WAAAAH!
DON'T GIMME THAT CRAP! YOU GOT NO OTHER CHOICE IF YOU FAILED ALL YER EXAMS!
MAYBE IF YOU HADN'T CALLED TO *TELL* ME I FAILED...!
HUH?! DON'T TRY TO PIN IT ON ME, DUMMY!
SENSEI ...

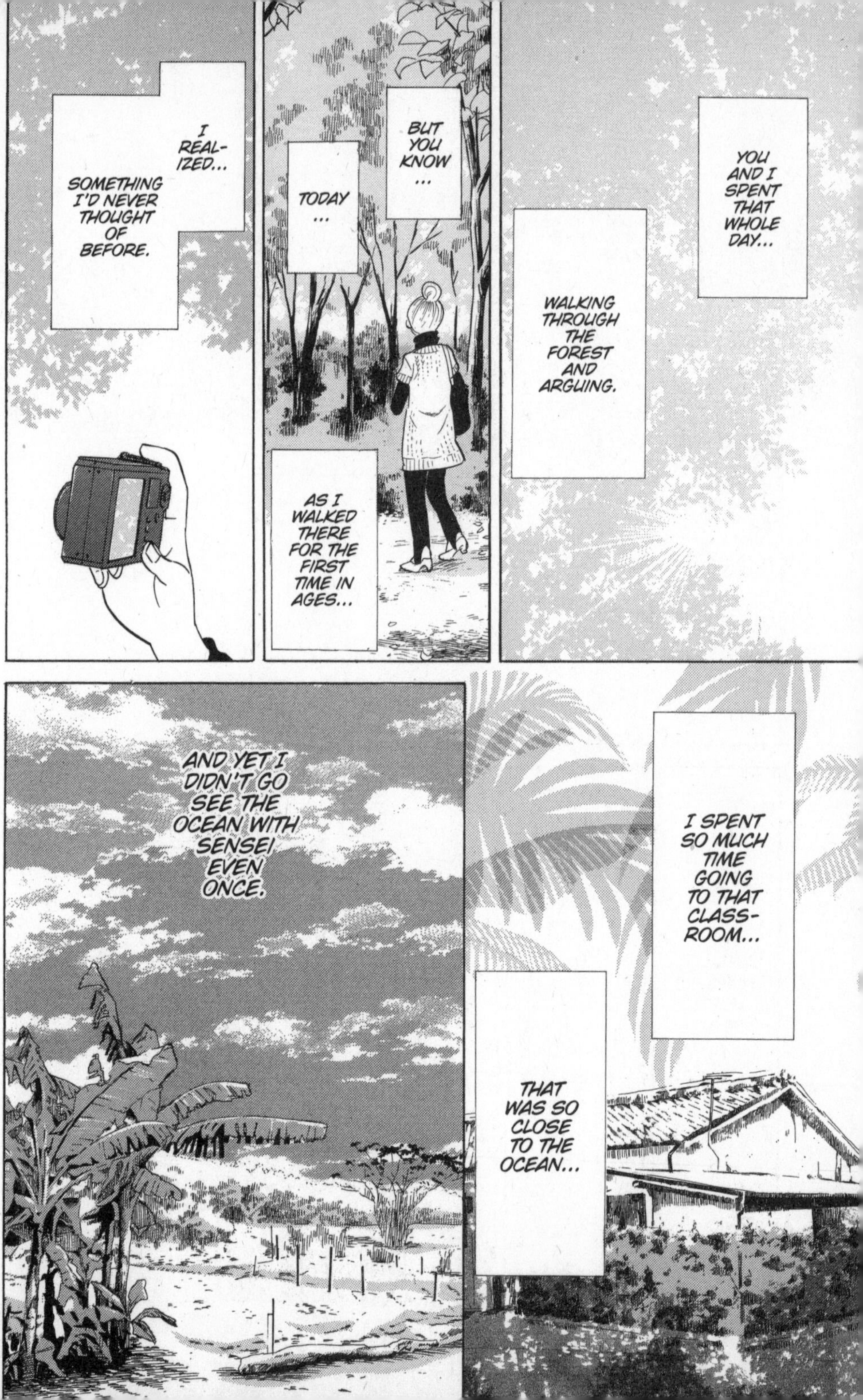
YOU AND I SPENT THAT WHOLE DAY...
WALKING THROUGH THE FOREST AND ARGUING.
BUT YOU KNOW...
TODAY...
AS I WALKED THERE FOR THE FIRST TIME IN AGES...
I REAL-IZED...
SOMETHING I'D NEVER THOUGHT OF BEFORE.
I SPENT SO MUCH TIME GOING TO THAT CLASS-ROOM...
THAT WAS SO CLOSE TO THE OCEAN...
AND YET I DIDN'T GO SEE THE OCEAN WITH SENSEI EVEN ONCE.

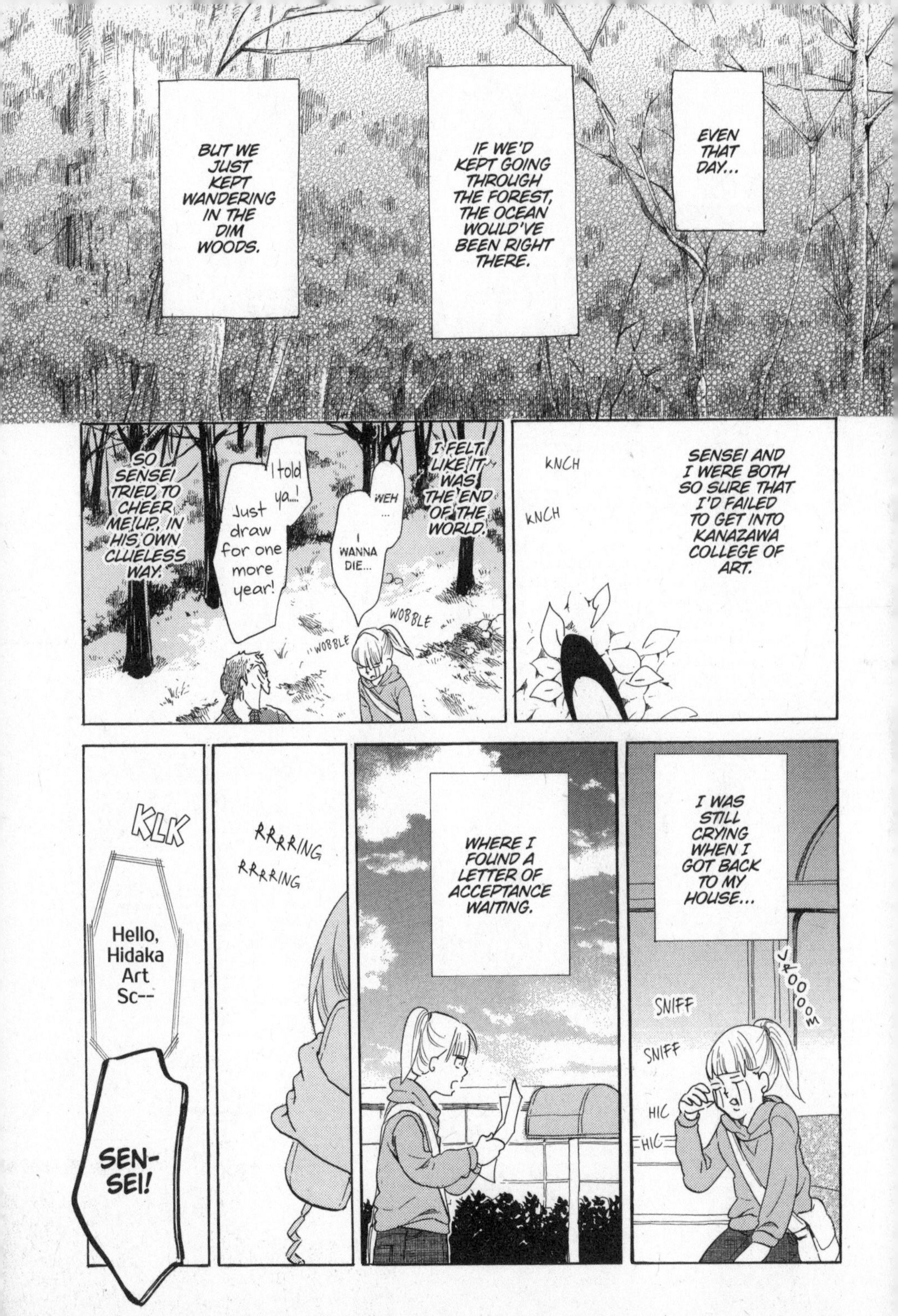
EVEN THAT DAY...
IF WE'D KEPT GOING THROUGH THE FOREST, THE OCEAN WOULD'VE BEEN RIGHT THERE.
BUT WE JUST KEPT WANDERING IN THE DIM WOODS.
SENSEI AND I WERE BOTH SO SURE THAT I'D FAILED TO GET INTO KANAZAWA COLLEGE OF ART.
KNCH
KNCH
I FELT LIKE IT WAS THE END OF THE WORLD.
WEH ...
I WANNA DIE...
I told ya...!
Just draw for one more year!
SO SENSEI TRIED TO CHEER ME UP, IN HIS OWN CLUELESS WAY.
WOBBLE
WOBBLE
I WAS STILL CRYING WHEN I GOT BACK TO MY HOUSE...
VROOOOOM
SNIFF
SNIFF
HIC
HIC
WHERE I FOUND A LETTER OF ACCEPTANCE WAITING.
RRRRING
RRRRING
KLK
Hello, Hidaka Art Sc--
SEN-SEI!

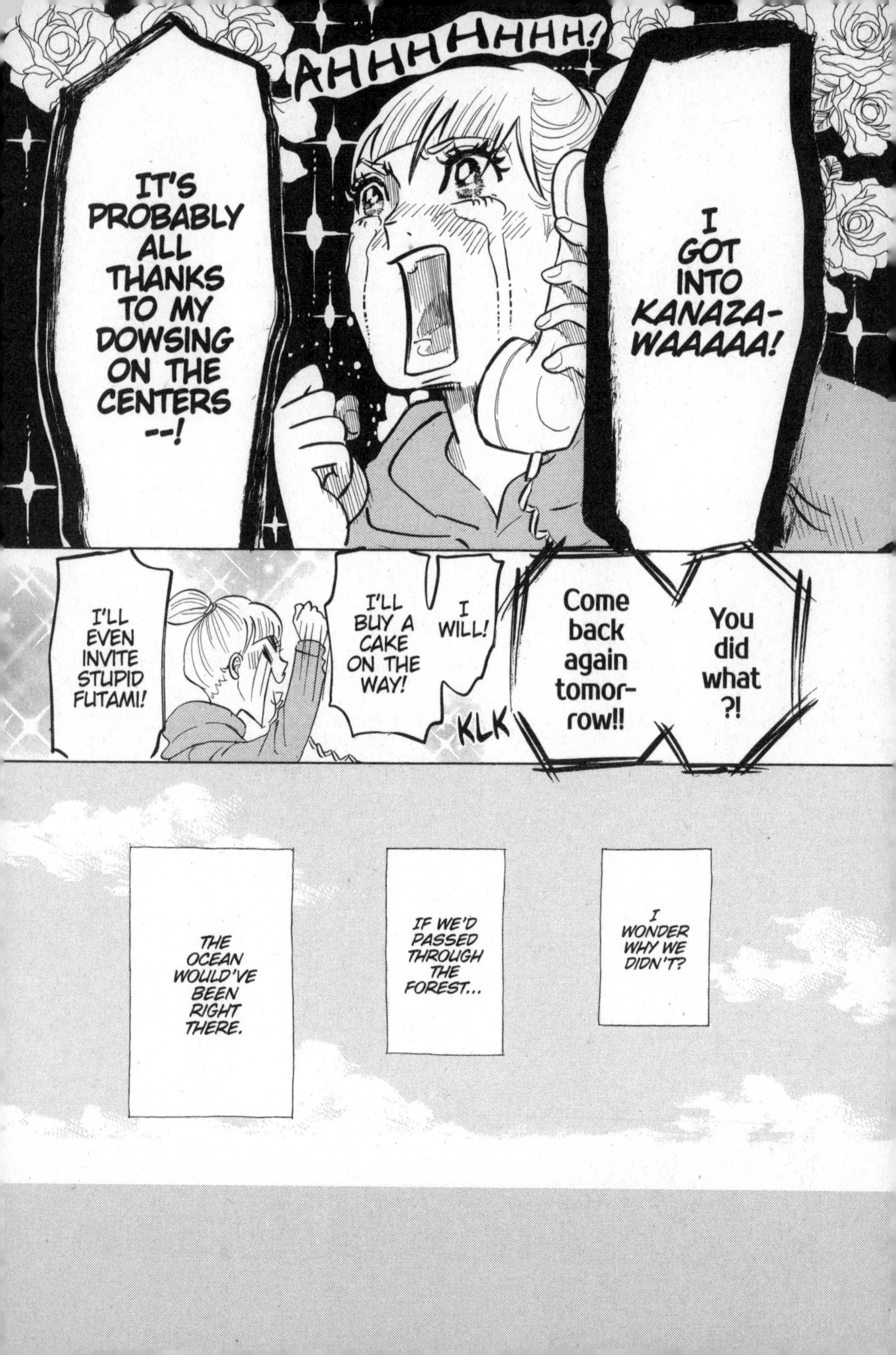
I GOT INTO KANAZA-WAAAAAA!
AHHHHHHHH!
IT'S PROBABLY ALL THANKS TO MY DOWSING ON THE CENTERS--!
You did what?!
Come back again tomorrow!!
KLK
I WILL!
I'LL BUY A CAKE ON THE WAY!
I'LL EVEN INVITE STUPID FUTAMI!
I WONDER WHY WE DIDN'T?
IF WE'D PASSED THROUGH THE FOREST...
THE OCEAN WOULD'VE BEEN RIGHT THERE.

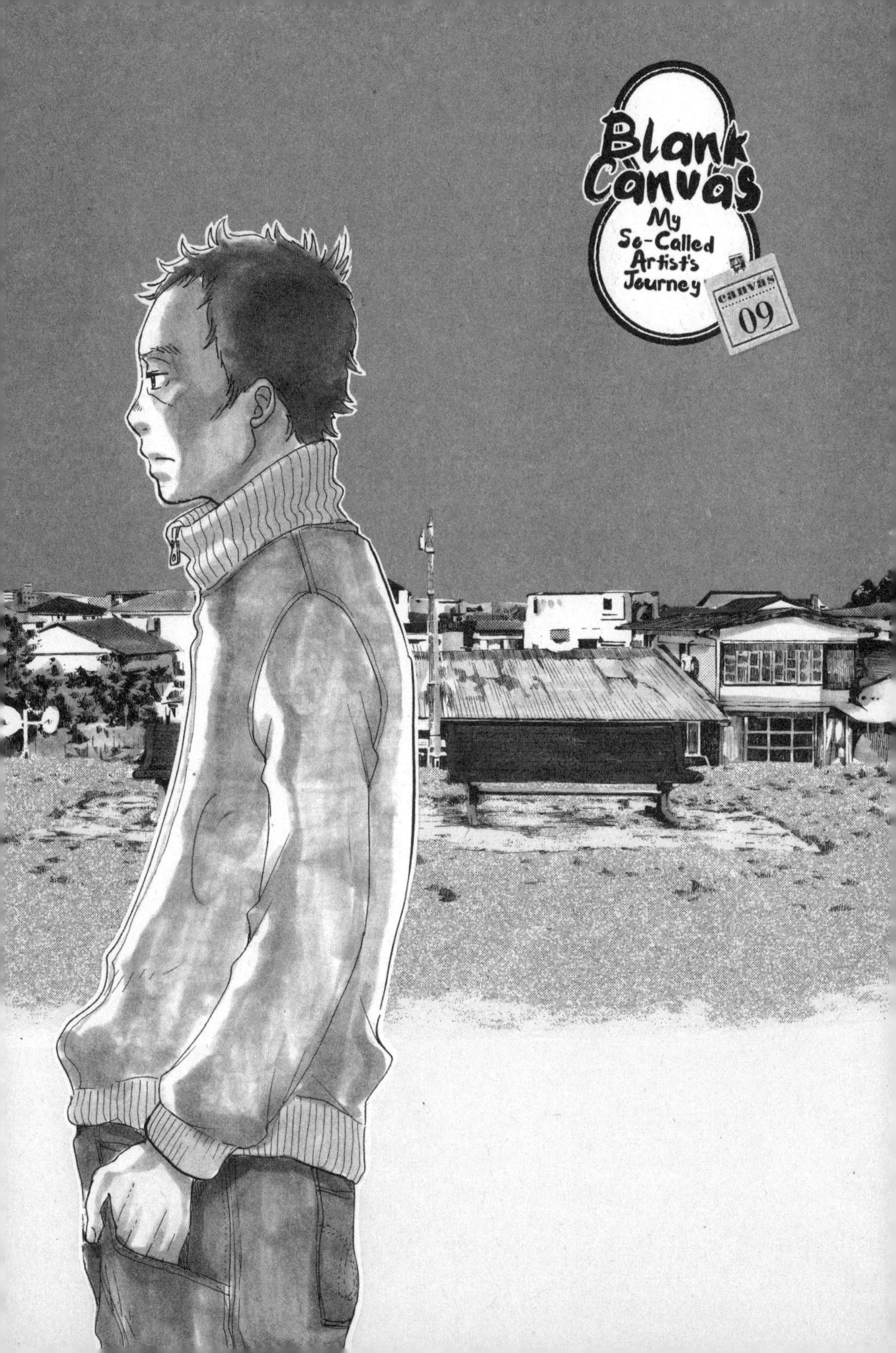

Blank Canvas
My So-Called Artist's Journey
canvas 09

Blank Canvas

My So-Called
Artist's Journey

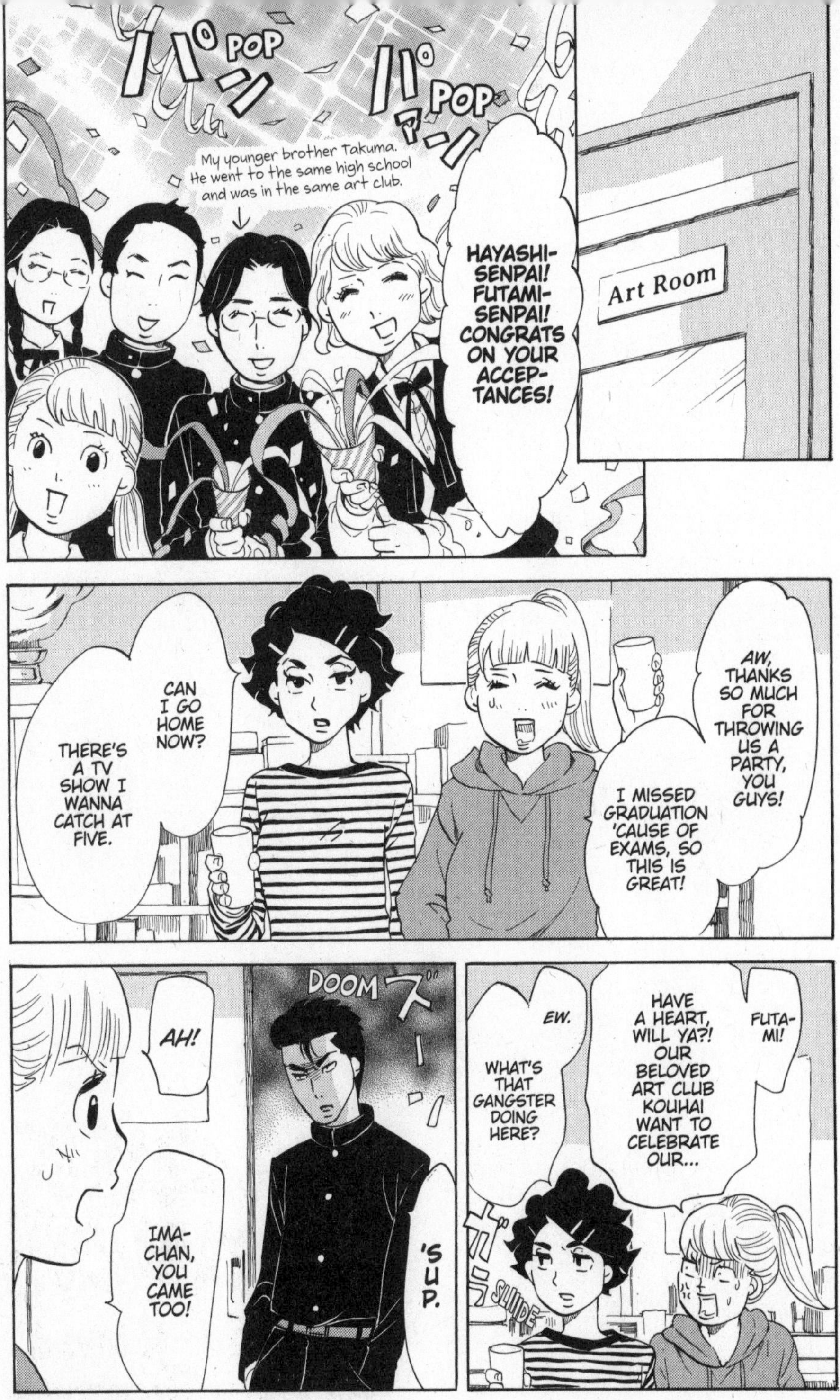
POP
POP
HAYASHI-SENPAI! FUTAMI-SENPAI! CONGRATS ON YOUR ACCEPTANCES!
Art Room
My younger brother Takuma. He went to the same high school and was in the same art club.
AW, THANKS SO MUCH FOR THROWING US A PARTY, YOU GUYS!
I MISSED GRADUATION 'CAUSE OF EXAMS, SO THIS IS GREAT!
CAN I GO HOME NOW?
THERE'S A TV SHOW I WANNA CATCH AT FIVE.
FUTA-MI!
HAVE A HEART, WILL YA?! OUR BELOVED ART CLUB KOUHAI WANT TO CELEBRATE OUR...
EW.
WHAT'S THAT GANGSTER DOING HERE?
SLIDE
DOOM
AH!
'SUP.
IMA-CHAN, YOU CAME TOO!

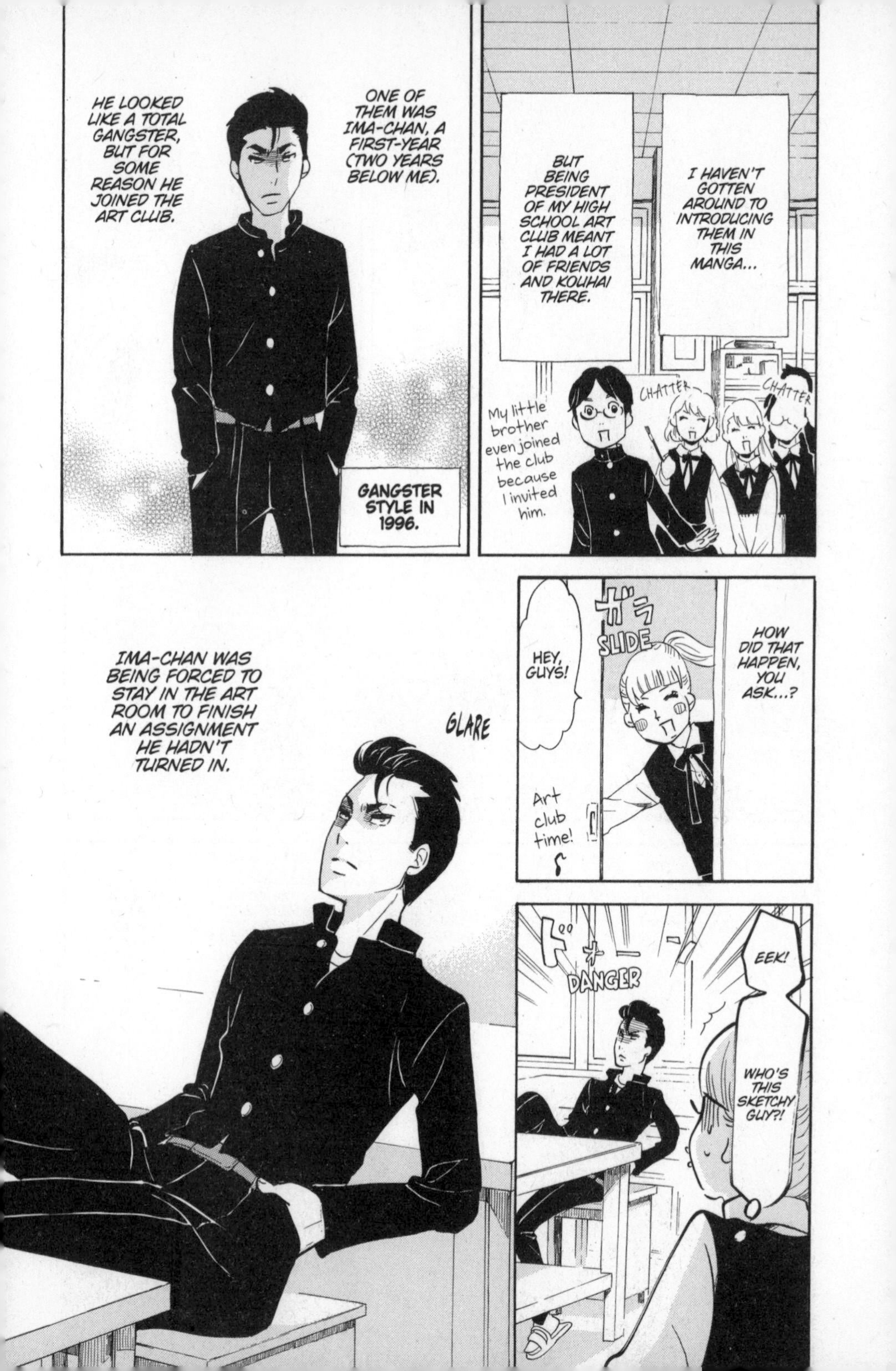
I HAVEN'T GOTTEN AROUND TO INTRODUCING THEM IN THIS MANGA...
BUT BEING PRESIDENT OF MY HIGH SCHOOL ART CLUB MEANT I HAD A LOT OF FRIENDS AND KOUHAI THERE.
CHATTER
CHATTER
My little brother even joined the club because I invited him.
ONE OF THEM WAS IMA-CHAN, A FIRST-YEAR (TWO YEARS BELOW ME).
HE LOOKED LIKE A TOTAL GANGSTER, BUT FOR SOME REASON HE JOINED THE ART CLUB.
GANGSTER STYLE IN 1996.
HOW DID THAT HAPPEN, YOU ASK...?
ガラ
SLIDE
HEY, GUYS!
Art club time!
EEK!
WHO'S THIS SKETCHY GUY?!
ドォー
DANGER
IMA-CHAN WAS BEING FORCED TO STAY IN THE ART ROOM TO FINISH AN ASSIGNMENT HE HADN'T TURNED IN.
GLARE

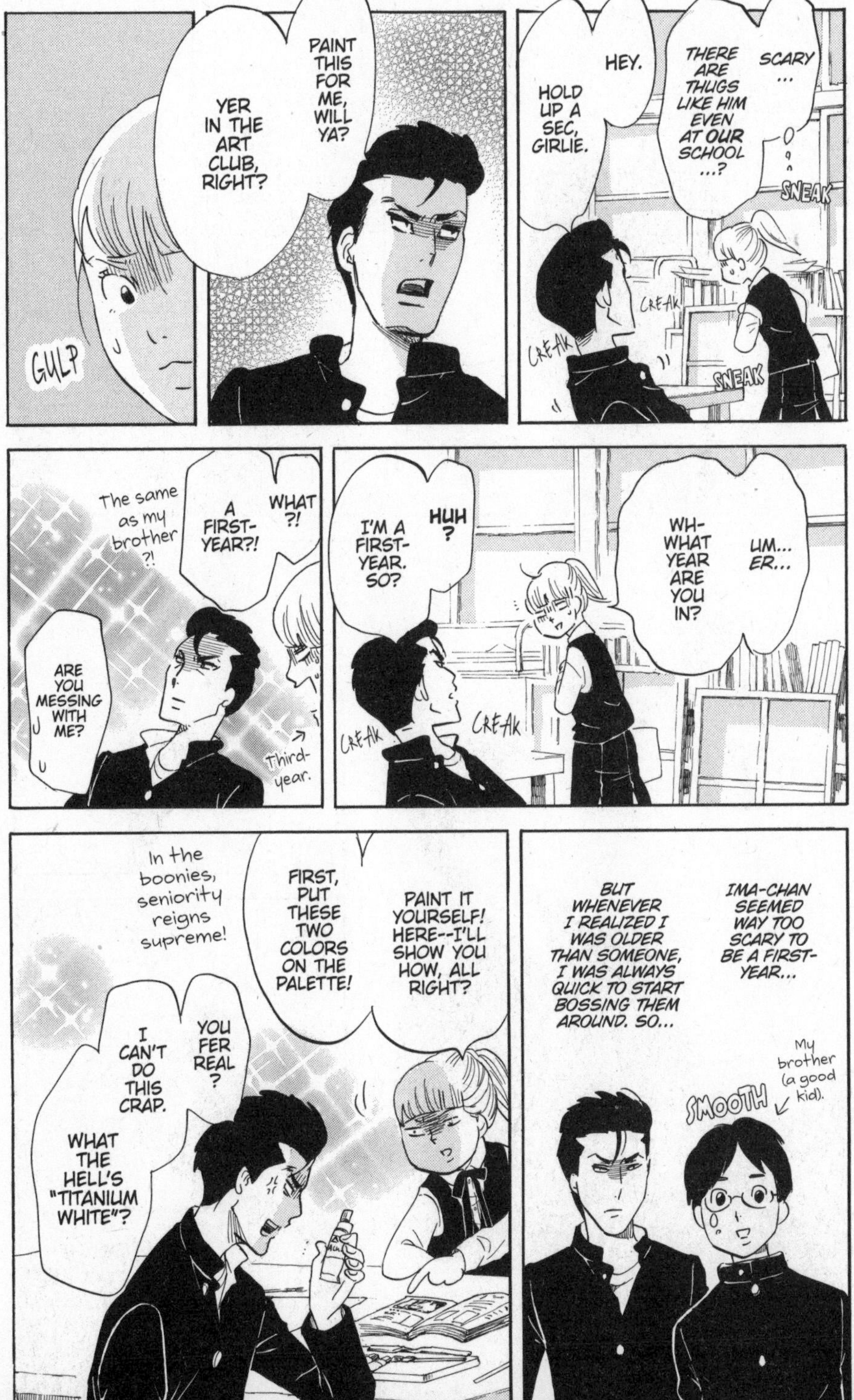
SCARY...
THERE ARE THUGS LIKE HIM EVEN AT OUR SCHOOL...?
SNEAK
HEY.
HOLD UP A SEC, GIRLIE.
CREAK
CREAK
SNEAK
PAINT THIS FOR ME, WILL YA?
YER IN THE ART CLUB, RIGHT?
GULP
UM... ER...
WH-WHAT YEAR ARE YOU IN?
HUH?
I'M A FIRST-YEAR. SO?
CREAK
CREAK
WHAT?!
A FIRST-YEAR?!
The same as my brother?!
ARE YOU MESSING WITH ME?
Third-year.
IMA-CHAN SEEMED WAY TOO SCARY TO BE A FIRST-YEAR...
BUT WHENEVER I REALIZED I WAS OLDER THAN SOMEONE, I WAS ALWAYS QUICK TO START BOSSING THEM AROUND. SO...
My brother (a good kid).
SMOOTH
PAINT IT YOURSELF! HERE--I'LL SHOW YOU HOW, ALL RIGHT?
FIRST, PUT THESE TWO COLORS ON THE PALETTE!
In the boonies, seniority reigns supreme!
YOU FER REAL?
I CAN'T DO THIS CRAP.
WHAT THE HELL'S "TITANIUM WHITE"?

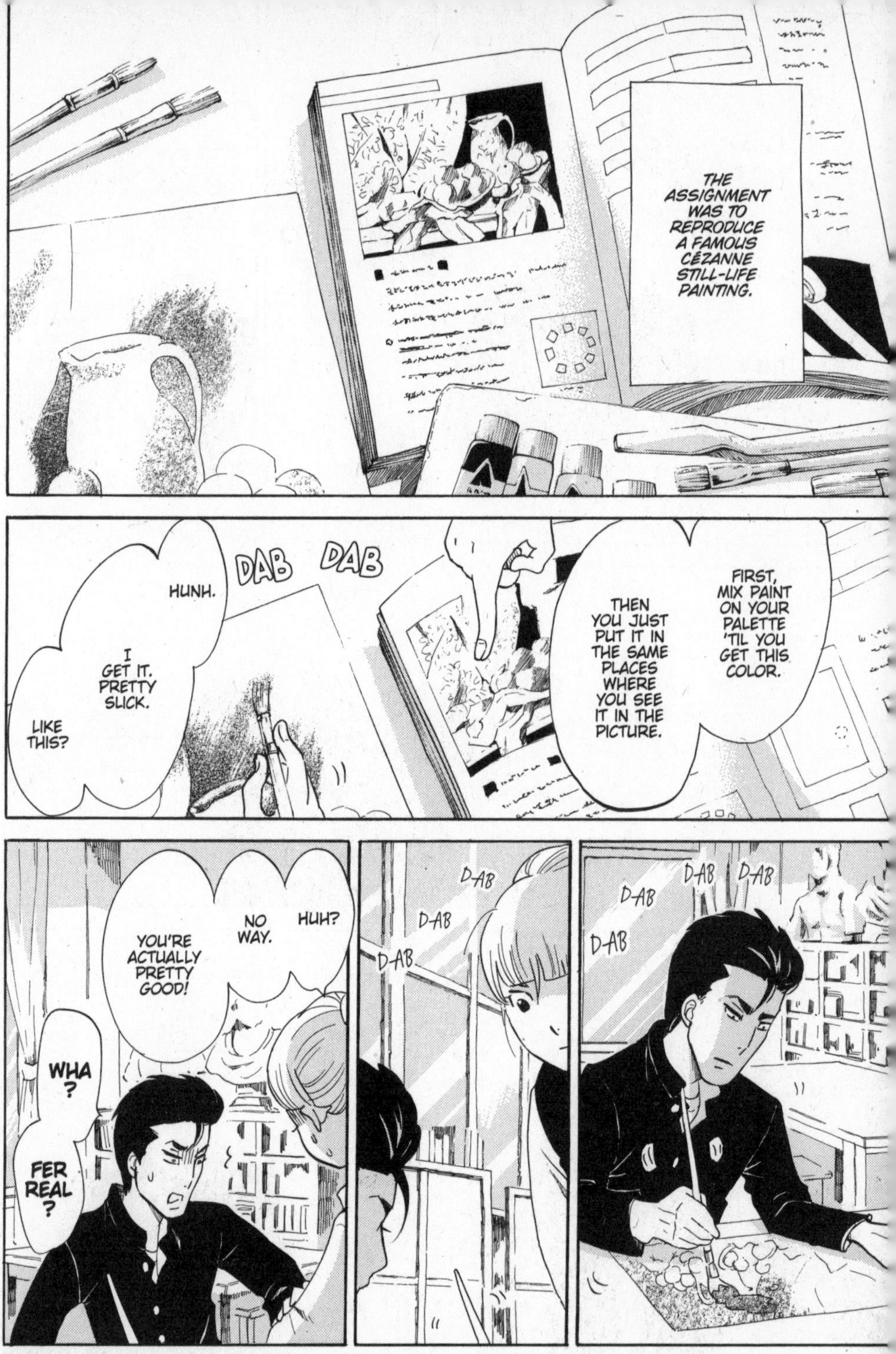
THE ASSIGNMENT WAS TO REPRODUCE A FAMOUS CÉZANNE STILL-LIFE PAINTING.
FIRST, MIX PAINT ON YOUR PALETTE 'TIL YOU GET THIS COLOR.
THEN YOU JUST PUT IT IN THE SAME PLACES WHERE YOU SEE IT IN THE PICTURE.
DAB DAB
HUNH.
I GET IT. PRETTY SLICK.
LIKE THIS?
D-AB D-AB
D-AB
D-AB
D-AB
D-AB
D-AB
HUH?
NO WAY.
YOU'RE ACTUALLY PRETTY GOOD!
WHA?
FER REAL?

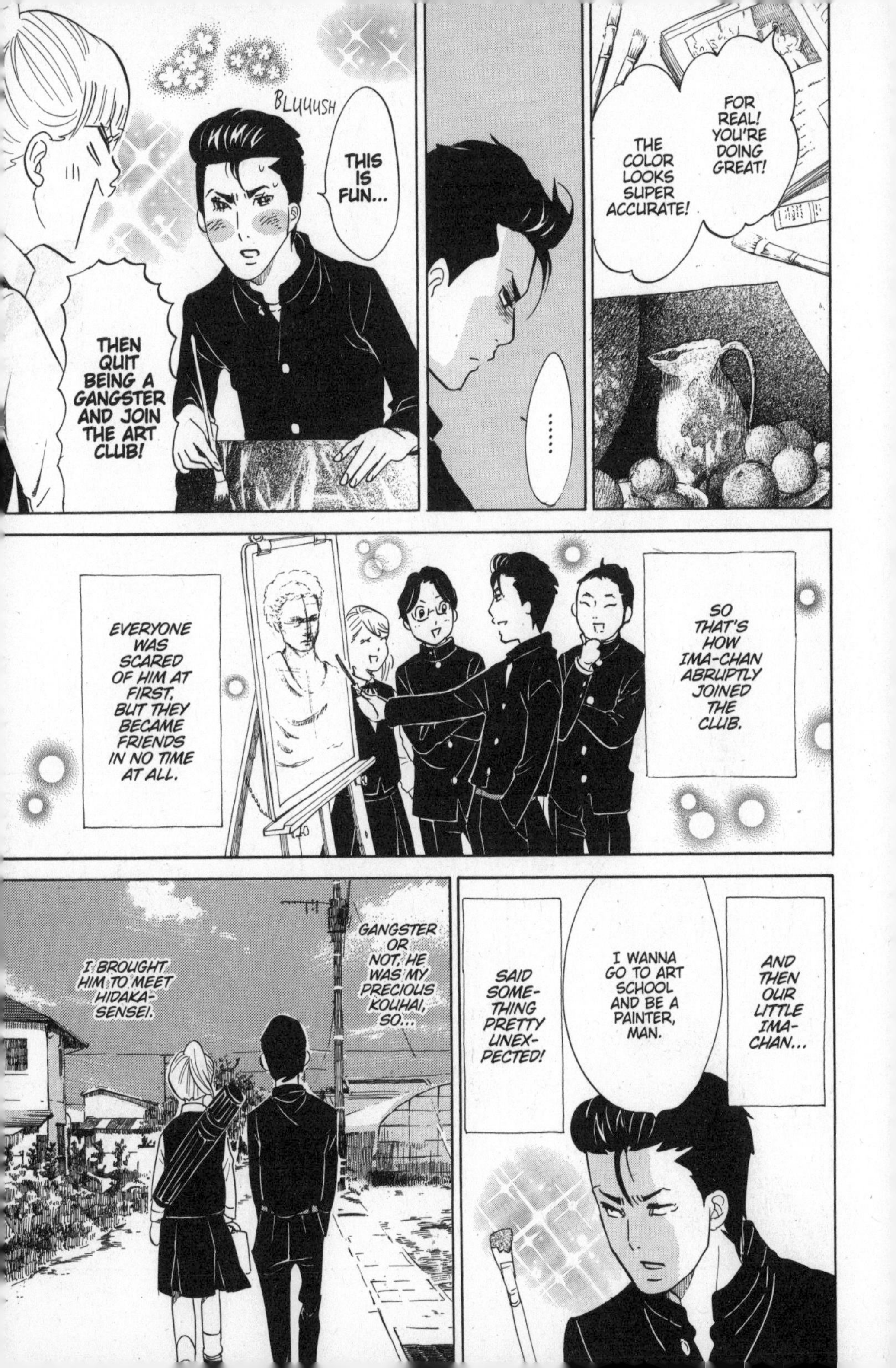
FOR REAL! YOU'RE DOING GREAT!
THE COLOR LOOKS SUPER ACCURATE!
......
BLUUUSH
THIS IS FUN...
THEN QUIT BEING A GANGSTER AND JOIN THE ART CLUB!
SO THAT'S HOW IMA-CHAN ABRUPTLY JOINED THE CLUB.
EVERYONE WAS SCARED OF HIM AT FIRST, BUT THEY BECAME FRIENDS IN NO TIME AT ALL.
AND THEN OUR LITTLE IMA-CHAN...
I WANNA GO TO ART SCHOOL AND BE A PAINTER, MAN.
SAID SOMETHING PRETTY UNEXPECTED!
GANGSTER OR NOT, HE WAS MY PRECIOUS KOUHAI, SO...
I BROUGHT HIM TO MEET HIDAKA-SENSEI.

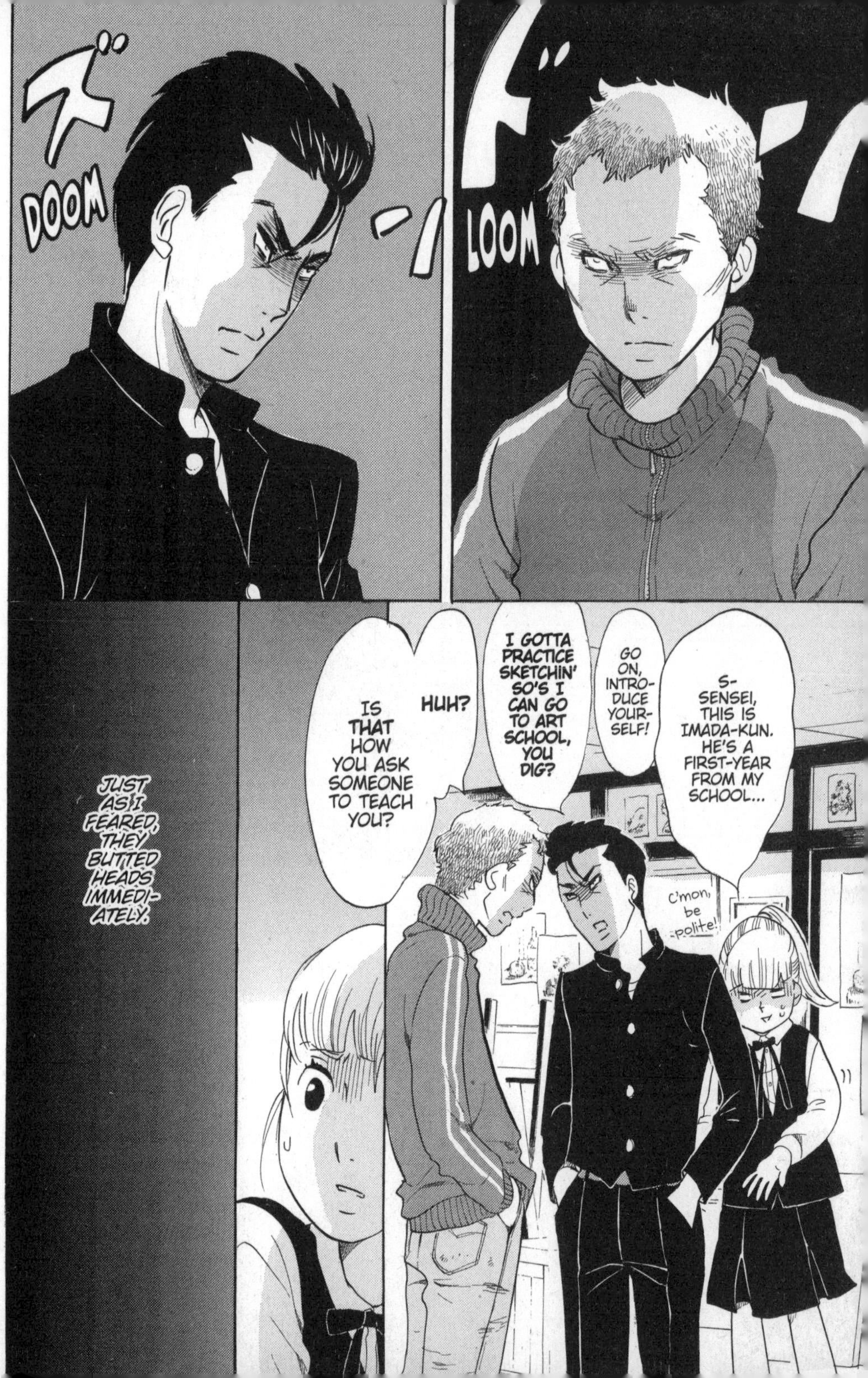
LOOM
DOOM
S-SENSEI, THIS IS IMADA-KUN. HE'S A FIRST-YEAR FROM MY SCHOOL...
GO ON, INTRODUCE YOURSELF!
I GOTTA PRACTICE SKETCHIN' SO'S I CAN GO TO ART SCHOOL, YOU DIG?
C'mon, be polite!
HUH?
IS THAT HOW YOU ASK SOMEONE TO TEACH YOU?
JUST AS I FEARED, THEY BUTTED HEADS IMMEDIATELY.

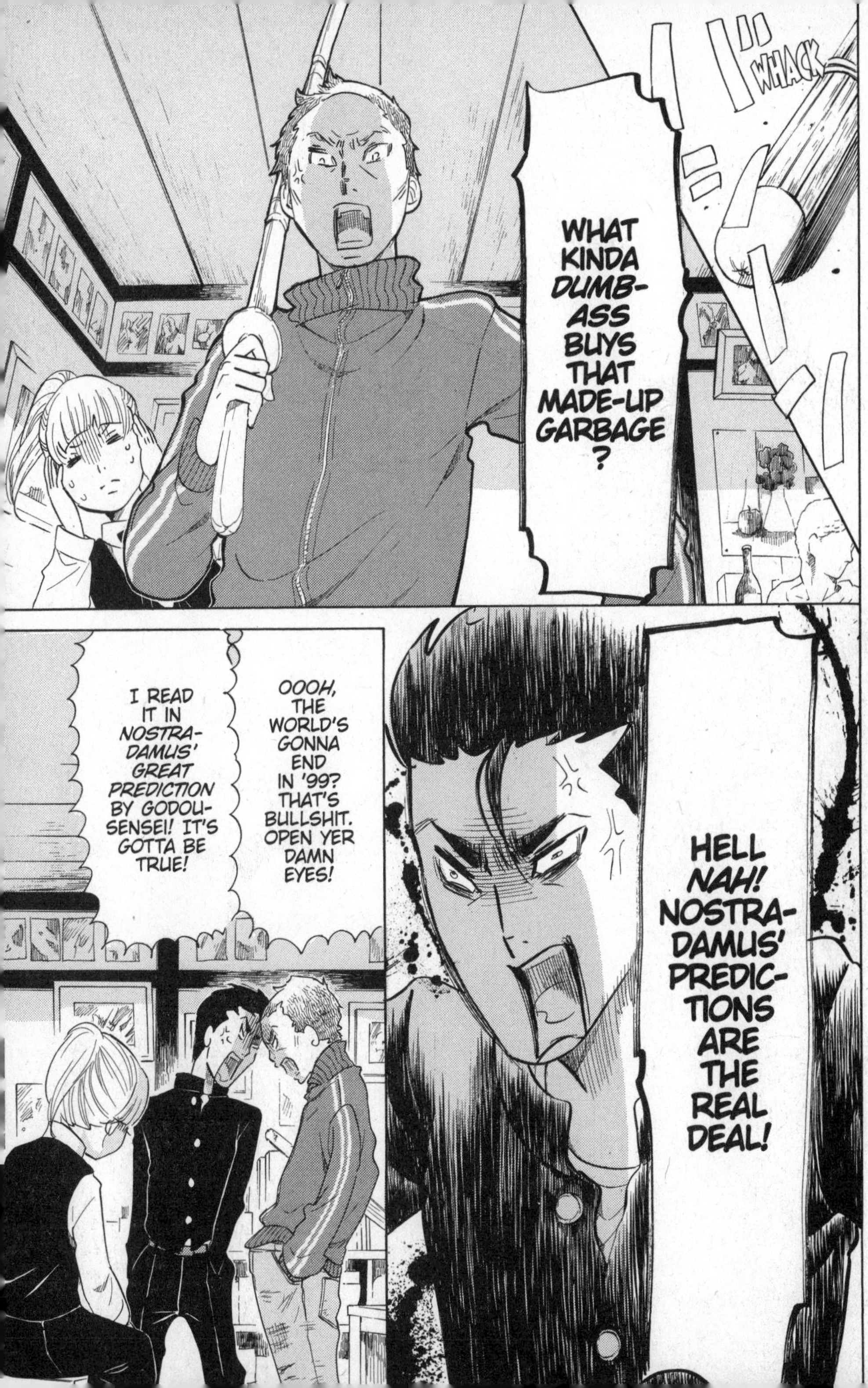
WHACK
WHAT KINDA DUMB-ASS BUYS THAT MADE-UP GARBAGE?
HELL NAH! NOSTRA-DAMUS' PREDIC-TIONS ARE THE REAL DEAL!
OOOH, THE WORLD'S GONNA END IN '99? THAT'S BULLSHIT. OPEN YER DAMN EYES!
I READ IT IN NOSTRA-DAMUS' GREAT PREDICTION BY GODOU-SENSEI! IT'S GOTTA BE TRUE!

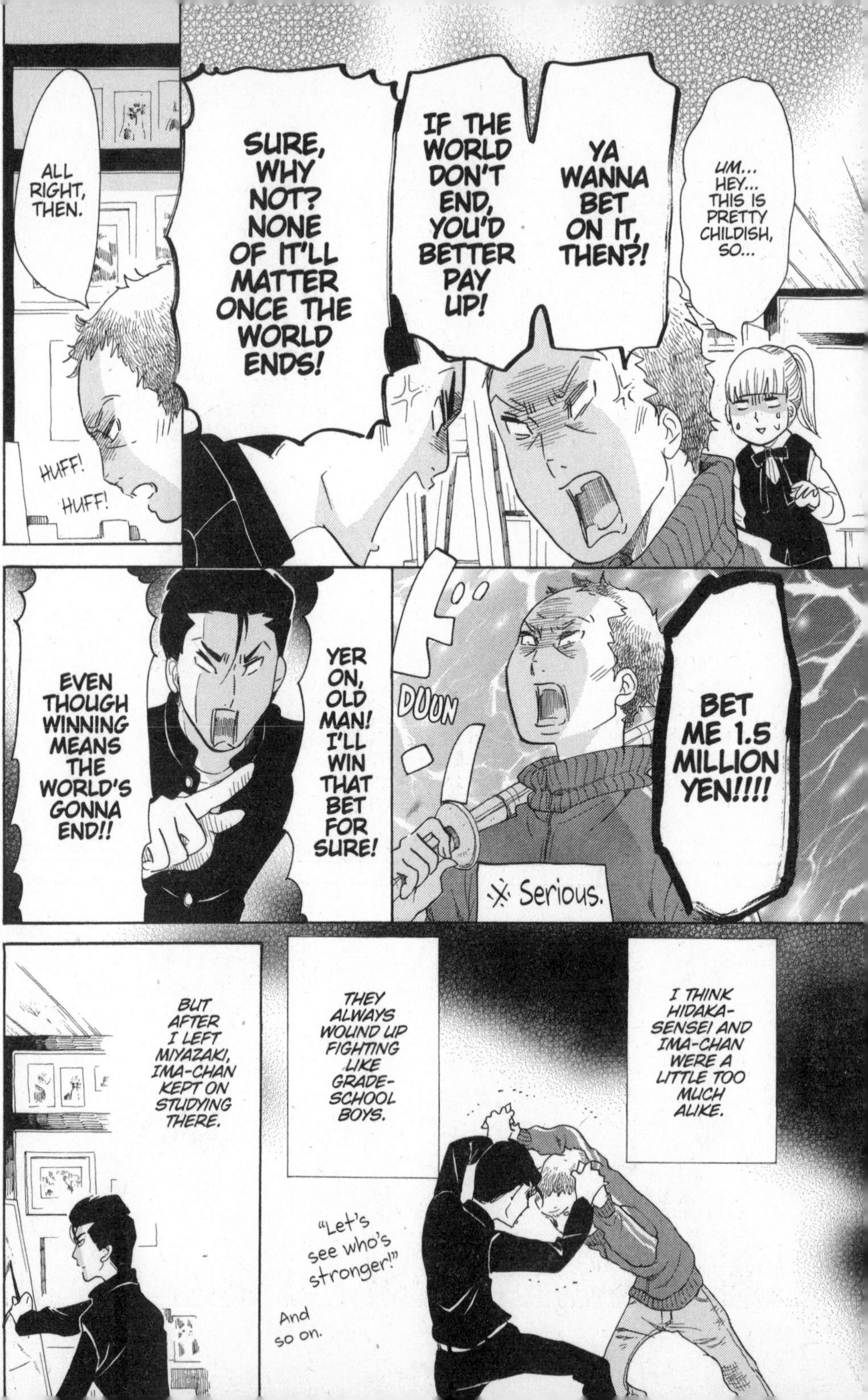
UM... HEY... THIS IS PRETTY CHILDISH, SO...
YA WANNA BET ON IT, THEN?!
IF THE WORLD DON'T END, YOU'D BETTER PAY UP!
SURE, WHY NOT? NONE OF IT'LL MATTER ONCE THE WORLD ENDS!
ALL RIGHT, THEN.
HUFF! HUFF!
BET ME 1.5 MILLION YEN!!!!
DUUN
※ Serious.
YER ON, OLD MAN! I'LL WIN THAT BET FOR SURE!
EVEN THOUGH WINNING MEANS THE WORLD'S GONNA END!!
I THINK HIDAKA-SENSEI AND IMA-CHAN WERE A LITTLE TOO MUCH ALIKE.
THEY ALWAYS WOUND UP FIGHTING LIKE GRADE-SCHOOL BOYS.
“Let's see who's stronger!”
And so on.
BUT AFTER I LEFT MIYAZAKI, IMA-CHAN KEPT ON STUDYING THERE.

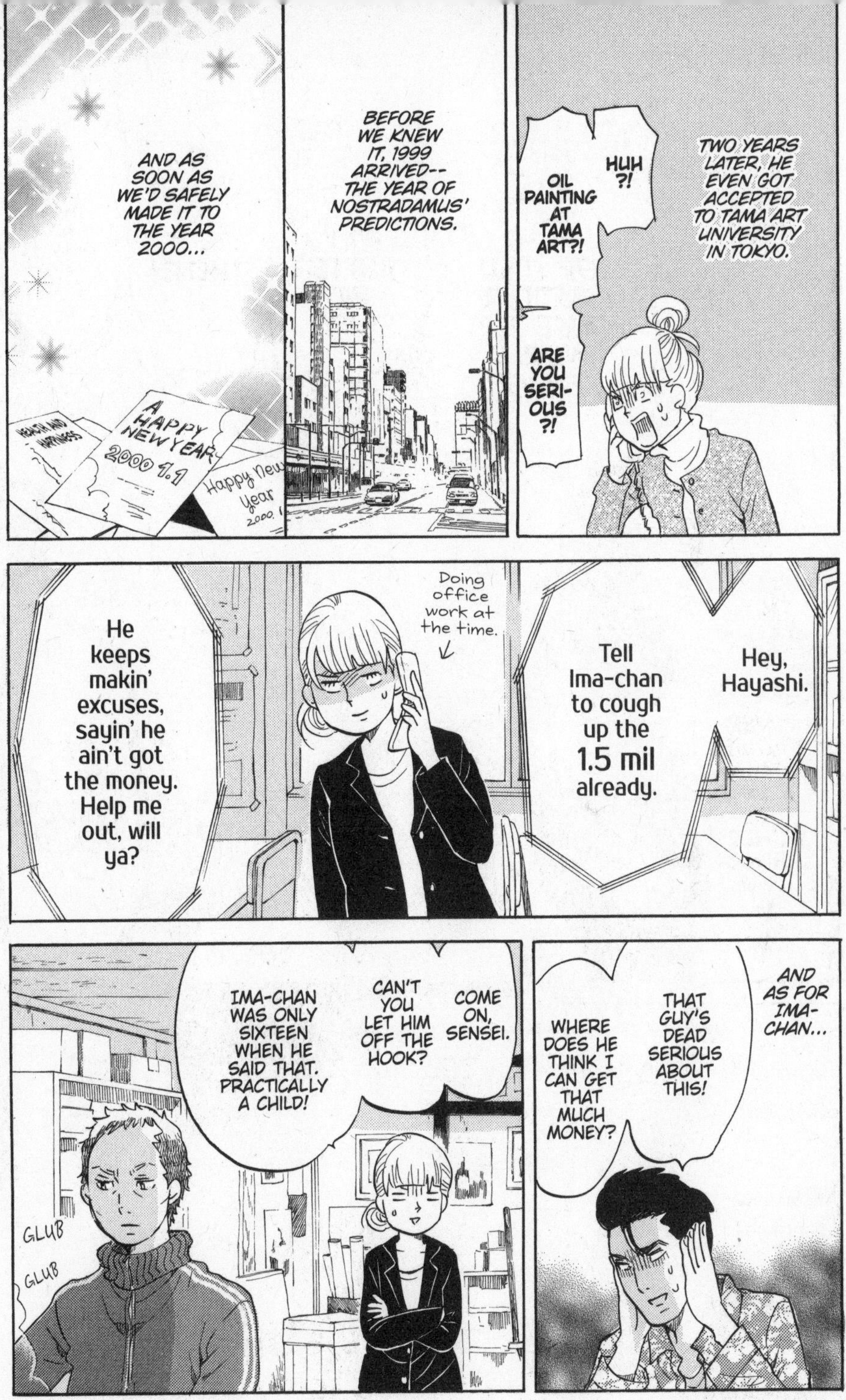
TWO YEARS LATER, HE EVEN GOT ACCEPTED TO TAMA ART UNIVERSITY IN TOKYO.
HUH?!
OIL PAINTING AT TAMA ART?!
ARE YOU SERIOUS?!
BEFORE WE KNEW IT, 1999 ARRIVED-- THE YEAR OF NOSTRADAMUS' PREDICTIONS.
AND AS SOON AS WE'D SAFELY MADE IT TO THE YEAR 2000...
HEALTH AND HAPPINESS
A HAPPY NEW YEAR 2000 1.1
Happy New Year 2000.
Hey, Hayashi.
Tell Ima-chan to cough up the 1.5 mil already.
Doing office work at the time.
He keeps makin' excuses, sayin' he ain't got the money. Help me out, will ya?
AND AS FOR IMA-CHAN...
THAT GUY'S DEAD SERIOUS ABOUT THIS!
WHERE DOES HE THINK I CAN GET THAT MUCH MONEY?
COME ON, SENSEI.
CAN'T YOU LET HIM OFF THE HOOK?
IMA-CHAN WAS ONLY SIXTEEN WHEN HE SAID THAT. PRACTICALLY A CHILD!
GLUB
GLUB

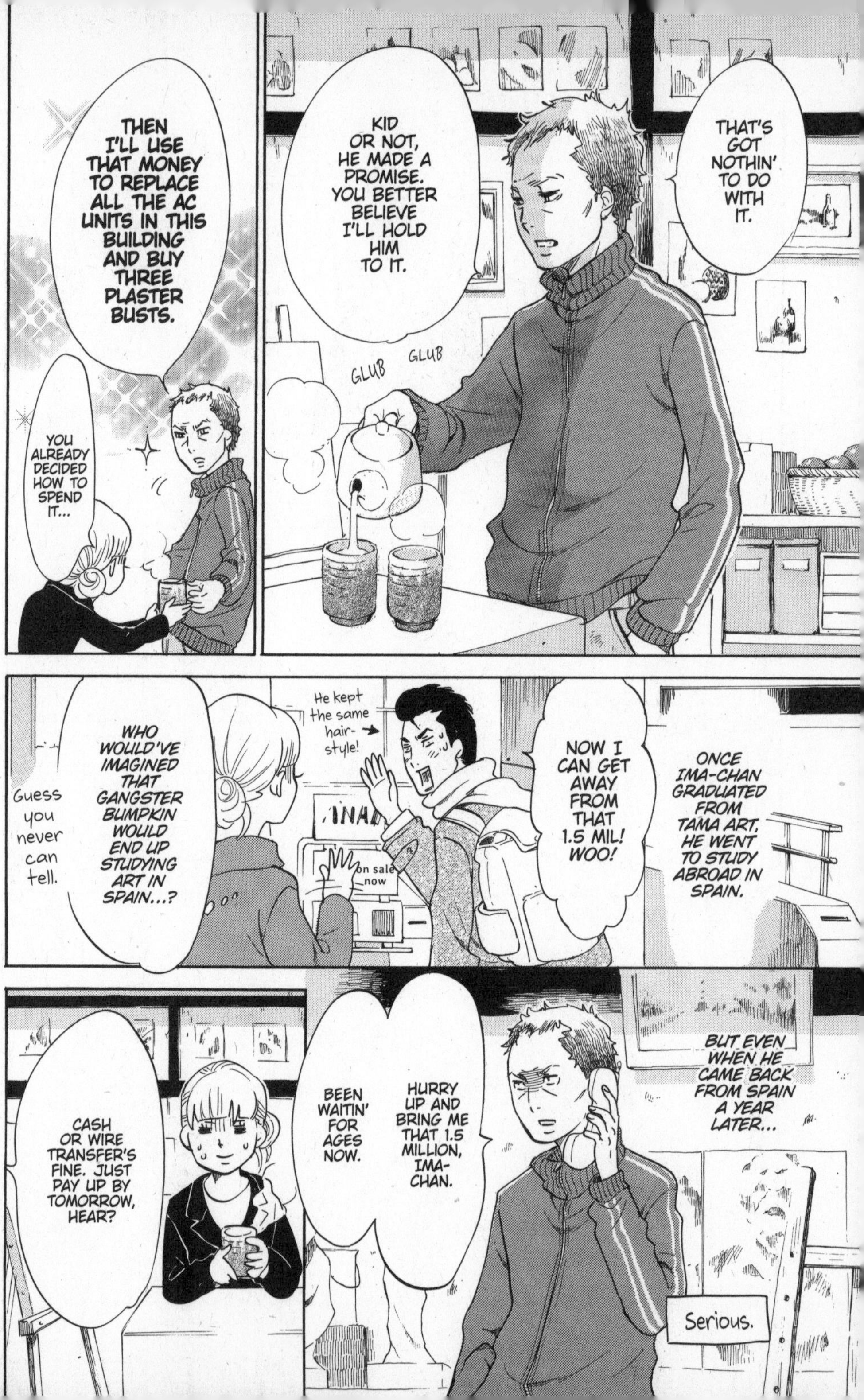
THAT'S GOT NOTHIN' TO DO WITH IT.
KID OR NOT, HE MADE A PROMISE. YOU BETTER BELIEVE I'LL HOLD HIM TO IT.
GLUB GLUB
THEN I'LL USE THAT MONEY TO REPLACE ALL THE AC UNITS IN THIS BUILDING AND BUY THREE PLASTER BUSTS.
YOU ALREADY DECIDED HOW TO SPEND IT...
ONCE IMA-CHAN GRADUATED FROM TAMA ART, HE WENT TO STUDY ABROAD IN SPAIN.
NOW I CAN GET AWAY FROM THAT 1.5 MIL! WOO!
He kept the same hair-style!
on sale now
WHO WOULD'VE IMAGINED THAT GANGSTER BUMPKIN WOULD END UP STUDYING ART IN SPAIN...?
Guess you never can tell.
BUT EVEN WHEN HE CAME BACK FROM SPAIN A YEAR LATER...
HURRY UP AND BRING ME THAT 1.5 MILLION, IMA-CHAN.
BEEN WAITIN' FOR AGES NOW.
CASH OR WIRE TRANSFER'S FINE. JUST PAY UP BY TOMORROW, HEAR?
Serious.

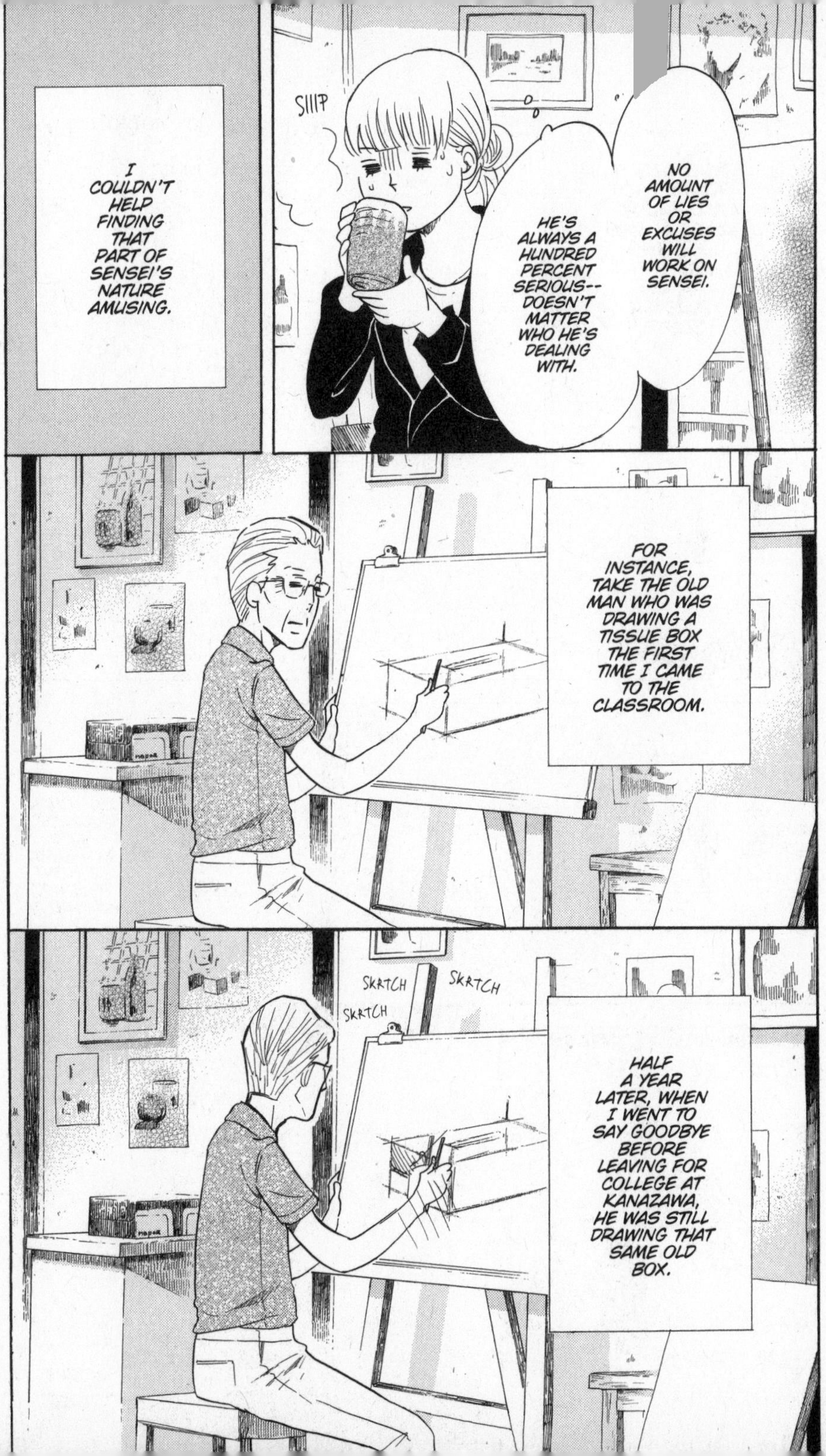
NO AMOUNT OF LIES OR EXCUSES WILL WORK ON SENSEI.
HE'S ALWAYS A HUNDRED PERCENT SERIOUS-- DOESN'T MATTER WHO HE'S DEALING WITH.
SIIIP
I COULDN'T HELP FINDING THAT PART OF SENSEI'S NATURE AMUSING.
FOR INSTANCE, TAKE THE OLD MAN WHO WAS DRAWING A TISSUE BOX THE FIRST TIME I CAME TO THE CLASSROOM.
HALF A YEAR LATER, WHEN I WENT TO SAY GOODBYE BEFORE LEAVING FOR COLLEGE AT KANAZAWA, HE WAS STILL DRAWING THAT SAME OLD BOX.
SKRTCH
SKRTCH
SKRTCH

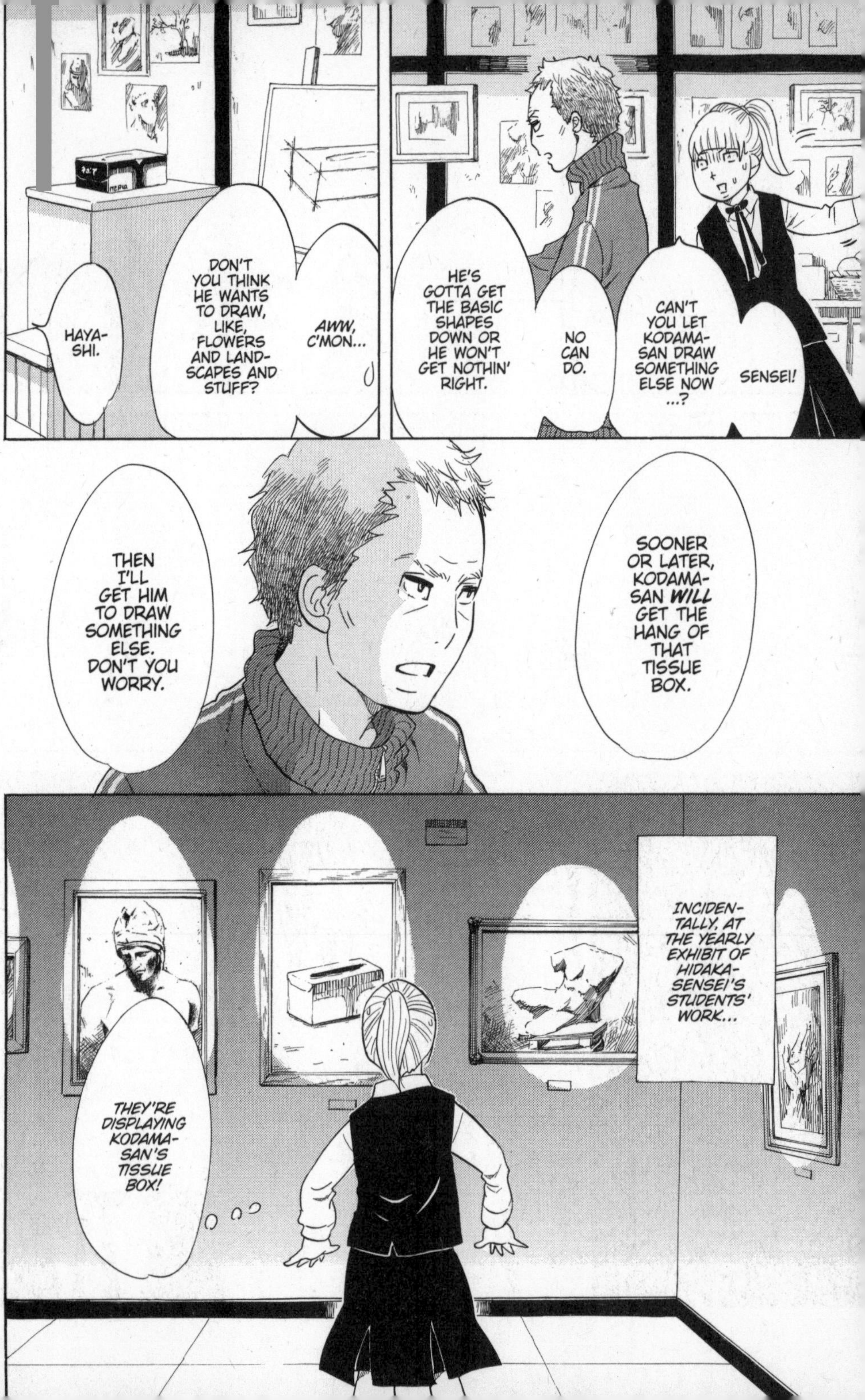
SENSEI!
CAN'T YOU LET KODAMA-SAN DRAW SOMETHING ELSE NOW ...?
NO CAN DO.
HE'S GOTTA GET THE BASIC SHAPES DOWN OR HE WON'T GET NOTHIN' RIGHT.
AWW, C'MON...
DON'T YOU THINK HE WANTS TO DRAW, LIKE, FLOWERS AND LAND-SCAPES AND STUFF?
HAYA-SHI.
SOONER OR LATER, KODAMA-SAN WILL GET THE HANG OF THAT TISSUE BOX.
THEN I'LL GET HIM TO DRAW SOMETHING ELSE. DON'T YOU WORRY.
INCIDEN-TALLY, AT THE YEARLY EXHIBIT OF HIDAKA-SENSEI'S STUDENTS' WORK...
THEY'RE DISPLAYING KODAMA-SAN'S TISSUE BOX!

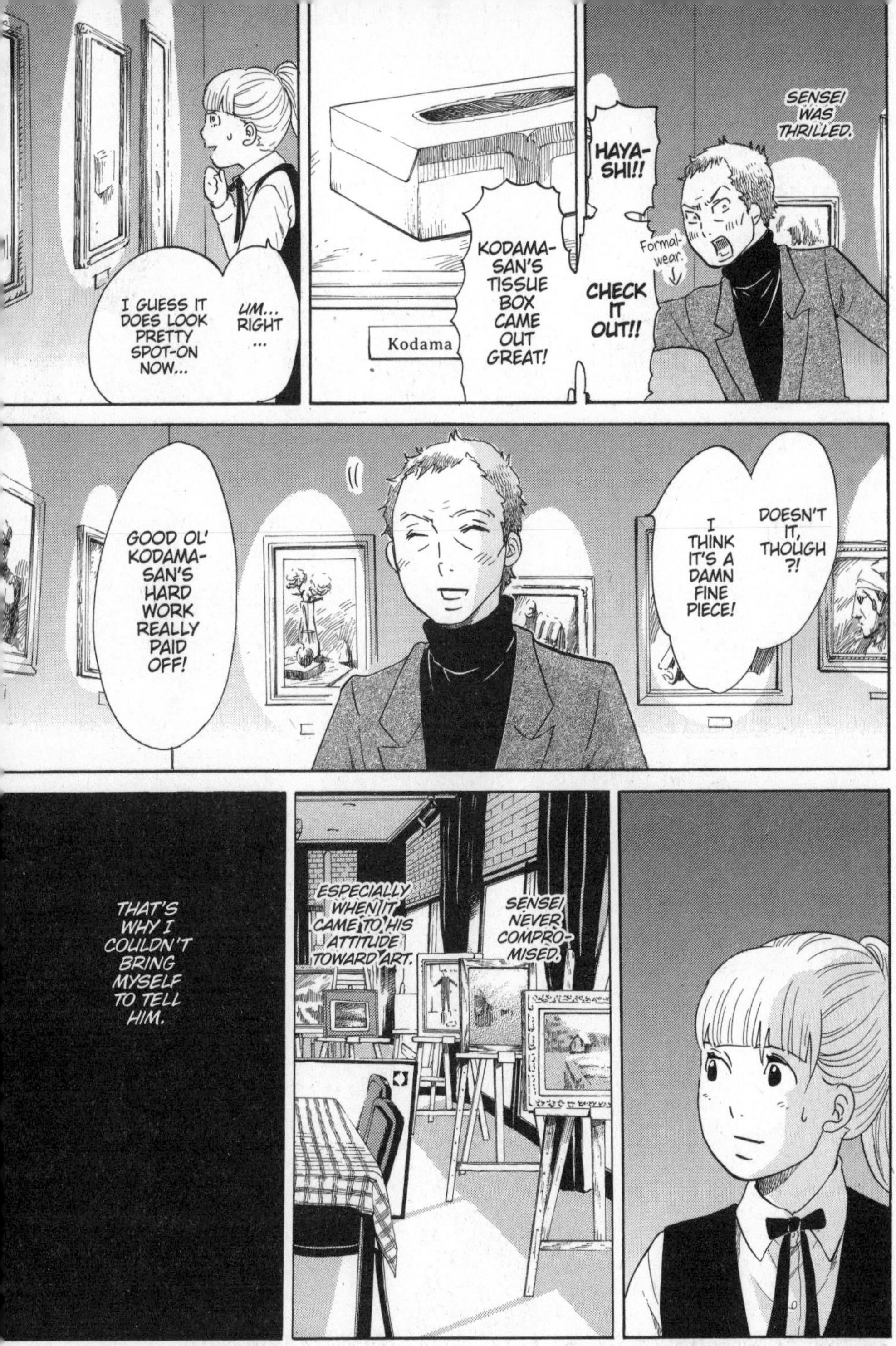
SENSEI WAS THRILLED.
HAYA-SHI!!
CHECK IT OUT!!
Formal-wear.
KODAMA-SAN'S TISSUE BOX CAME OUT GREAT!
Kodama
UM... RIGHT ...
I GUESS IT DOES LOOK PRETTY SPOT-ON NOW...
DOESN'T IT, THOUGH ?!
I THINK IT'S A DAMN FINE PIECE!
GOOD OL' KODAMA-SAN'S HARD WORK REALLY PAID OFF!
SENSEI NEVER COMPROMISED.
ESPECIALLY WHEN IT CAME TO HIS ATTITUDE TOWARD ART.
THAT'S WHY I COULDN'T BRING MYSELF TO TELL HIM.

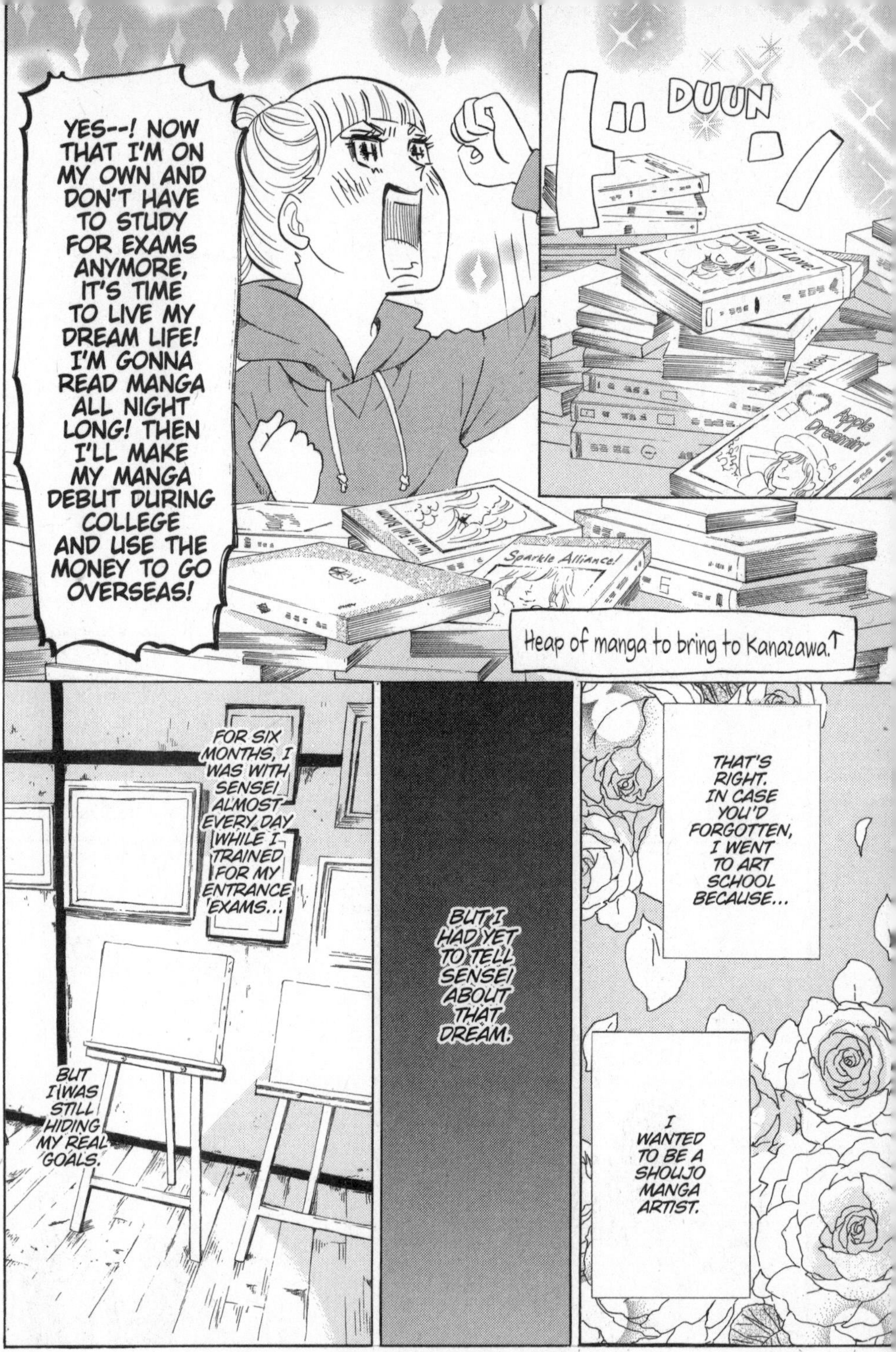
DUUN
Full of Love!
Apple Dreamin'
Sparkle Alliance!
YES--! NOW THAT I'M ON MY OWN AND DON'T HAVE TO STUDY FOR EXAMS ANYMORE, IT'S TIME TO LIVE MY DREAM LIFE! I'M GONNA READ MANGA ALL NIGHT LONG! THEN I'LL MAKE MY MANGA DEBUT DURING COLLEGE AND USE THE MONEY TO GO OVERSEAS!
Heap of manga to bring to Kanazawa.↑
THAT'S RIGHT. IN CASE YOU'D FORGOTTEN, I WENT TO ART SCHOOL BECAUSE...
I WANTED TO BE A SHOUJO MANGA ARTIST.
BUT I HAD YET TO TELL SENSEI ABOUT THAT DREAM.
FOR SIX MONTHS, I WAS WITH SENSEI ALMOST EVERY DAY WHILE I TRAINED FOR MY ENTRANCE EXAMS...
BUT I WAS STILL HIDING MY REAL GOALS.

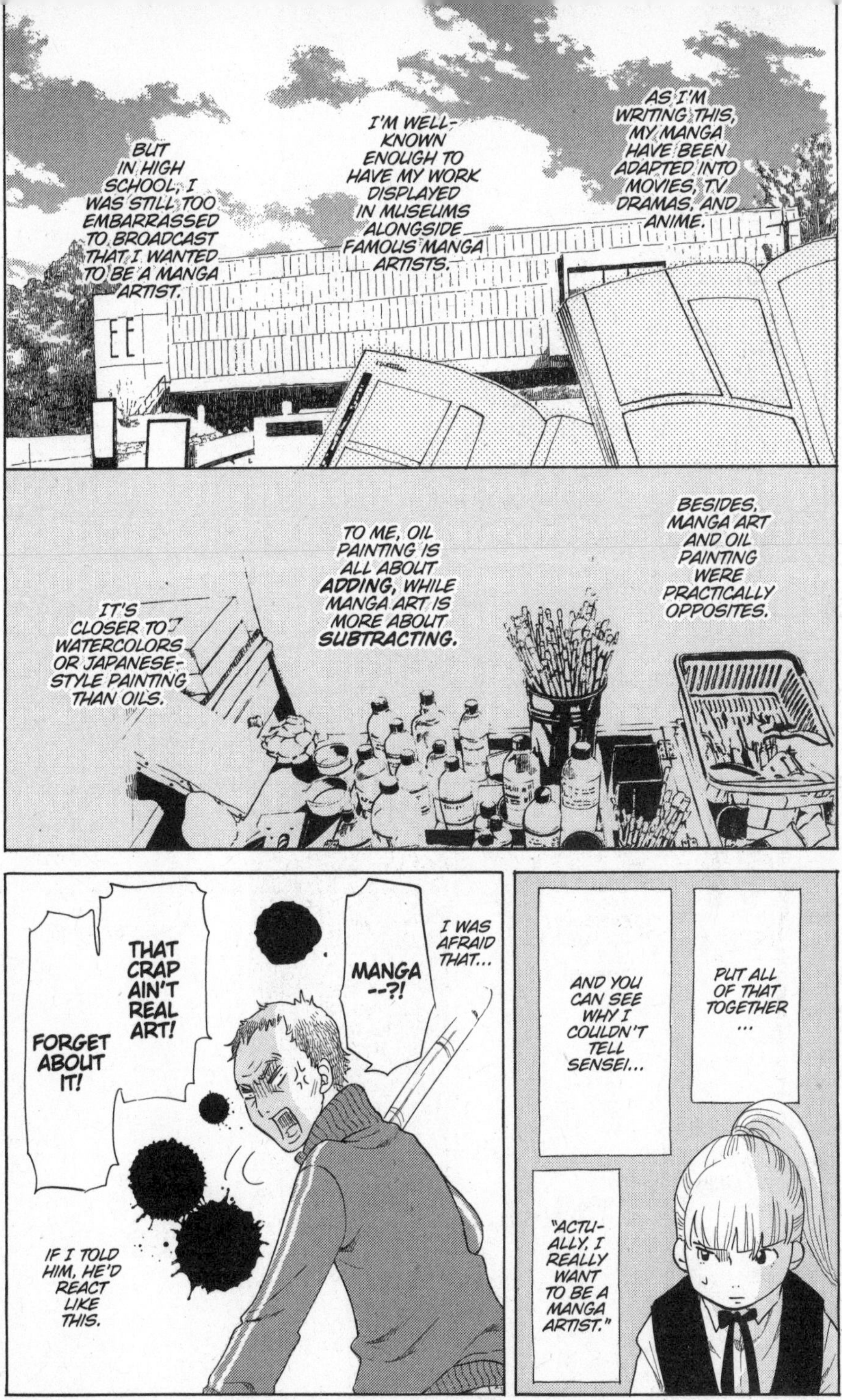
AS I'M WRITING THIS, MY MANGA HAVE BEEN ADAPTED INTO MOVIES, TV DRAMAS, AND ANIME.
I'M WELL-KNOWN ENOUGH TO HAVE MY WORK DISPLAYED IN MUSEUMS ALONGSIDE FAMOUS MANGA ARTISTS.
BUT IN HIGH SCHOOL, I WAS STILL TOO EMBARRASSED TO BROADCAST THAT I WANTED TO BE A MANGA ARTIST.
BESIDES, MANGA ART AND OIL PAINTING WERE PRACTICALLY OPPOSITES.
TO ME, OIL PAINTING IS ALL ABOUT **ADDING**, WHILE MANGA ART IS MORE ABOUT **SUBTRACTING**.
IT'S CLOSER TO WATERCOLORS OR JAPANESE-STYLE PAINTING THAN OILS.
PUT ALL OF THAT TOGETHER ...
AND YOU CAN SEE WHY I COULDN'T TELL SENSEI...
"ACTU-ALLY, I REALLY WANT TO BE A MANGA ARTIST."
I WAS AFRAID THAT...
MANGA --?!
THAT CRAP AIN'T REAL ART!
FORGET ABOUT IT!
IF I TOLD HIM, HE'D REACT LIKE THIS.

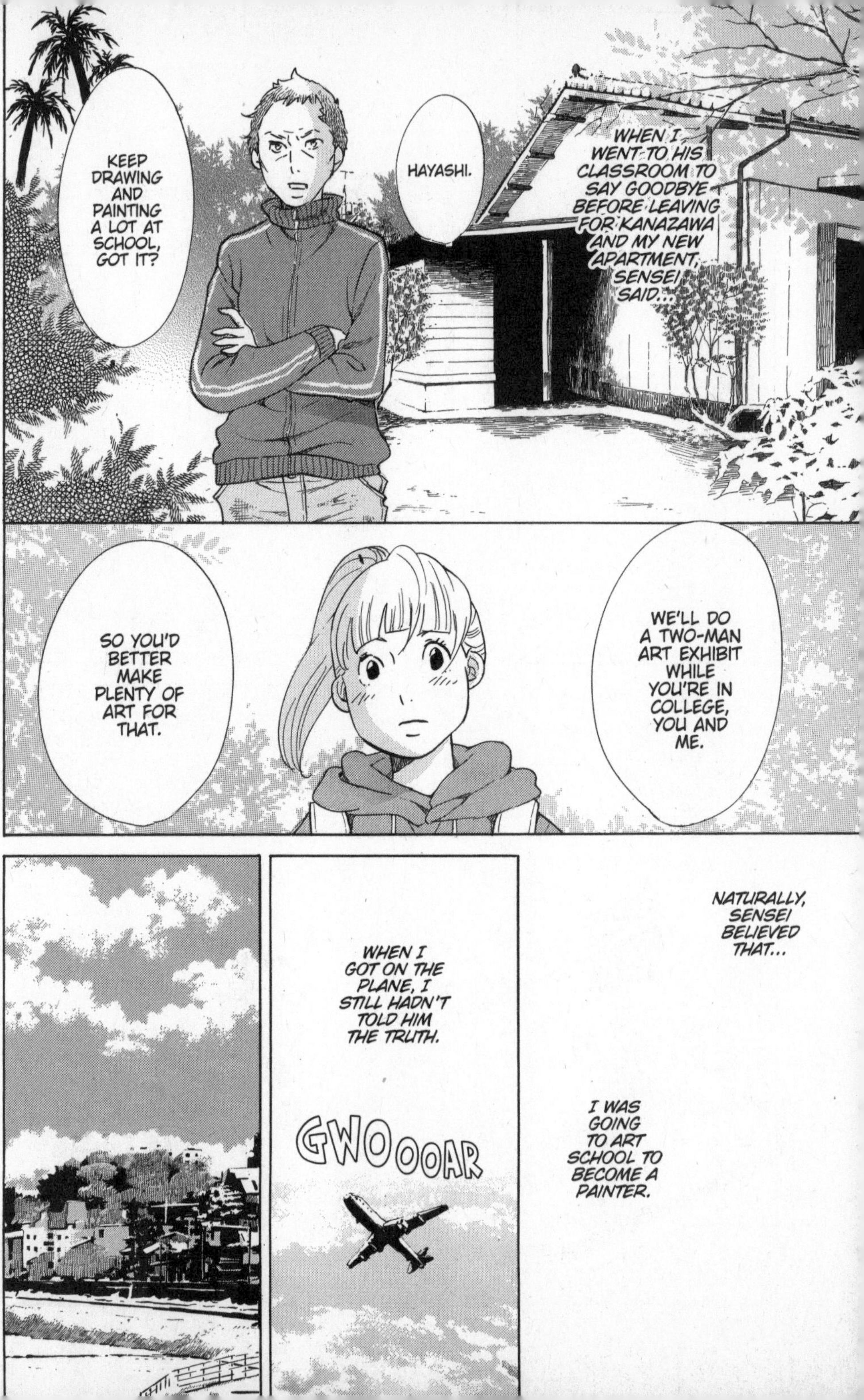
WHEN I WENT TO HIS CLASSROOM TO SAY GOODBYE BEFORE LEAVING FOR KANAZAWA AND MY NEW APARTMENT, SENSEI SAID...
HAYASHI.
KEEP DRAWING AND PAINTING A LOT AT SCHOOL, GOT IT?
WE'LL DO A TWO-MAN ART EXHIBIT WHILE YOU'RE IN COLLEGE, YOU AND ME.
SO YOU'D BETTER MAKE PLENTY OF ART FOR THAT.
NATURALLY, SENSEI BELIEVED THAT...
I WAS GOING TO ART SCHOOL TO BECOME A PAINTER.
WHEN I GOT ON THE PLANE, I STILL HADN'T TOLD HIM THE TRUTH.
GWOoooAR

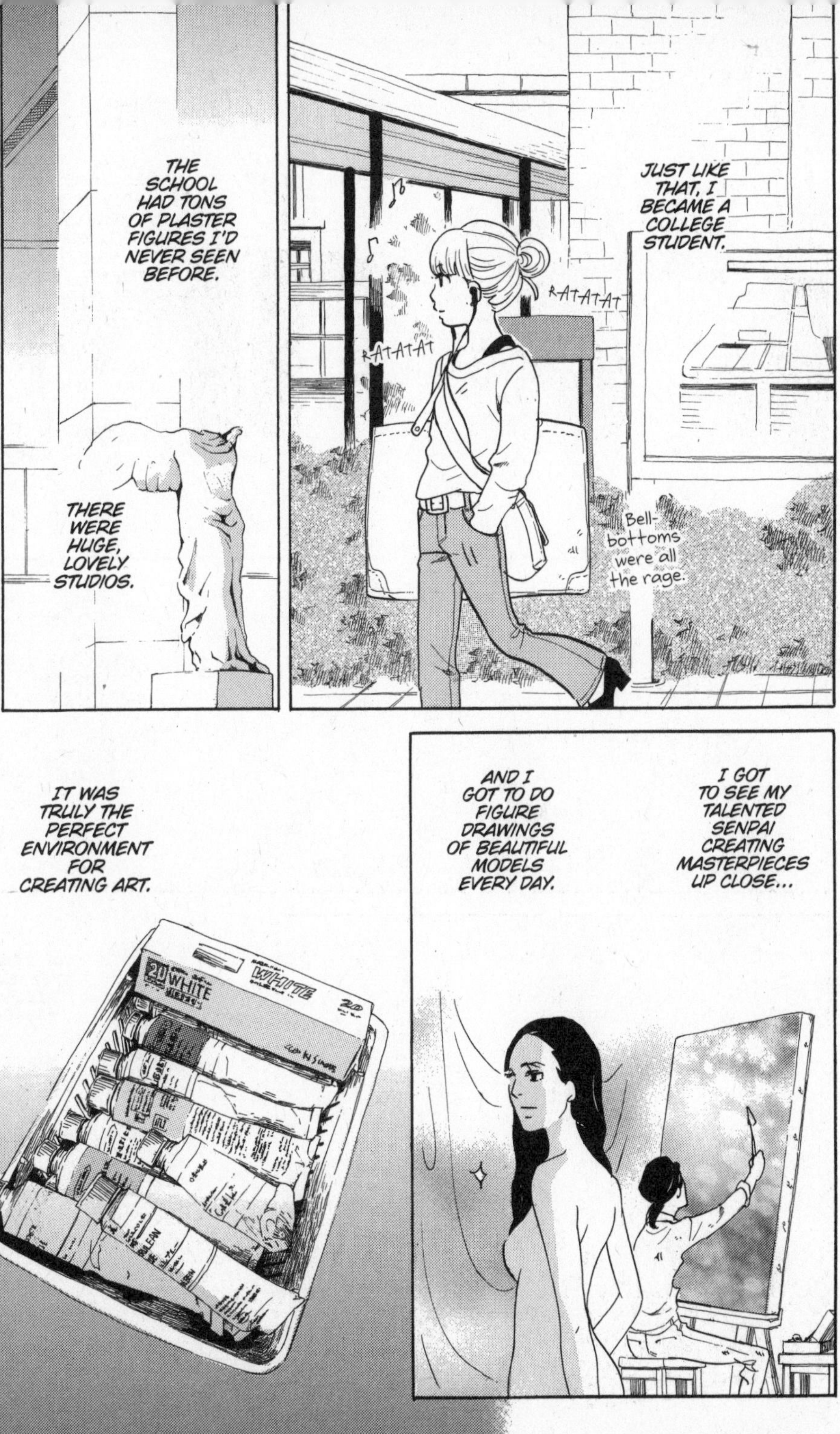
JUST LIKE THAT, I BECAME A COLLEGE STUDENT.
RATATAT
RATATAT
Bell-bottoms were all the rage.
THE SCHOOL HAD TONS OF PLASTER FIGURES I'D NEVER SEEN BEFORE.
THERE WERE HUGE, LOVELY STUDIOS.
I GOT TO SEE MY TALENTED SENPAI CREATING MASTERPIECES UP CLOSE...
AND I GOT TO DO FIGURE DRAWINGS OF BEAUTIFUL MODELS EVERY DAY.
IT WAS TRULY THE PERFECT ENVIRONMENT FOR CREATING ART.
WHITE

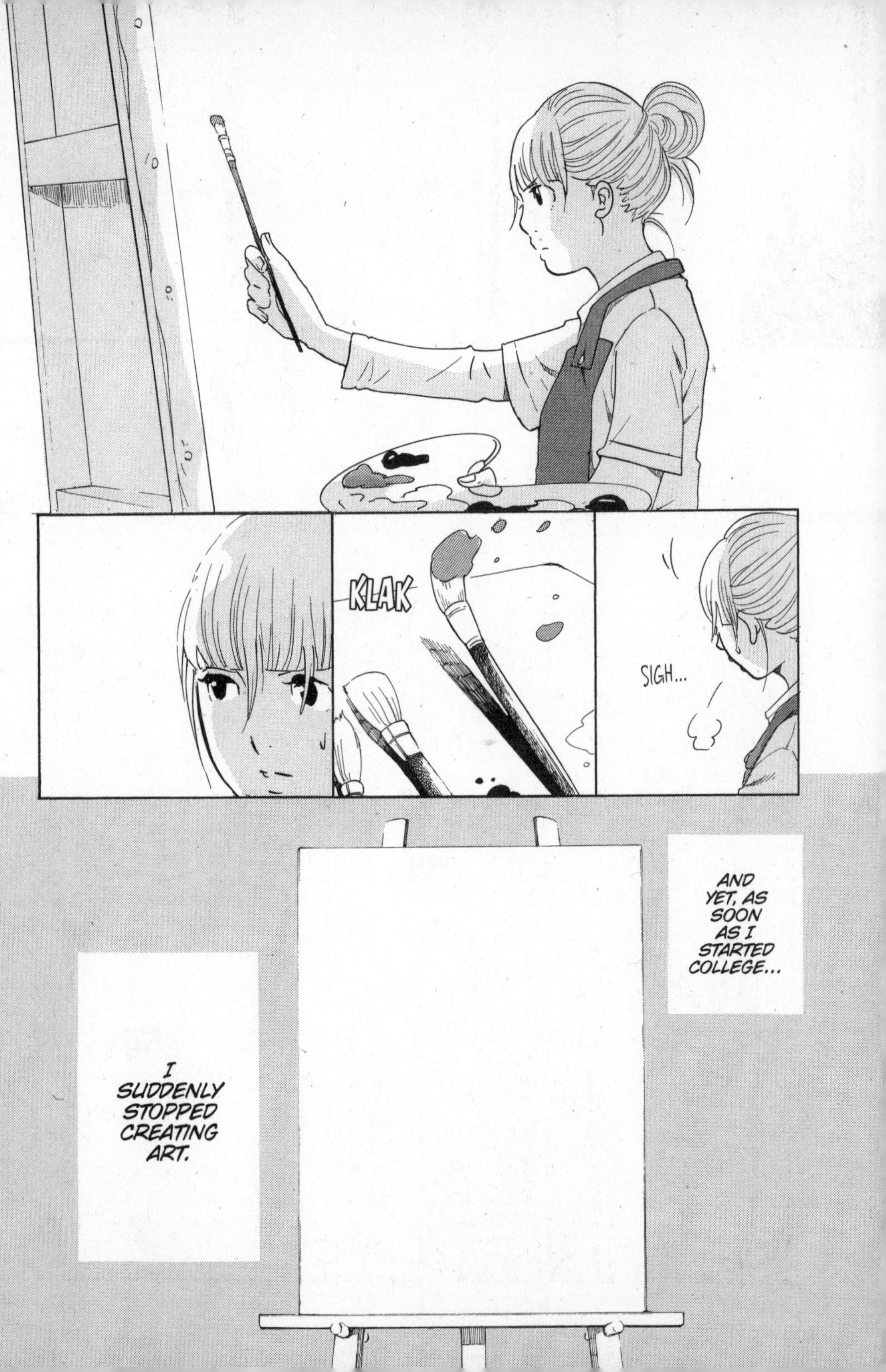
SIGH...
KLAK
AND YET, AS SOON AS I STARTED COLLEGE...
I SUDDENLY STOPPED CREATING ART.

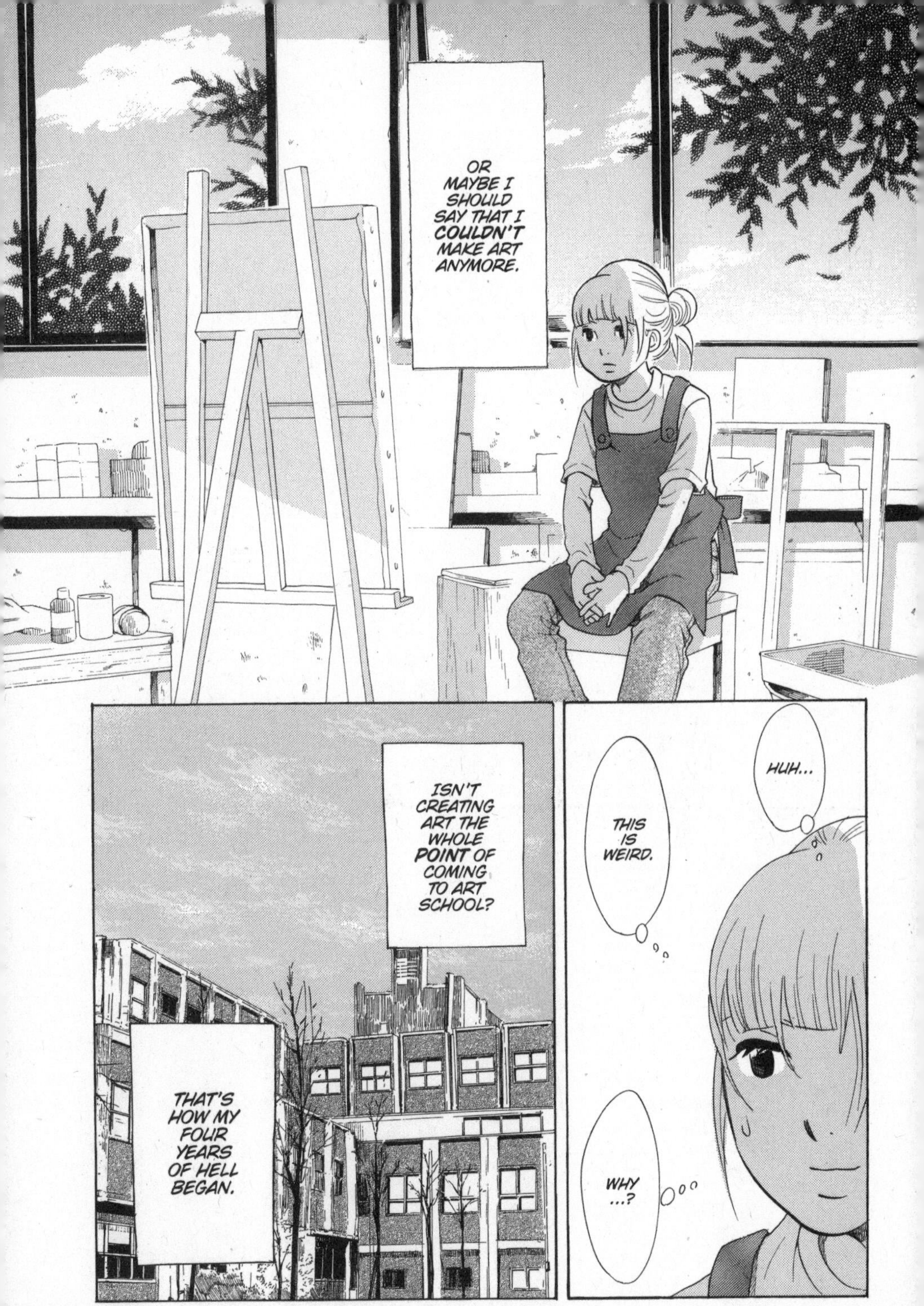
OR MAYBE I SHOULD SAY THAT I COULDN'T MAKE ART ANYMORE.
HUH...
THIS IS WEIRD.
WHY ...?
ISN'T CREATING ART THE WHOLE POINT OF COMING TO ART SCHOOL?
THAT'S HOW MY FOUR YEARS OF HELL BEGAN.

Blank Canvas

My So-Called
Artist's Journey

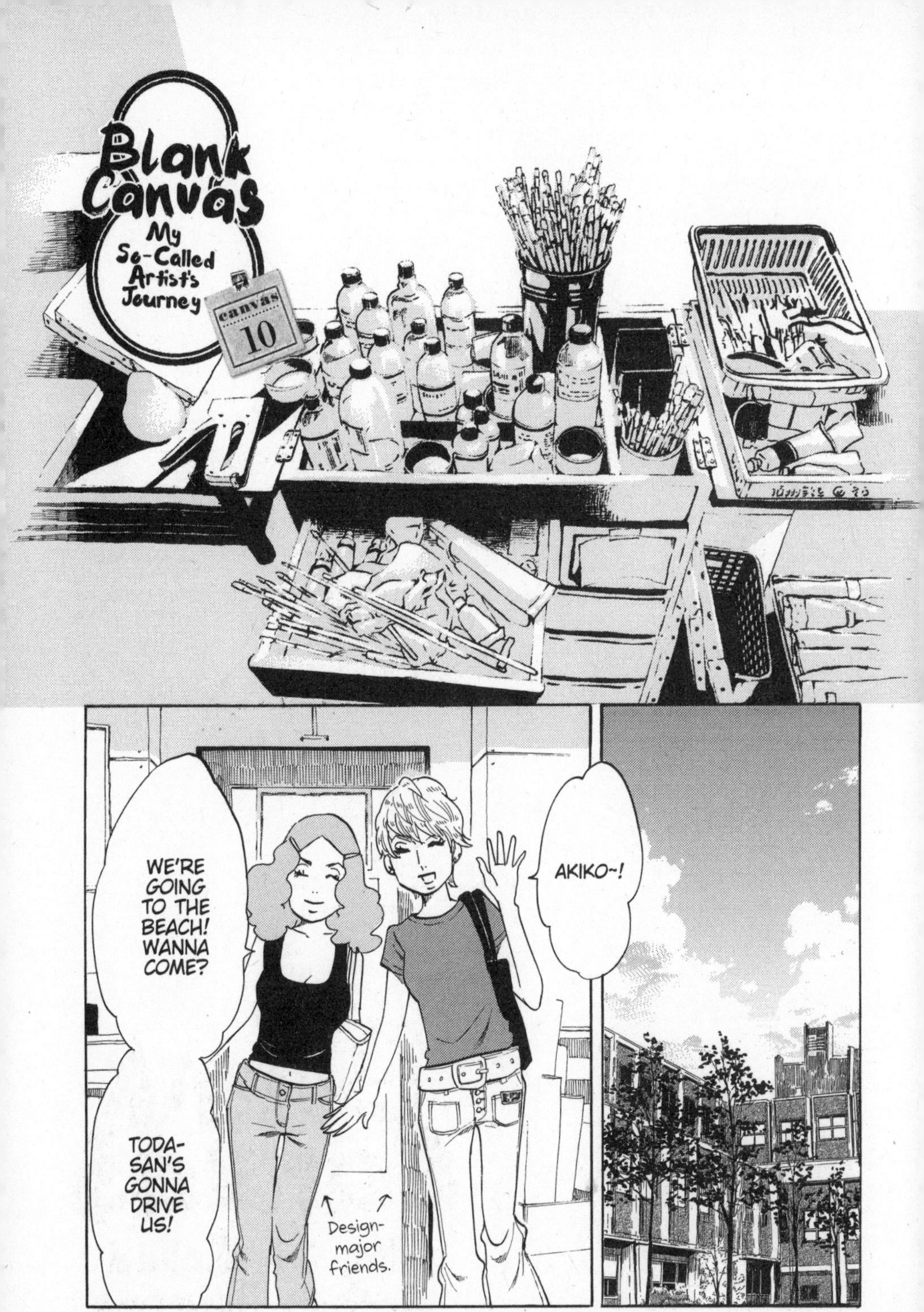
Blank Canvas
My So-Called Artist's Journey
canvas 10
AKIKO~!
WE'RE GOING TO THE BEACH! WANNA COME?
TODA-SAN'S GONNA DRIVE US!
Design-major friends.

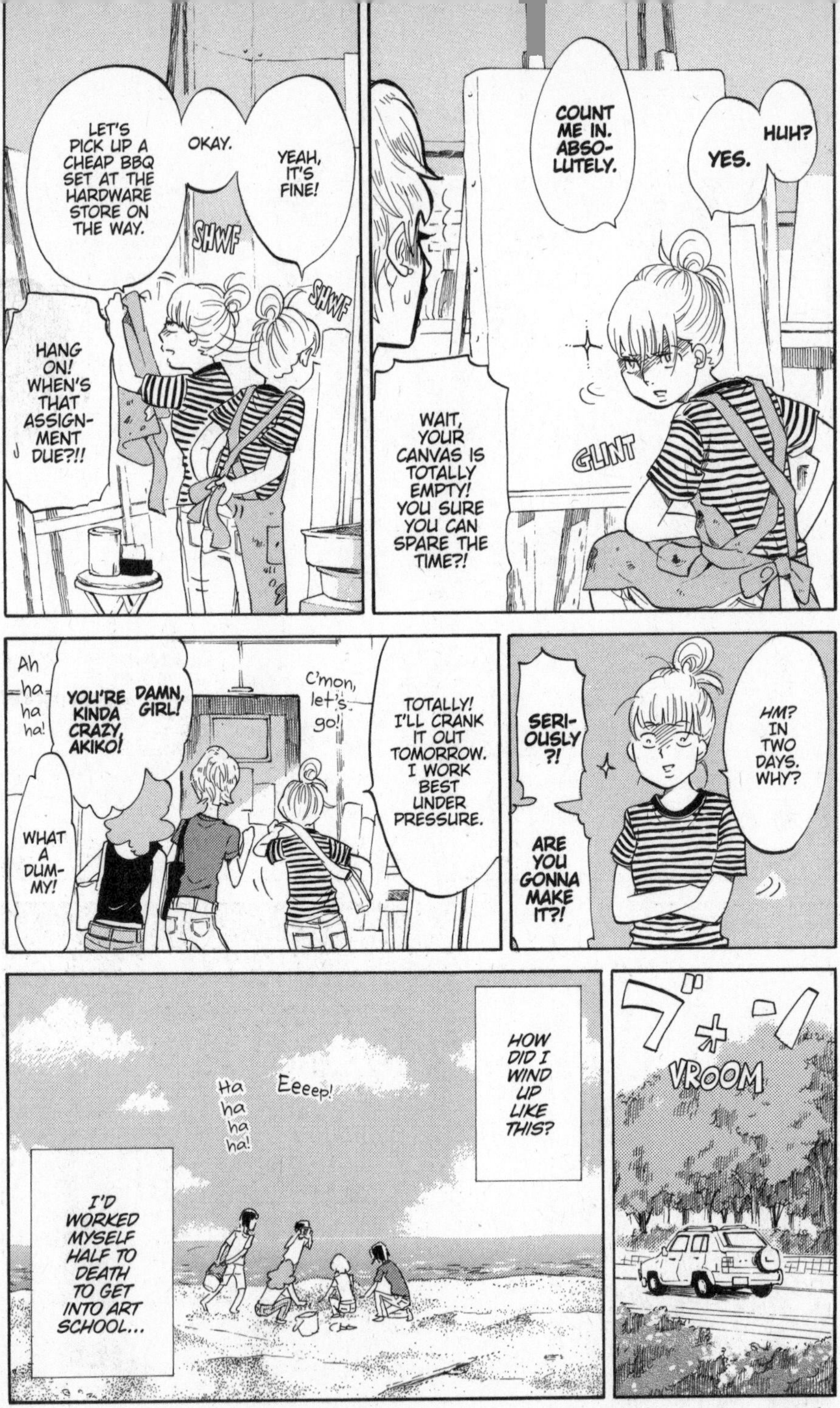
HUH?
YES.
COUNT ME IN. ABSOLUTELY.
WAIT, YOUR CANVAS IS TOTALLY EMPTY! YOU SURE YOU CAN SPARE THE TIME?!
GLINT
YEAH, IT'S FINE!
OKAY.
LET'S PICK UP A CHEAP BBQ SET AT THE HARDWARE STORE ON THE WAY.
SHWF
SHWF
HANG ON! WHEN'S THAT ASSIGNMENT DUE?!!
HM? IN TWO DAYS. WHY?
SERIOUSLY?!
ARE YOU GONNA MAKE IT?!
TOTALLY! I'LL CRANK IT OUT TOMORROW. I WORK BEST UNDER PRESSURE.
C'mon, let's go!
DAMN, GIRL!
YOU'RE KINDA CRAZY, AKIKO!
Ah ha ha ha!
WHAT A DUMMY!
ブォーン
VROOM
HOW DID I WIND UP LIKE THIS?
Eeeep!
Ha ha ha ha!
I'D WORKED MYSELF HALF TO DEATH TO GET INTO ART SCHOOL...

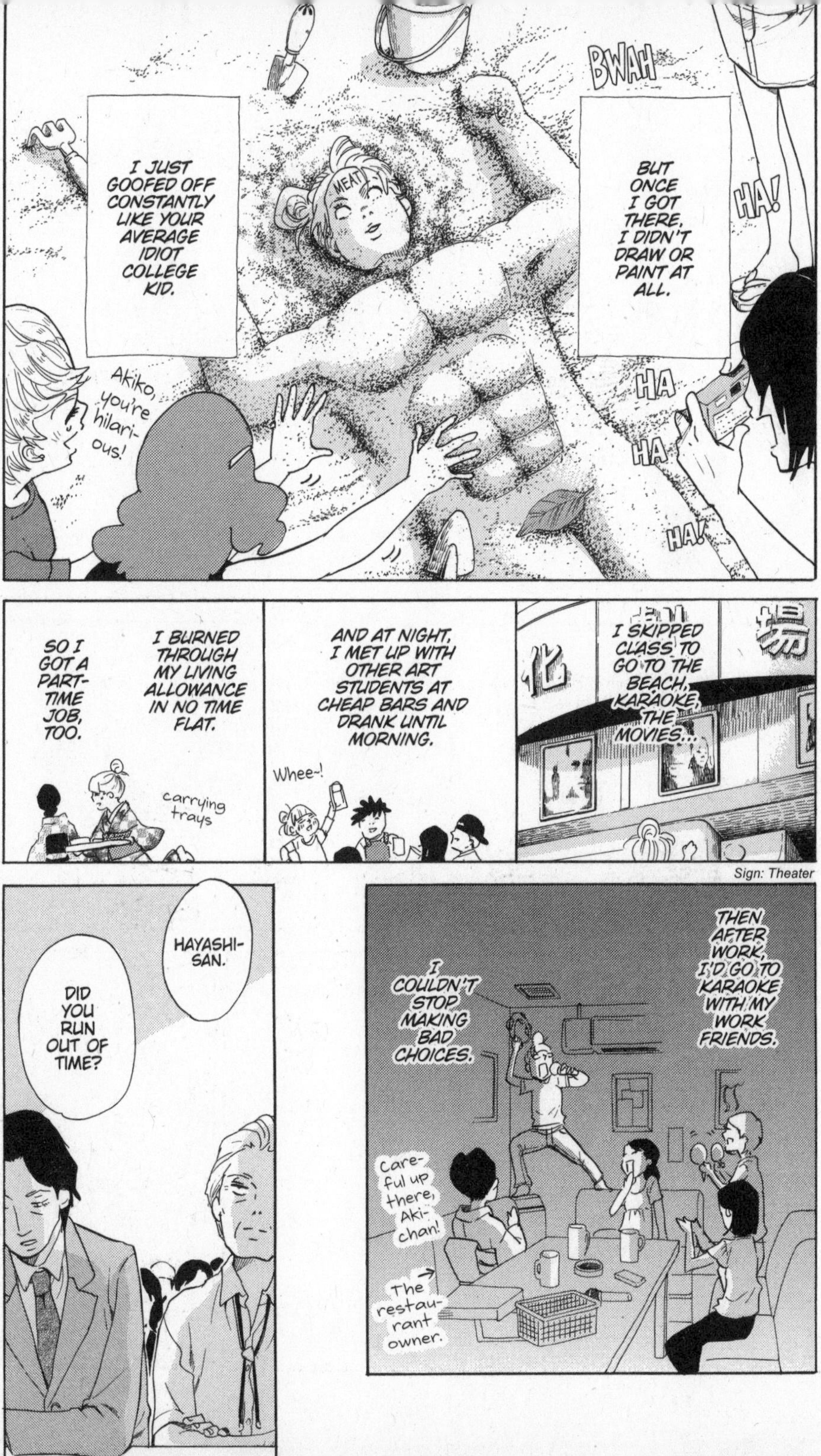
BWAH
BUT ONCE I GOT THERE, I DIDN'T DRAW OR PAINT AT ALL.
HA!
I JUST GOOFED OFF CONSTANTLY LIKE YOUR AVERAGE IDIOT COLLEGE KID.
MEAT
HA
HA
HA!
Akiko, you're hilarious!
I SKIPPED CLASS TO GO TO THE BEACH, KARAOKE, THE MOVIES...
AND AT NIGHT, I MET UP WITH OTHER ART STUDENTS AT CHEAP BARS AND DRANK UNTIL MORNING.
Whee-!
I BURNED THROUGH MY LIVING ALLOWANCE IN NO TIME FLAT.
SO I GOT A PART-TIME JOB, TOO.
carrying trays
Sign: Theater
THEN AFTER WORK, I'D GO TO KARAOKE WITH MY WORK FRIENDS.
I COULDN'T STOP MAKING BAD CHOICES.
Careful up there, Aki-chan!
The restaurant owner.
HAYASHI-SAN.
DID YOU RUN OUT OF TIME?

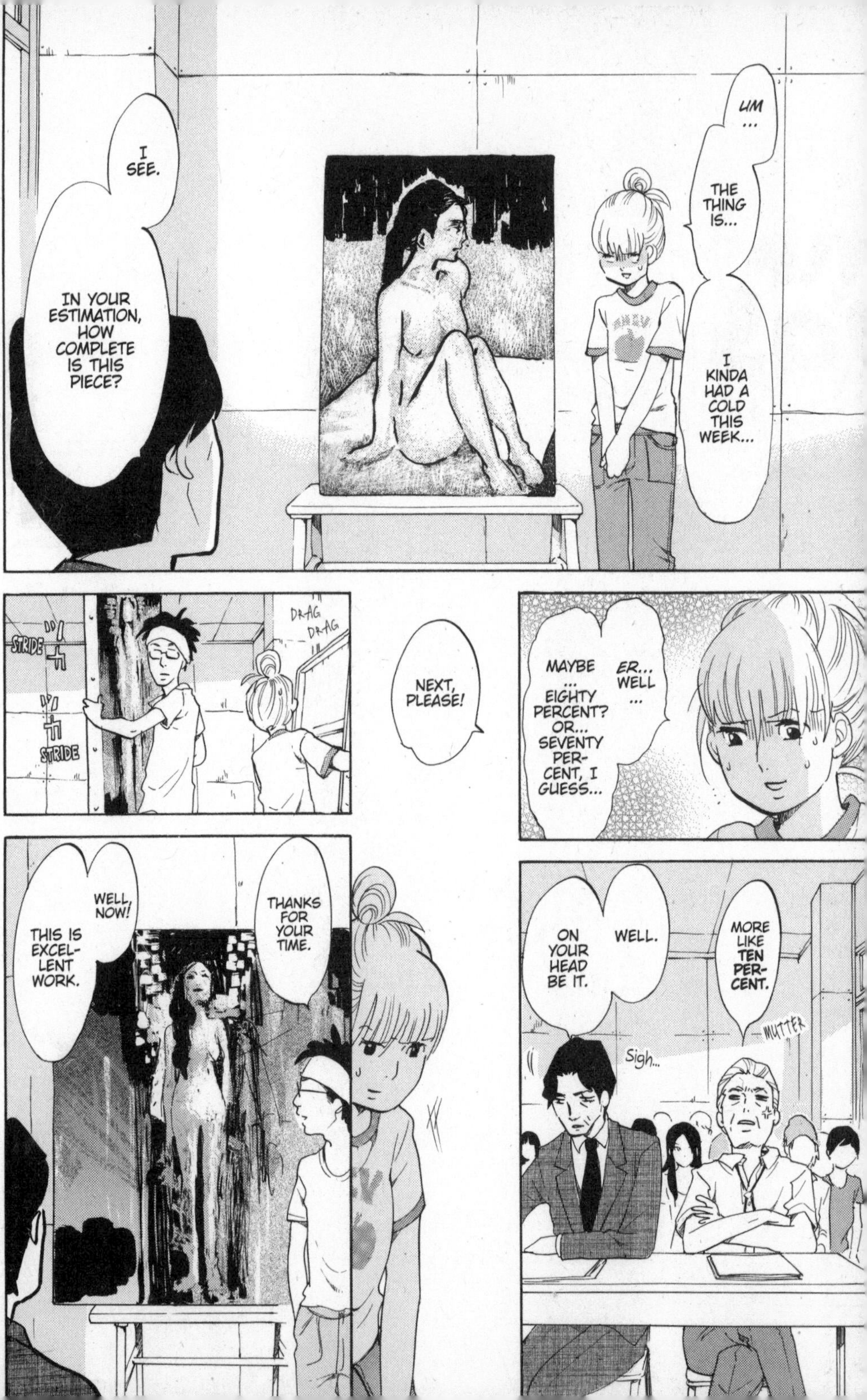

UM...
THE THING IS...
I KINDA HAD A COLD THIS WEEK...
I SEE.
IN YOUR ESTIMATION, HOW COMPLETE IS THIS PIECE?
ER... WELL...
MAYBE... EIGHTY PERCENT? OR... SEVENTY PERCENT, I GUESS...
NEXT, PLEASE!
DRAG DRAG
STRIDE
STRIDE
MORE LIKE TEN PERCENT.
MUTTER
WELL.
ON YOUR HEAD BE IT.
Sigh...
THANKS FOR YOUR TIME.
WELL, NOW!
THIS IS EXCELLENT WORK.

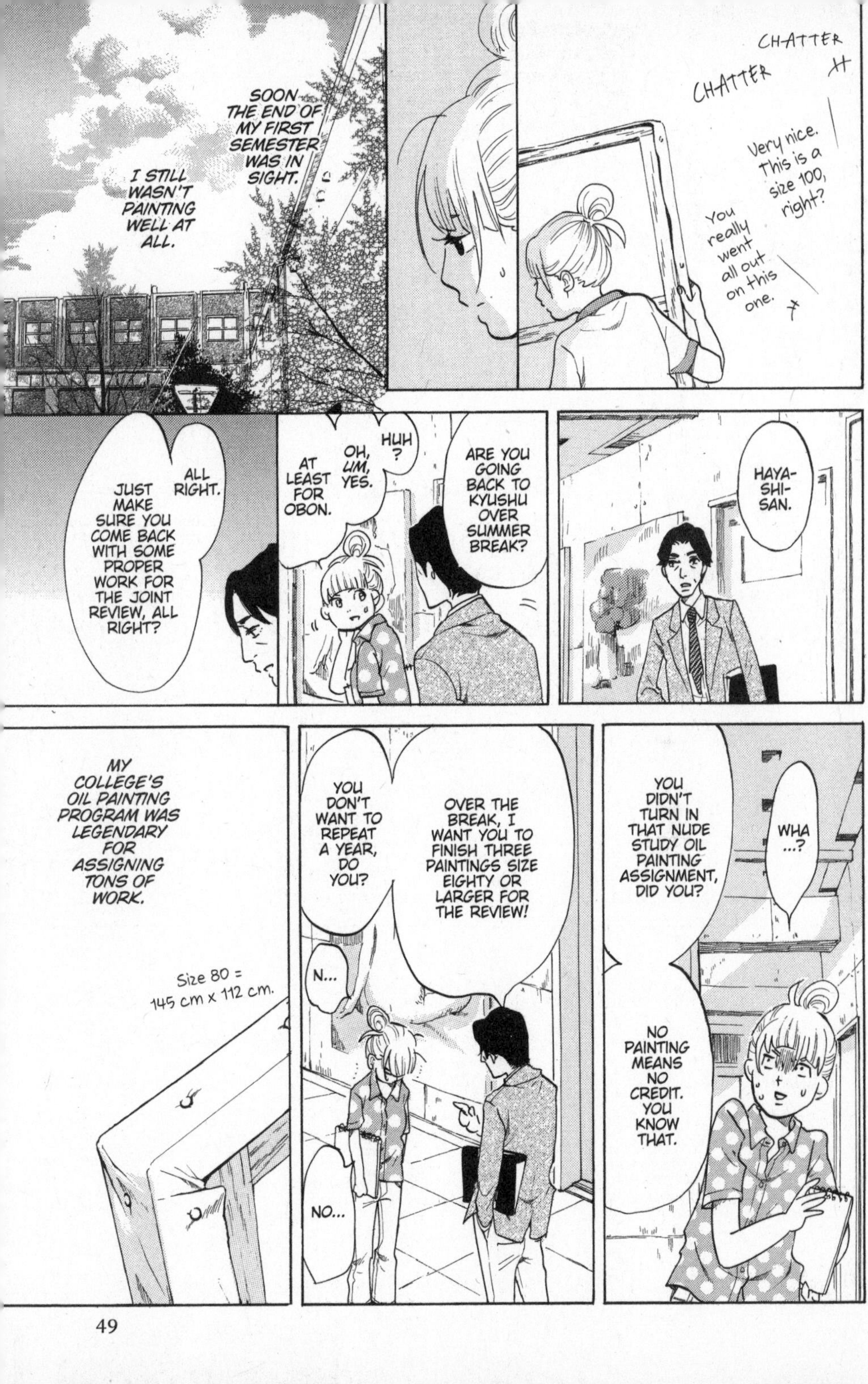
CHATTER
CHATTER
Very nice. This is a size 100, right?
You really went all out on this one.
SOON THE END OF MY FIRST SEMESTER WAS IN SIGHT.
I STILL WASN'T PAINTING WELL AT ALL.
HAYA-SHI-SAN.
ARE YOU GOING BACK TO KYUSHU OVER SUMMER BREAK?
HUH?
OH, UM, YES.
AT LEAST FOR OBON.
ALL RIGHT.
JUST MAKE SURE YOU COME BACK WITH SOME PROPER WORK FOR THE JOINT REVIEW, ALL RIGHT?
WHA...?
YOU DIDN'T TURN IN THAT NUDE STUDY OIL PAINTING ASSIGNMENT, DID YOU?
NO PAINTING MEANS NO CREDIT. YOU KNOW THAT.
OVER THE BREAK, I WANT YOU TO FINISH THREE PAINTINGS SIZE EIGHTY OR LARGER FOR THE REVIEW!
YOU DON'T WANT TO REPEAT A YEAR, DO YOU?
N...
NO...
MY COLLEGE'S OIL PAINTING PROGRAM WAS LEGENDARY FOR ASSIGNING TONS OF WORK.
Size 80 = 145 cm x 112 cm.

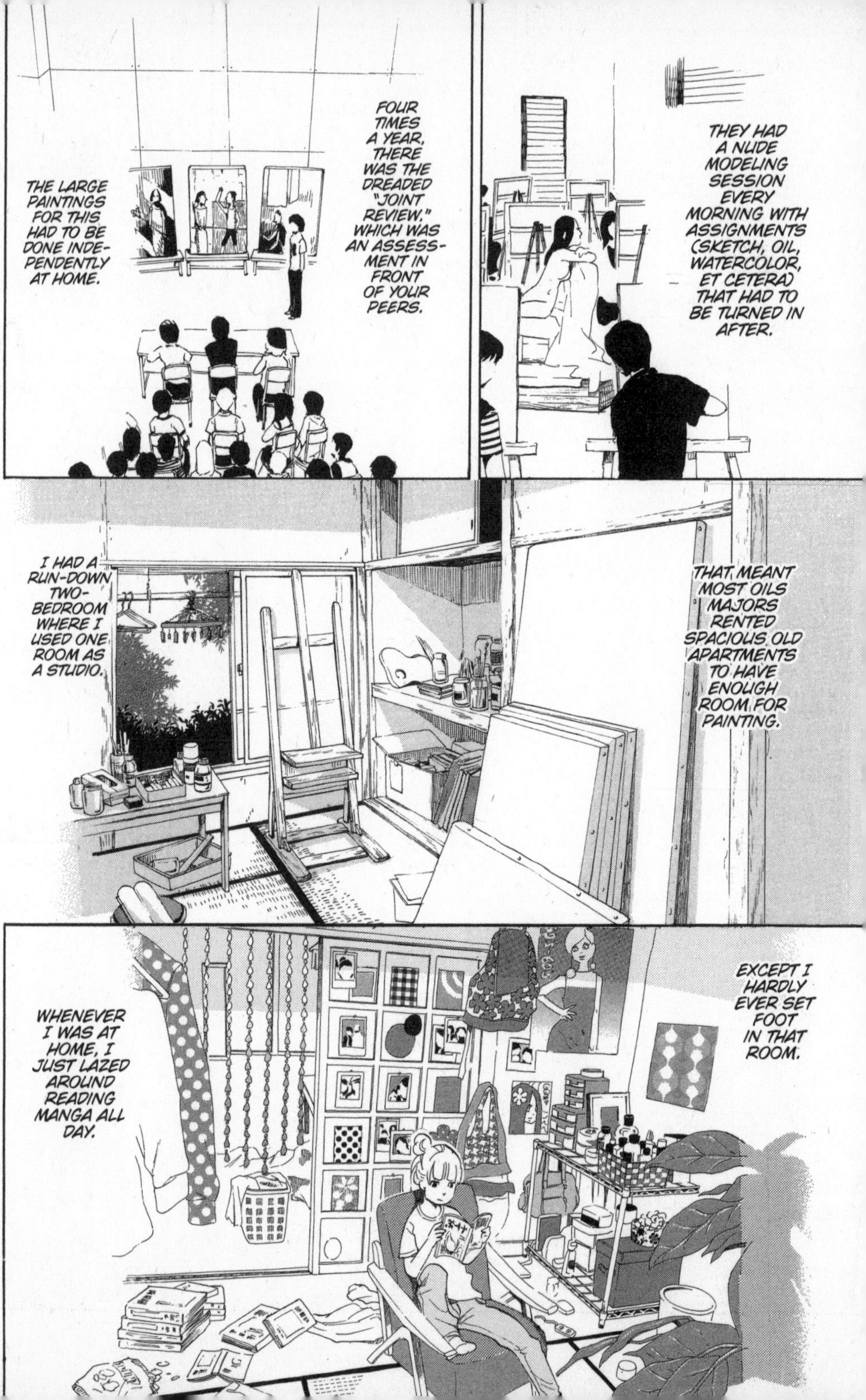
THEY HAD A NUDE MODELING SESSION EVERY MORNING WITH ASSIGNMENTS (SKETCH, OIL, WATERCOLOR, ET CETERA) THAT HAD TO BE TURNED IN AFTER.
FOUR TIMES A YEAR, THERE WAS THE DREADED "JOINT REVIEW," WHICH WAS AN ASSESS-MENT IN FRONT OF YOUR PEERS.
THE LARGE PAINTINGS FOR THIS HAD TO BE DONE INDE-PENDENTLY AT HOME.
THAT MEANT MOST OILS MAJORS RENTED SPACIOUS OLD APARTMENTS TO HAVE ENOUGH ROOM FOR PAINTING.
I HAD A RUN-DOWN TWO-BEDROOM WHERE I USED ONE ROOM AS A STUDIO.
EXCEPT I HARDLY EVER SET FOOT IN THAT ROOM.
WHENEVER I WAS AT HOME, I JUST LAZED AROUND READING MANGA ALL DAY.

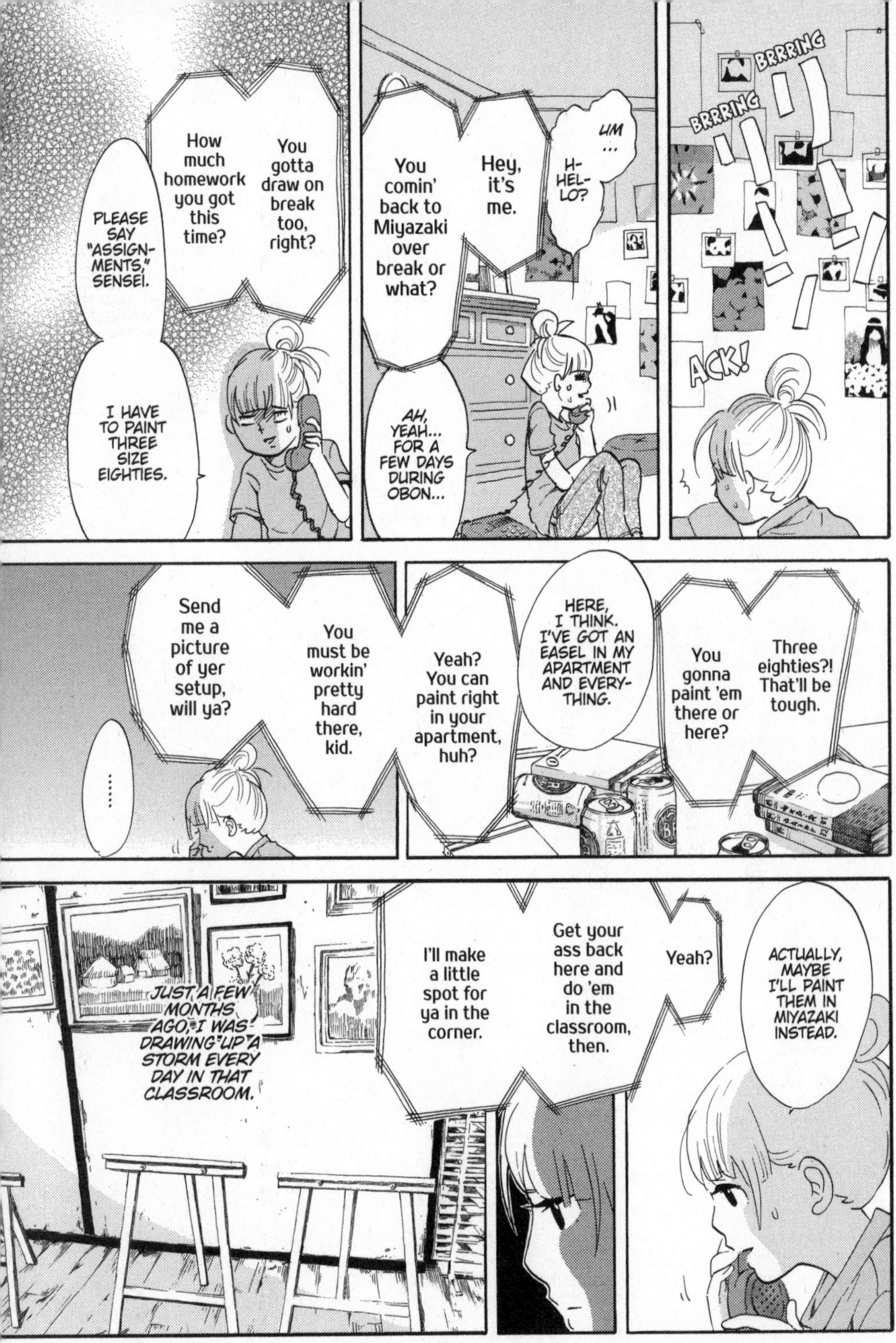
BRRRING
BRRRING
ACK!
H-HELLO?
UM...
Hey, it's me.
You comin' back to Miyazaki over break or what?
AH, YEAH... FOR A FEW DAYS DURING OBON...
You gotta draw on break too, right?
How much homework you got this time?
PLEASE SAY "ASSIGNMENTS," SENSEI.
I HAVE TO PAINT THREE SIZE EIGHTIES.
Three eighties?! That'll be tough.
You gonna paint 'em there or here?
HERE, I THINK. I'VE GOT AN EASEL IN MY APARTMENT AND EVERYTHING.
Yeah? You can paint right in your apartment, huh?
You must be workin' pretty hard there, kid.
Send me a picture of yer setup, will ya?
......
ACTUALLY, MAYBE I'LL PAINT THEM IN MIYAZAKI INSTEAD.
Yeah?
Get your ass back here and do 'em in the classroom, then.
I'll make a little spot for ya in the corner.
JUST A FEW MONTHS AGO, I WAS DRAWING UP A STORM EVERY DAY IN THAT CLASSROOM.

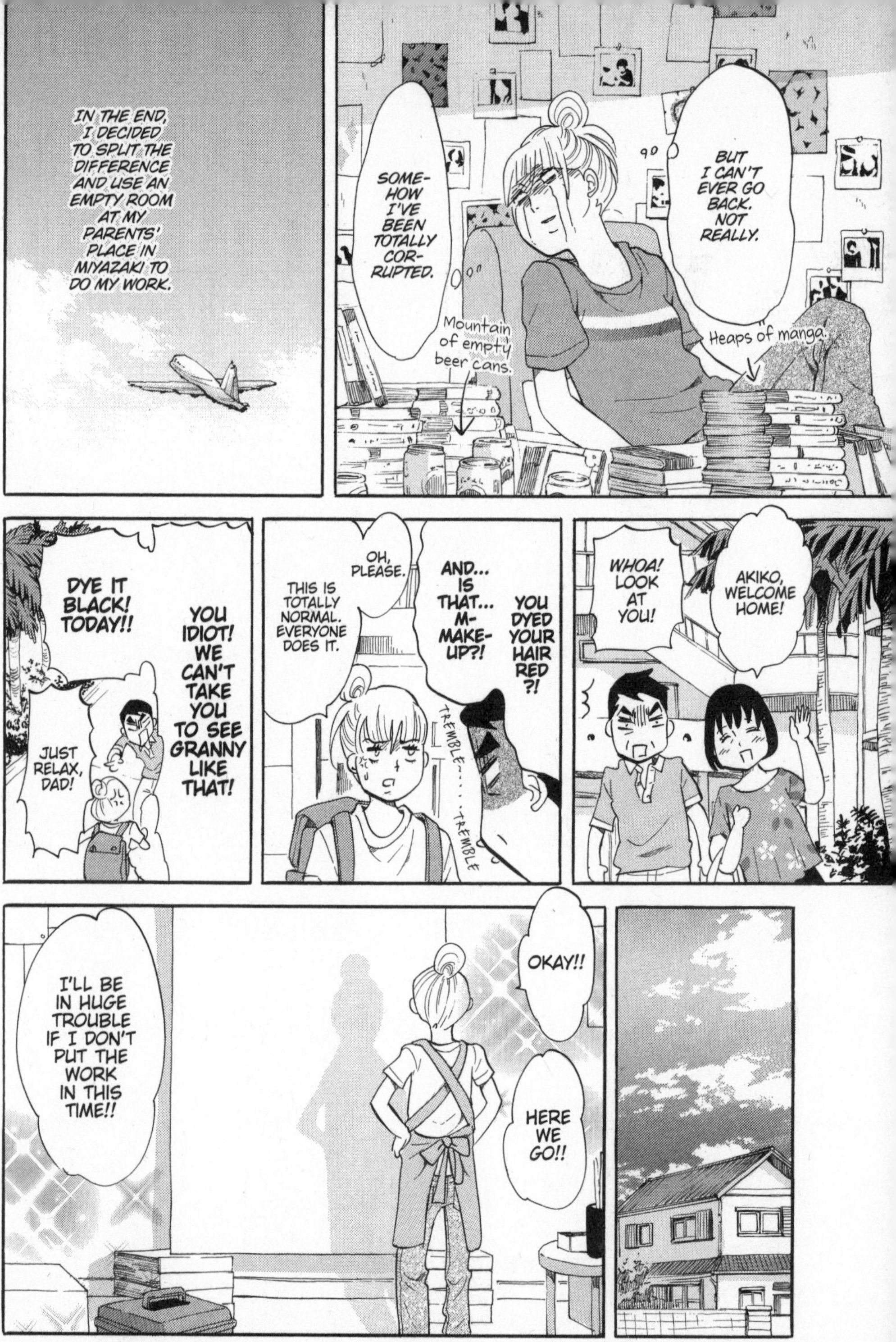
BUT I CAN'T EVER GO BACK. NOT REALLY.
SOME-HOW I'VE BEEN TOTALLY COR-RUPTED.
Heaps of manga.
Mountain of empty beer cans.
IN THE END, I DECIDED TO SPLIT THE DIFFERENCE AND USE AN EMPTY ROOM AT MY PARENTS' PLACE IN MIYAZAKI TO DO MY WORK.
AKIKO, WELCOME HOME!
WHOA! LOOK AT YOU!
YOU DYED YOUR HAIR RED?!
AND... IS THAT... M-MAKE-UP?!
OH, PLEASE.
THIS IS TOTALLY NORMAL. EVERYONE DOES IT.
TREMBLE... TREMBLE
YOU IDIOT! WE CAN'T TAKE YOU TO SEE GRANNY LIKE THAT!
DYE IT BLACK! TODAY!!
JUST RELAX, DAD!
OKAY!!
HERE WE GO!!
I'LL BE IN HUGE TROUBLE IF I DON'T PUT THE WORK IN THIS TIME!!

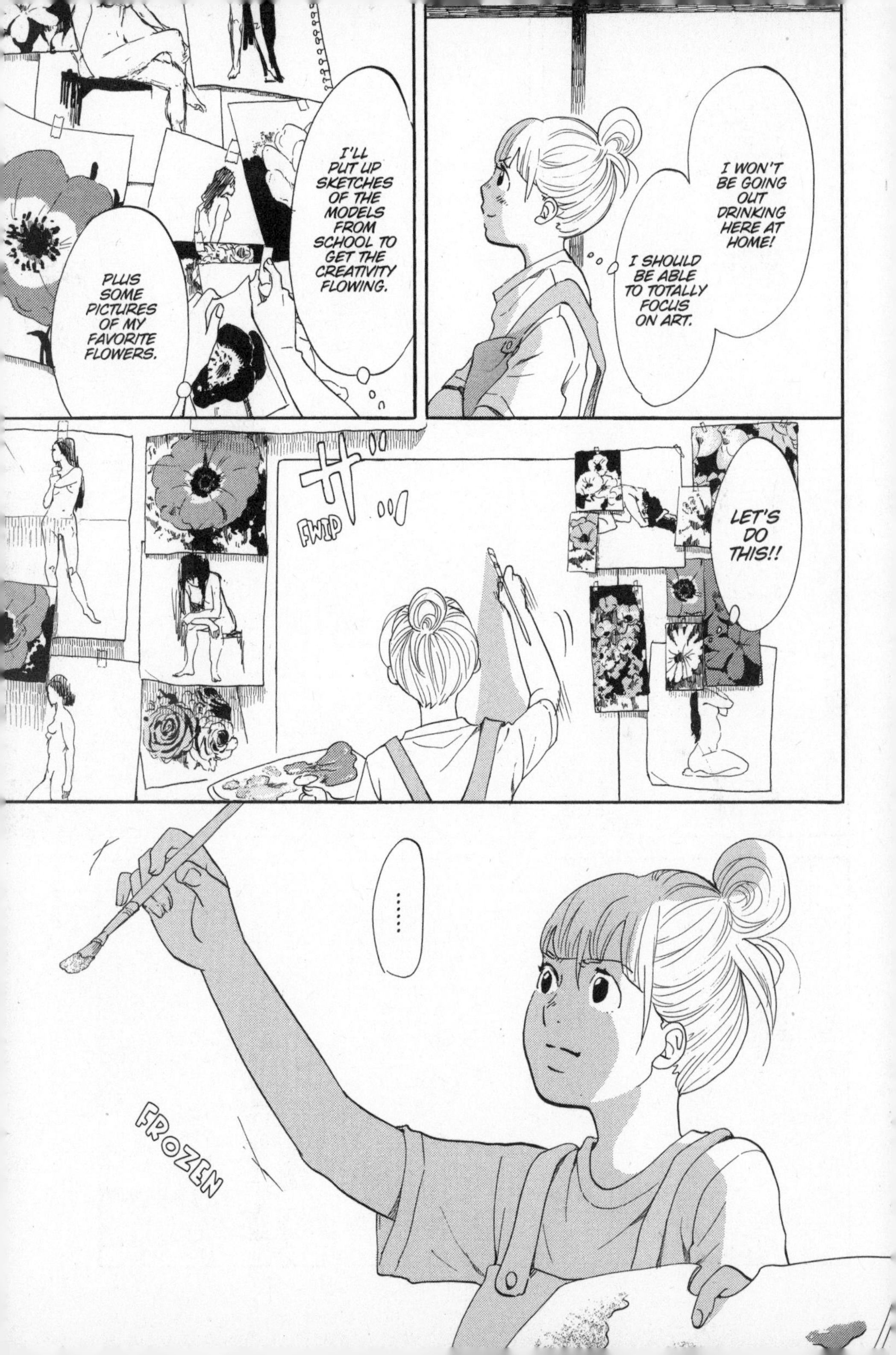
I WON'T BE GOING OUT DRINKING HERE AT HOME!
I SHOULD BE ABLE TO TOTALLY FOCUS ON ART.
I'LL PUT UP SKETCHES OF THE MODELS FROM SCHOOL TO GET THE CREATIVITY FLOWING.
PLUS SOME PICTURES OF MY FAVORITE FLOWERS.
LET'S DO THIS!!
FWIP
......
FROZEN

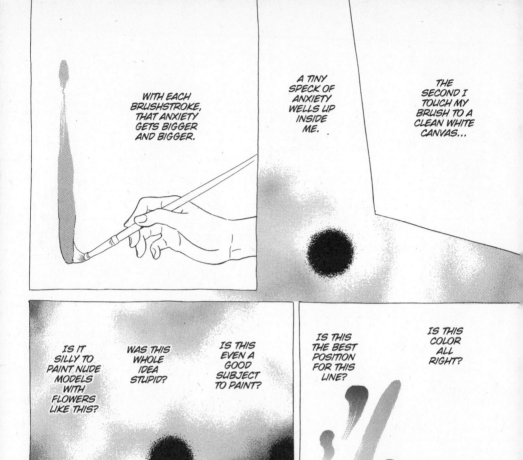

THE SECOND I TOUCH MY BRUSH TO A CLEAN WHITE CANVAS...
A TINY SPECK OF ANXIETY WELLS UP INSIDE ME.
WITH EACH BRUSHSTROKE, THAT ANXIETY GETS BIGGER AND BIGGER.
IS THIS COLOR ALL RIGHT?
IS THIS THE BEST POSITION FOR THIS LINE?
IS THIS EVEN A GOOD SUBJECT TO PAINT?
WAS THIS WHOLE IDEA STUPID?
IS IT SILLY TO PAINT NUDE MODELS WITH FLOWERS LIKE THIS?
SOON MY HAND JUST STOPS.
I CAN'T MOVE ANYMORE.
DURING THOSE FEW MONTHS AT SCHOOL, I REPEATED THIS CYCLE OVER AND OVER.

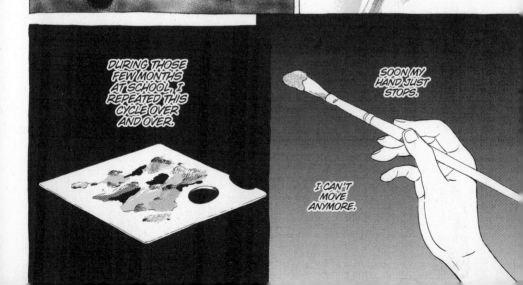

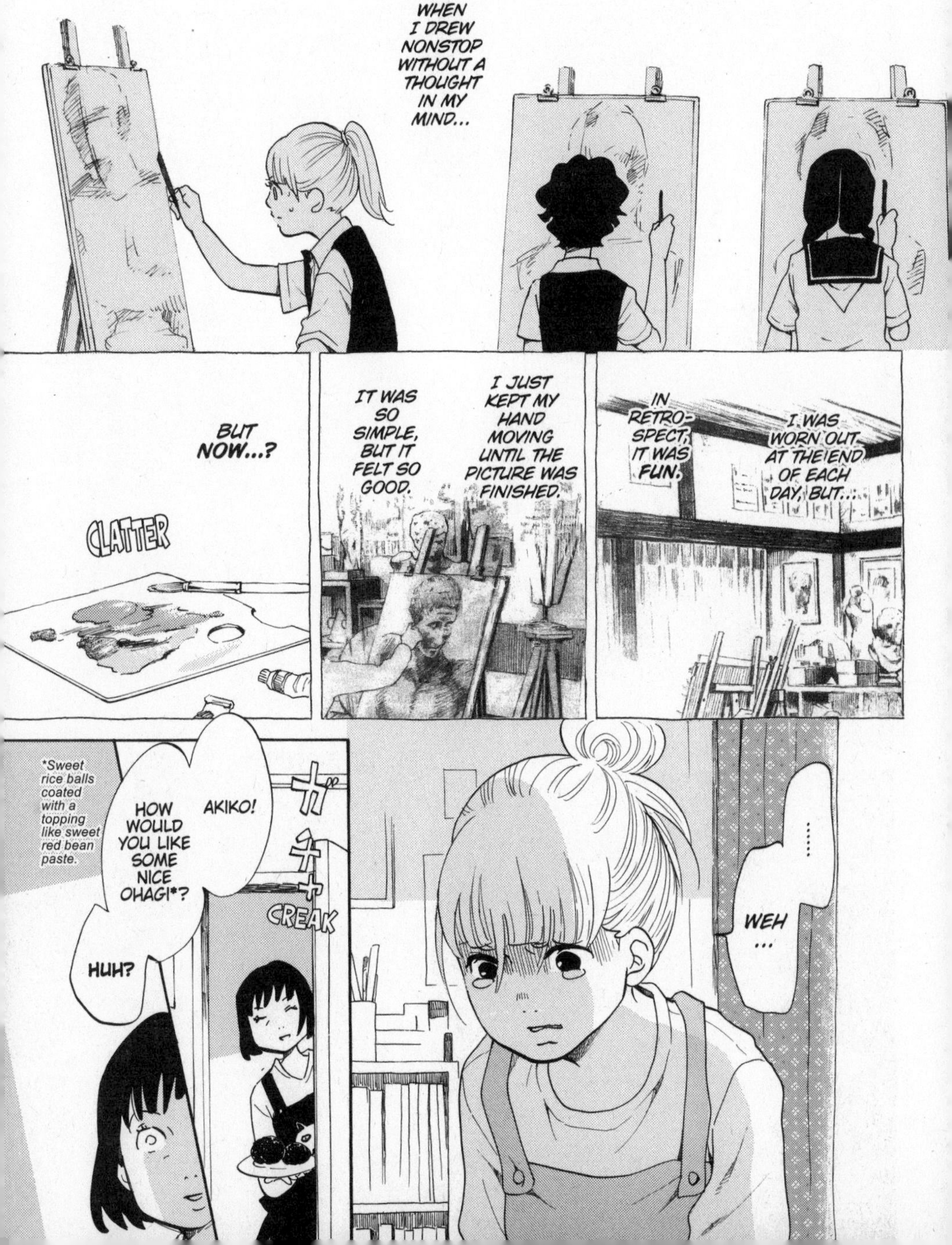
BACK WHEN I DREW NONSTOP WITHOUT A THOUGHT IN MY MIND...
I WAS WORN OUT AT THE END OF EACH DAY, BUT...
IN RETROSPECT, IT WAS FUN.
I JUST KEPT MY HAND MOVING UNTIL THE PICTURE WAS FINISHED.
IT WAS SO SIMPLE, BUT IT FELT SO GOOD.
BUT NOW...?
CLATTER
......
WEH ...
ガチャ
CREAK
AKIKO!
HOW WOULD YOU LIKE SOME NICE OHAGI*?
HUH?
*Sweet rice balls coated with a topping like sweet red bean paste.

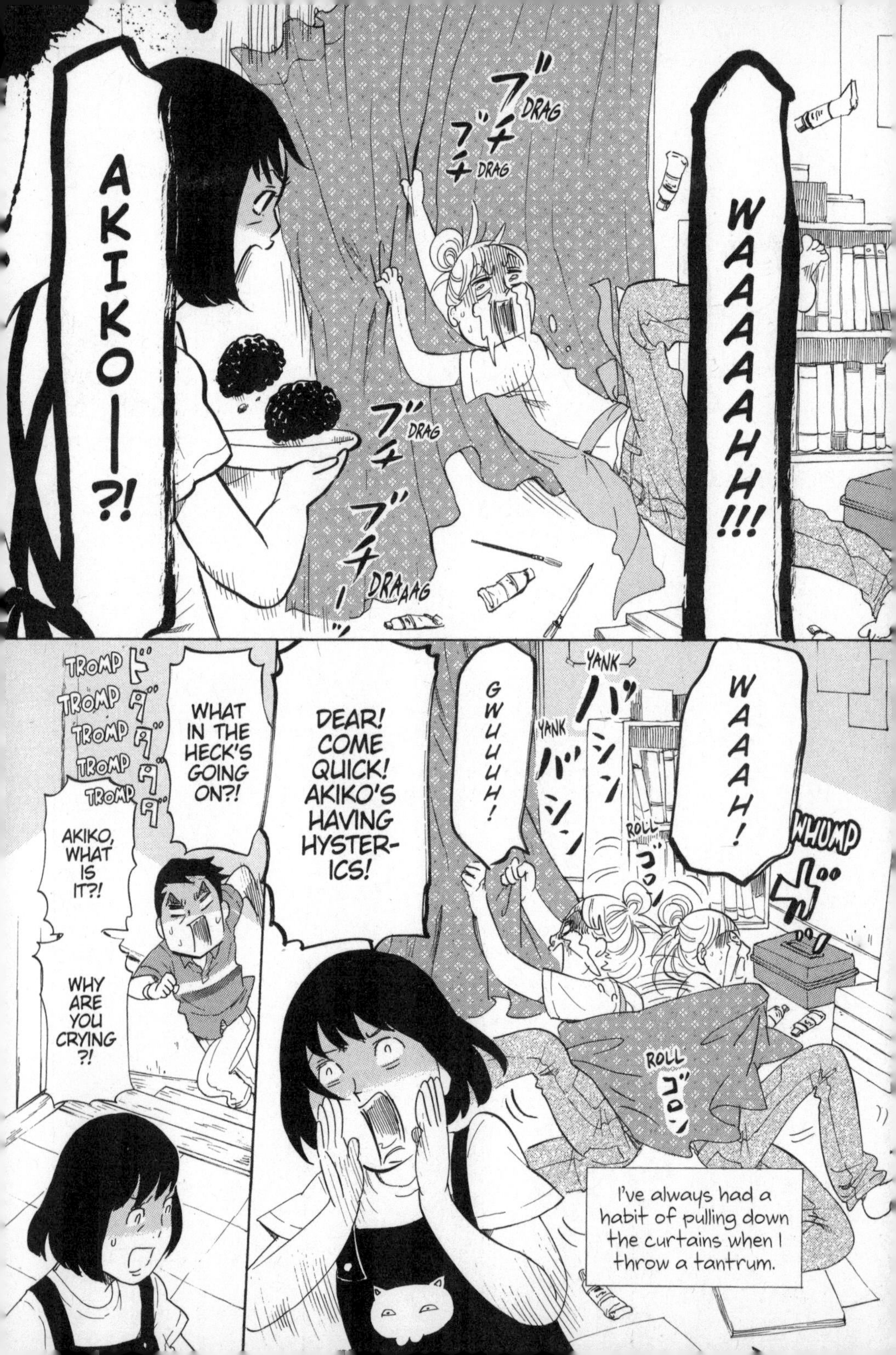

WAAAAAAHH!!!
DRAG
DRAG
DRAG
DRAAAG
AKIKO—?!
WAAAAH!
YANK
YANK
GWUUUH!
ROLL
WHUMP
ROLL
DEAR! COME QUICK! AKIKO'S HAVING HYSTER-ICS!
I've always had a habit of pulling down the curtains when I throw a tantrum.
WHAT IN THE HECK'S GOING ON?!
TROMP
TROMP
TROMP
TROMP
TROMP
AKIKO, WHAT IS IT?!
WHY ARE YOU CRYING?!

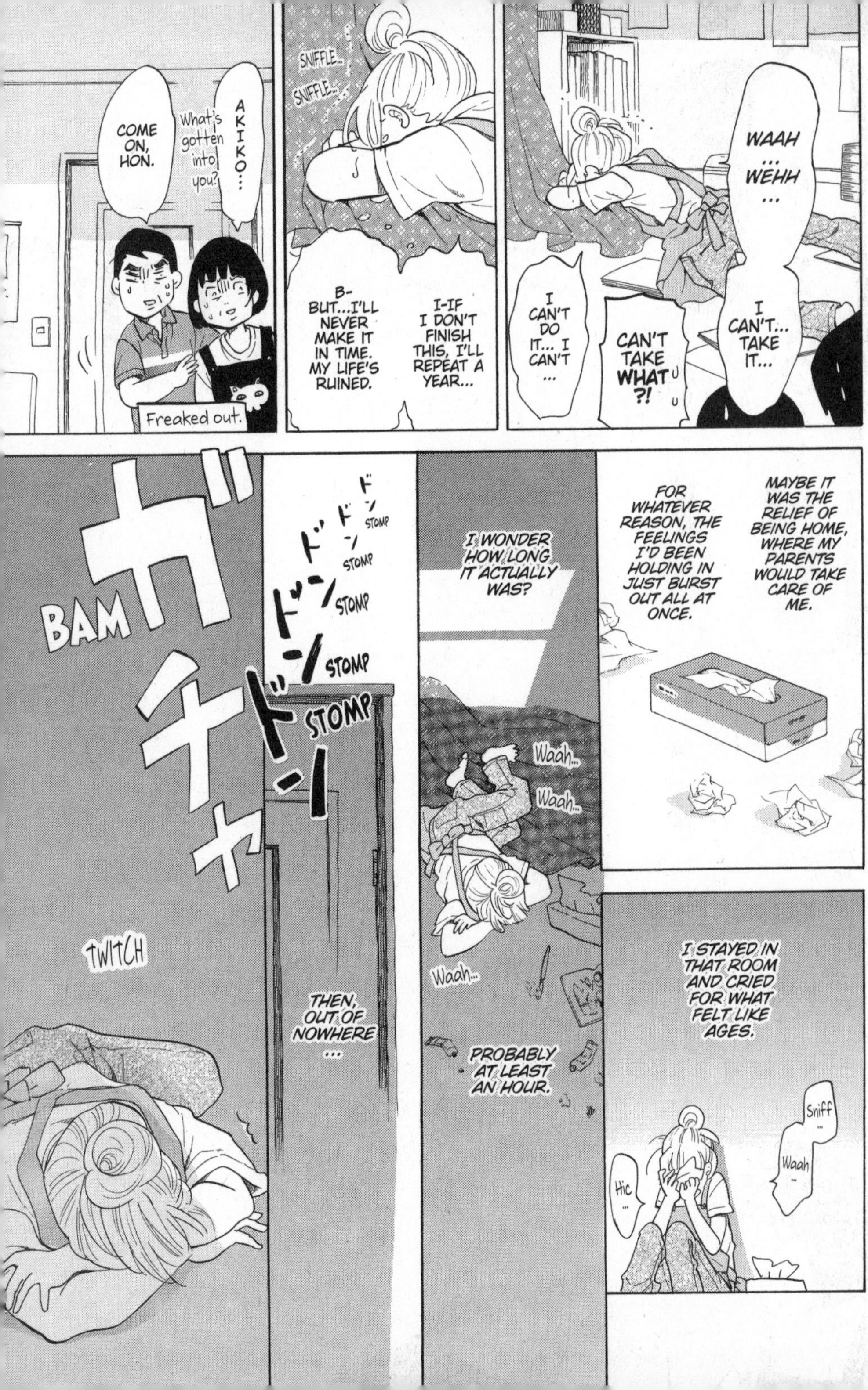
WAAH... WEHH...
I CAN'T... TAKE IT...
CAN'T TAKE WHAT?!
I CAN'T DO IT... I CAN'T...
SNIFFLE...
SNIFFLE...
I-IF I DON'T FINISH THIS, I'LL REPEAT A YEAR...
B-BUT...I'LL NEVER MAKE IT IN TIME. MY LIFE'S RUINED.
AKIKO...
What's gotten into you?
COME ON, HON.
Freaked out.
MAYBE IT WAS THE RELIEF OF BEING HOME, WHERE MY PARENTS WOULD TAKE CARE OF ME.
FOR WHATEVER REASON, THE FEELINGS I'D BEEN HOLDING IN JUST BURST OUT ALL AT ONCE.
I STAYED IN THAT ROOM AND CRIED FOR WHAT FELT LIKE AGES.
Sniff...
Waah...
Hic...
I WONDER HOW LONG IT ACTUALLY WAS?
Waah...
Waah...
Waah...
PROBABLY AT LEAST AN HOUR.
ドン STOMP
ドン STOMP
ドーン STOMP
ドーン STOMP
ドーン STOMP
THEN, OUT OF NOWHERE...
ガチャ BAM
TWITCH

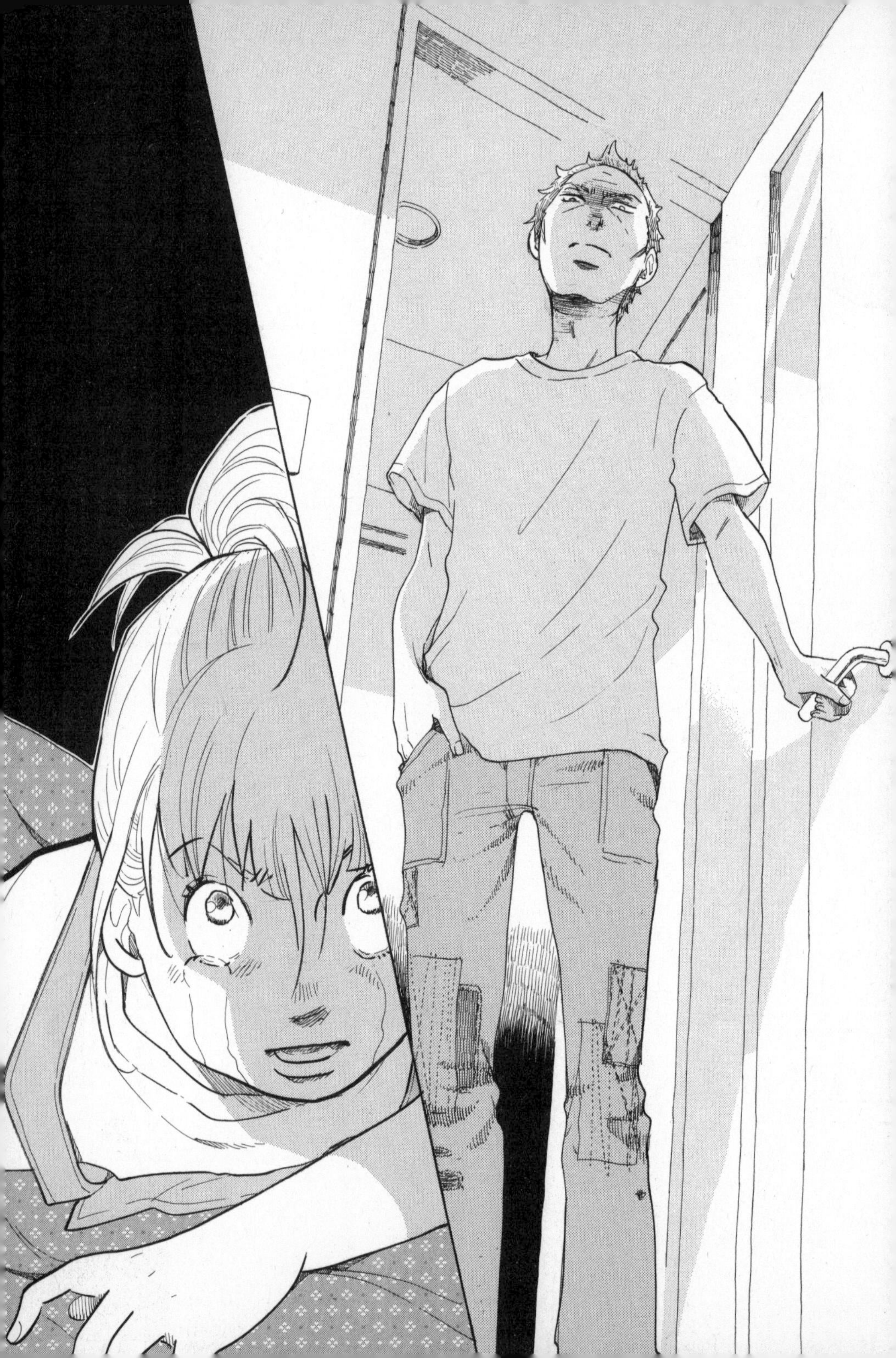

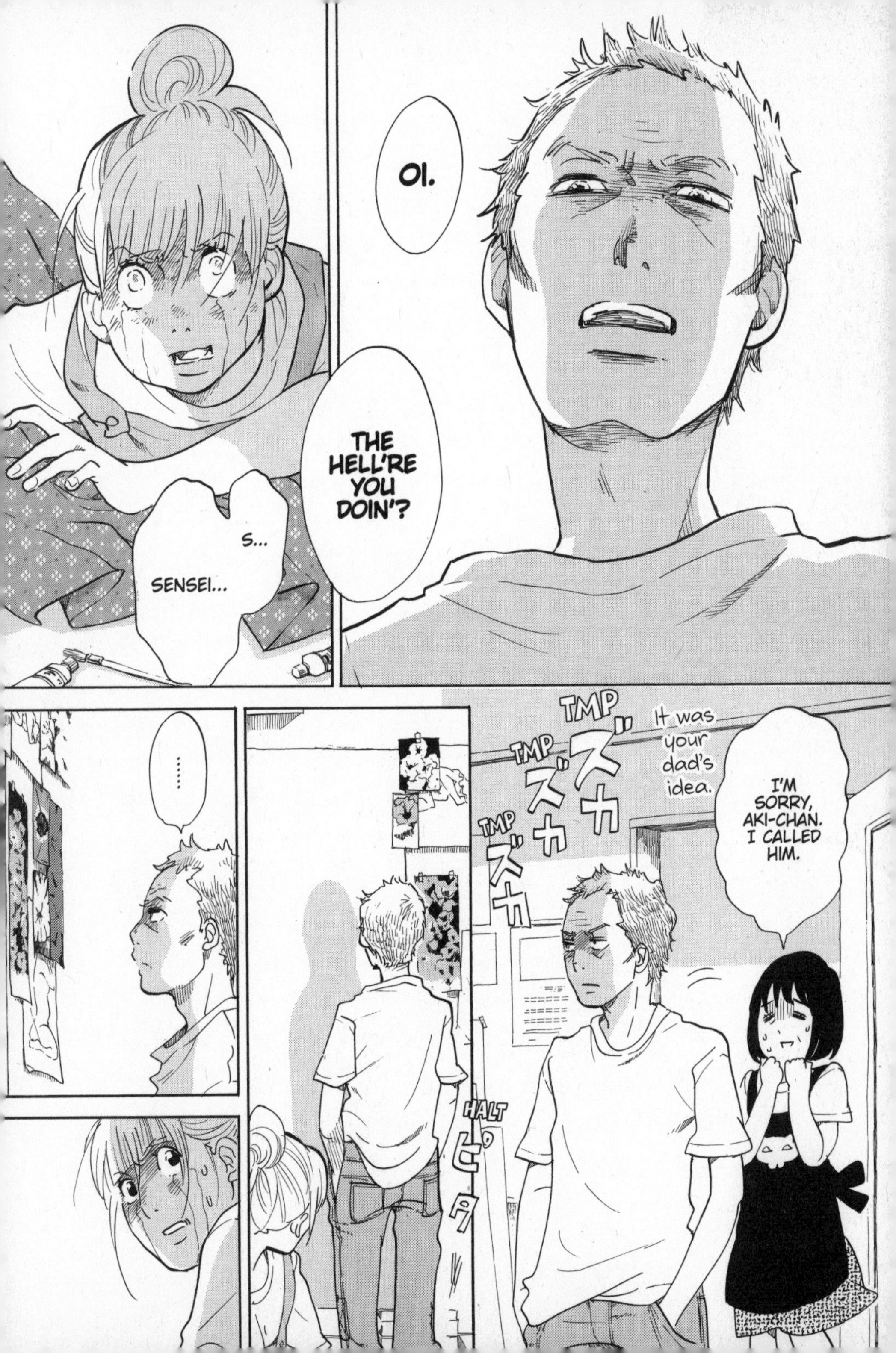

OI.
THE HELL'RE YOU DOIN'?
S... SENSEI...
I'M SORRY, AKI-CHAN. I CALLED HIM.
It was your dad's idea.
TMP ズカ
TMP ズカ
TMP ズカ
HALT ピタ
......

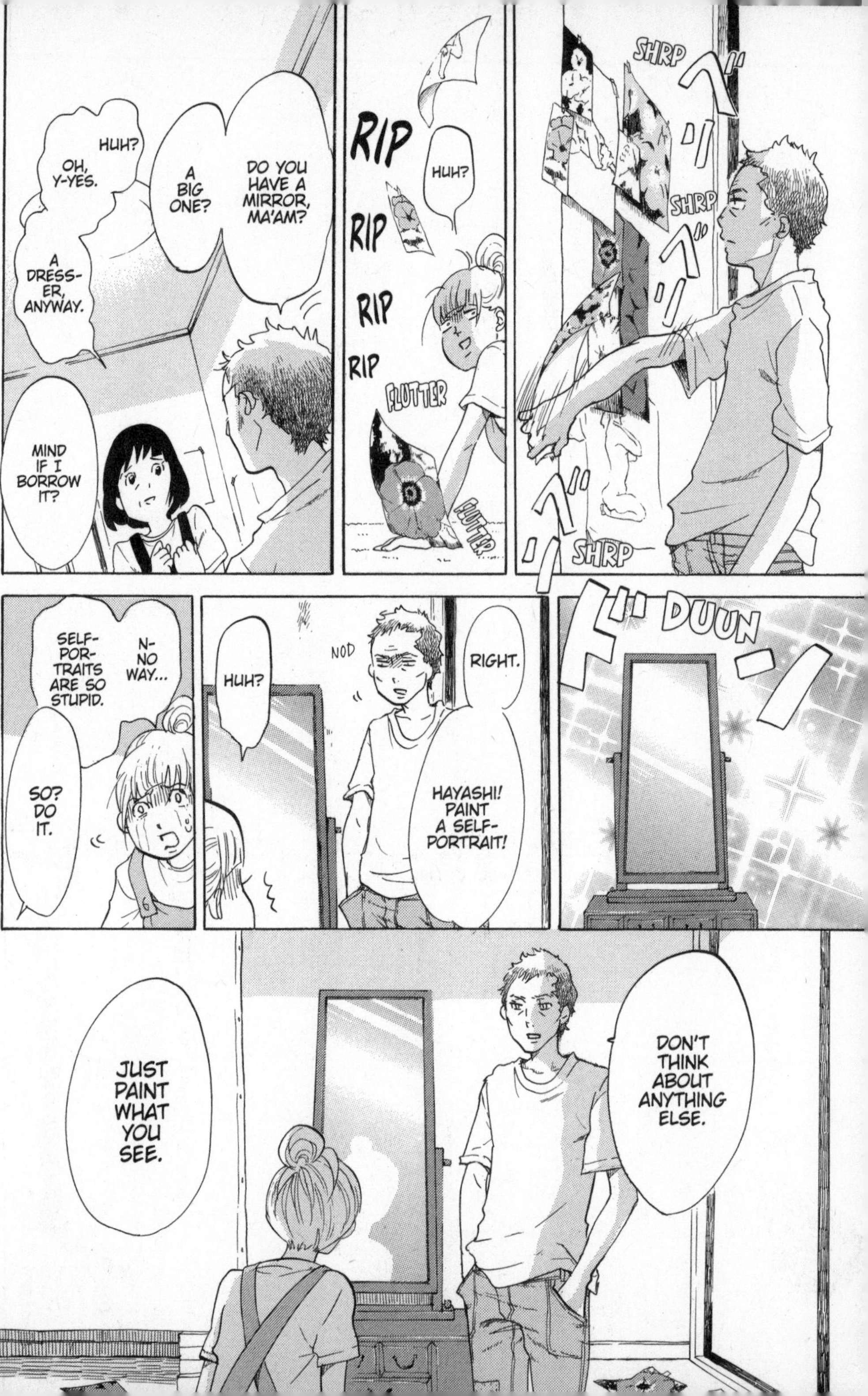
SHRP
SHRP
SHRP
RIP
RIP
RIP
RIP
HUH?
FLUTTER
FLUTTER
DO YOU HAVE A MIRROR, MA'AM?
A BIG ONE?
HUH?
OH, Y-YES.
A DRESSER, ANYWAY.
MIND IF I BORROW IT?
DUUN
RIGHT.
HUH?
NOD
HAYASHI! PAINT A SELF-PORTRAIT!
N-NO WAY...
SELF-PORTRAITS ARE SO STUPID.
SO? DO IT.
DON'T THINK ABOUT ANYTHING ELSE.
JUST PAINT WHAT YOU SEE.

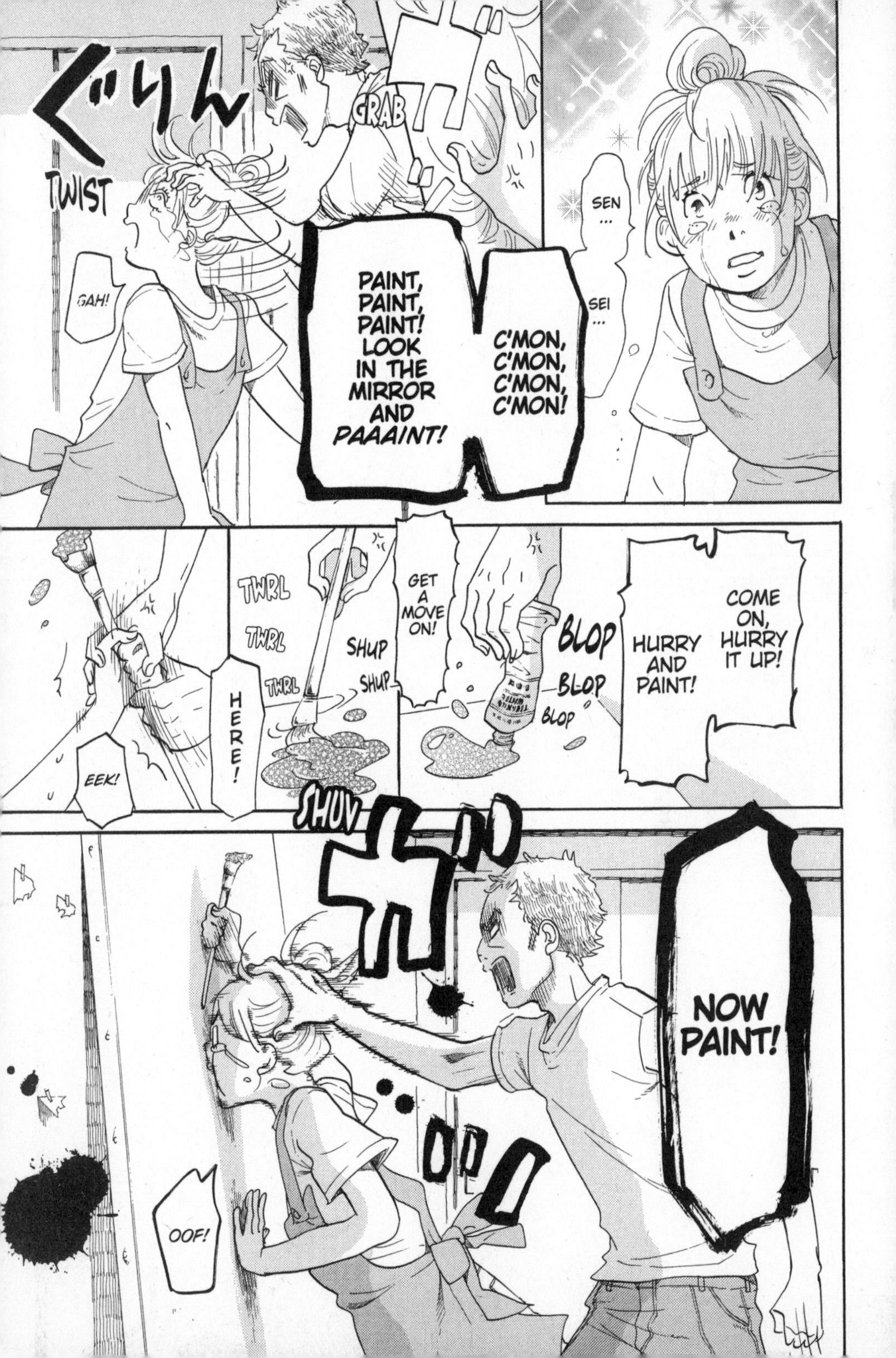
SEN ...
SEI ...
GRAB
C'MON, C'MON, C'MON, C'MON!
PAINT, PAINT, PAINT! LOOK IN THE MIRROR AND PAAAINT!
ぐりん
TWIST
GAH!
COME ON, HURRY IT UP!
HURRY AND PAINT!
GET A MOVE ON!
BLOP
BLOP
BLOP
SHUP
SHUP
TWRL
TWRL
TWRL
HERE!
EEK!
NOW PAINT!
SHUV
OOF!

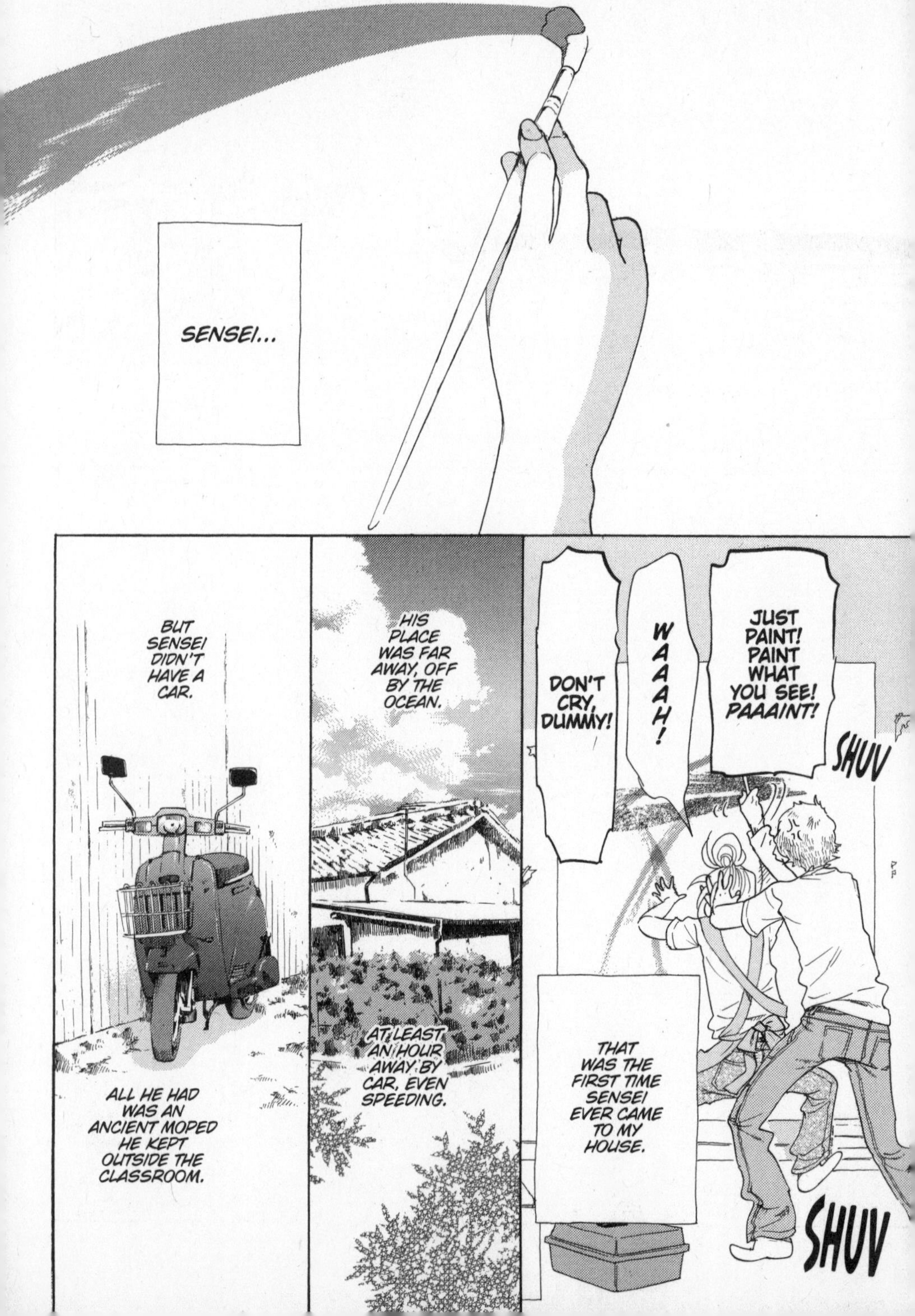
SENSEI...
JUST PAINT! PAINT WHAT YOU SEE! PAAAINT!
WAAAAH!
DON'T CRY, DUMMY!
SHUV
SHUV
THAT WAS THE FIRST TIME SENSEI EVER CAME TO MY HOUSE.
HIS PLACE WAS FAR AWAY, OFF BY THE OCEAN.
AT LEAST AN HOUR AWAY BY CAR, EVEN SPEEDING.
BUT SENSEI DIDN'T HAVE A CAR.
ALL HE HAD WAS AN ANCIENT MOPED HE KEPT OUTSIDE THE CLASSROOM.

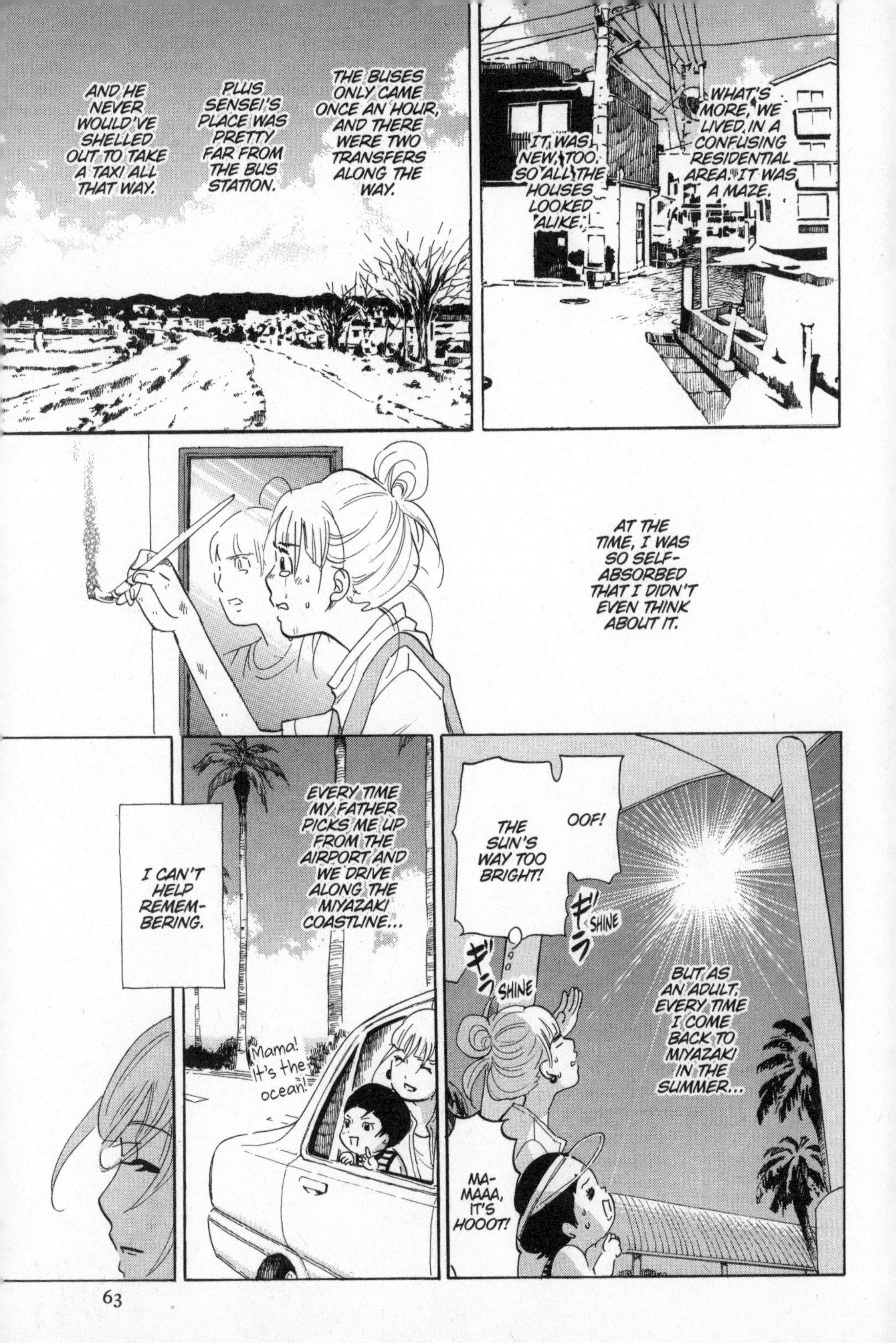
WHAT'S MORE, WE LIVED IN A CONFUSING RESIDENTIAL AREA. IT WAS A MAZE.
IT WAS NEW, TOO, SO ALL THE HOUSES LOOKED ALIKE.
THE BUSES ONLY CAME ONCE AN HOUR, AND THERE WERE TWO TRANSFERS ALONG THE WAY.
PLUS SENSEI'S PLACE WAS PRETTY FAR FROM THE BUS STATION.
AND HE NEVER WOULD'VE SHELLED OUT TO TAKE A TAXI ALL THAT WAY.
AT THE TIME, I WAS SO SELF-ABSORBED THAT I DIDN'T EVEN THINK ABOUT IT.
OOF!
THE SUN'S WAY TOO BRIGHT!
SHINE
SHINE
BUT AS AN ADULT, EVERY TIME I COME BACK TO MIYAZAKI IN THE SUMMER...
MA-MAAA, IT'S HOOOT!
EVERY TIME MY FATHER PICKS ME UP FROM THE AIRPORT AND WE DRIVE ALONG THE MIYAZAKI COASTLINE...
Mama! It's the ocean!
I CAN'T HELP REMEMBERING.

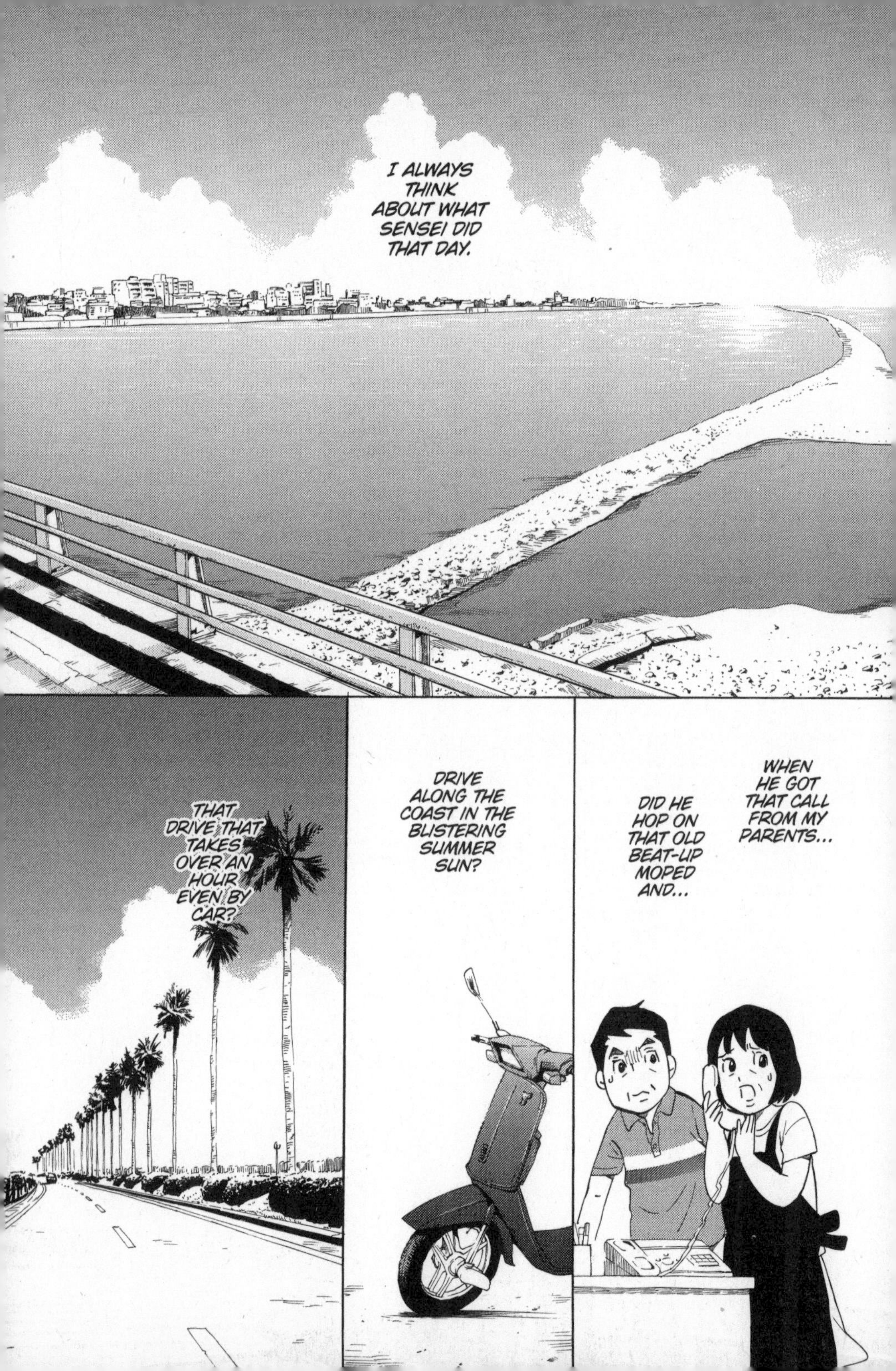
I ALWAYS THINK ABOUT WHAT SENSEI DID THAT DAY.
WHEN HE GOT THAT CALL FROM MY PARENTS...
DID HE HOP ON THAT OLD BEAT-UP MOPED AND...
DRIVE ALONG THE COAST IN THE BLISTERING SUMMER SUN?
THAT DRIVE THAT TAKES OVER AN HOUR EVEN BY CAR?

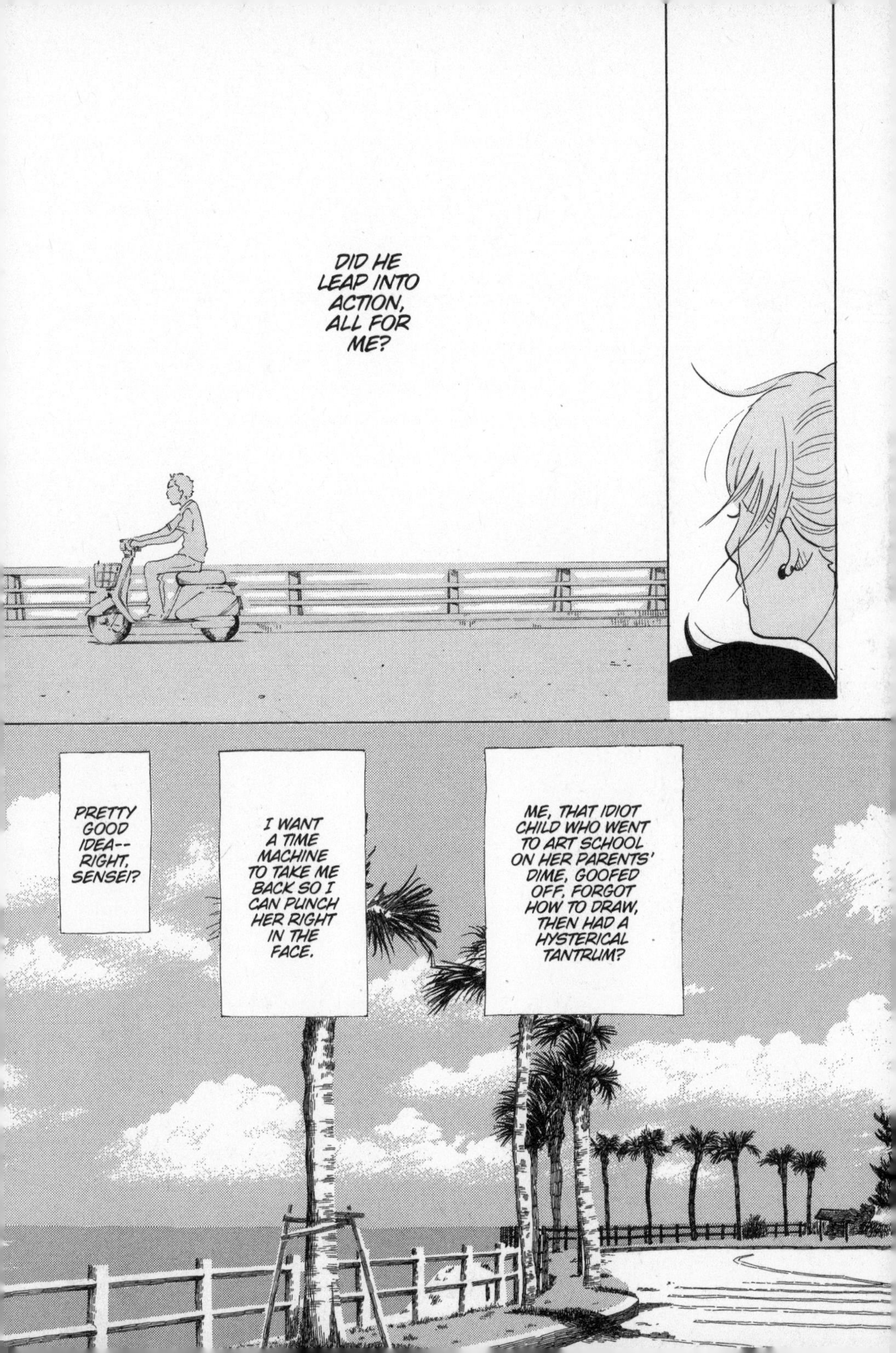
DID HE LEAP INTO ACTION, ALL FOR ME?
ME, THAT IDIOT CHILD WHO WENT TO ART SCHOOL ON HER PARENTS' DIME, GOOFED OFF, FORGOT HOW TO DRAW, THEN HAD A HYSTERICAL TANTRUM?
I WANT A TIME MACHINE TO TAKE ME BACK SO I CAN PUNCH HER RIGHT IN THE FACE.
PRETTY GOOD IDEA-- RIGHT, SENSEI?

Blank Canvas

My So-Called Artist's Journey

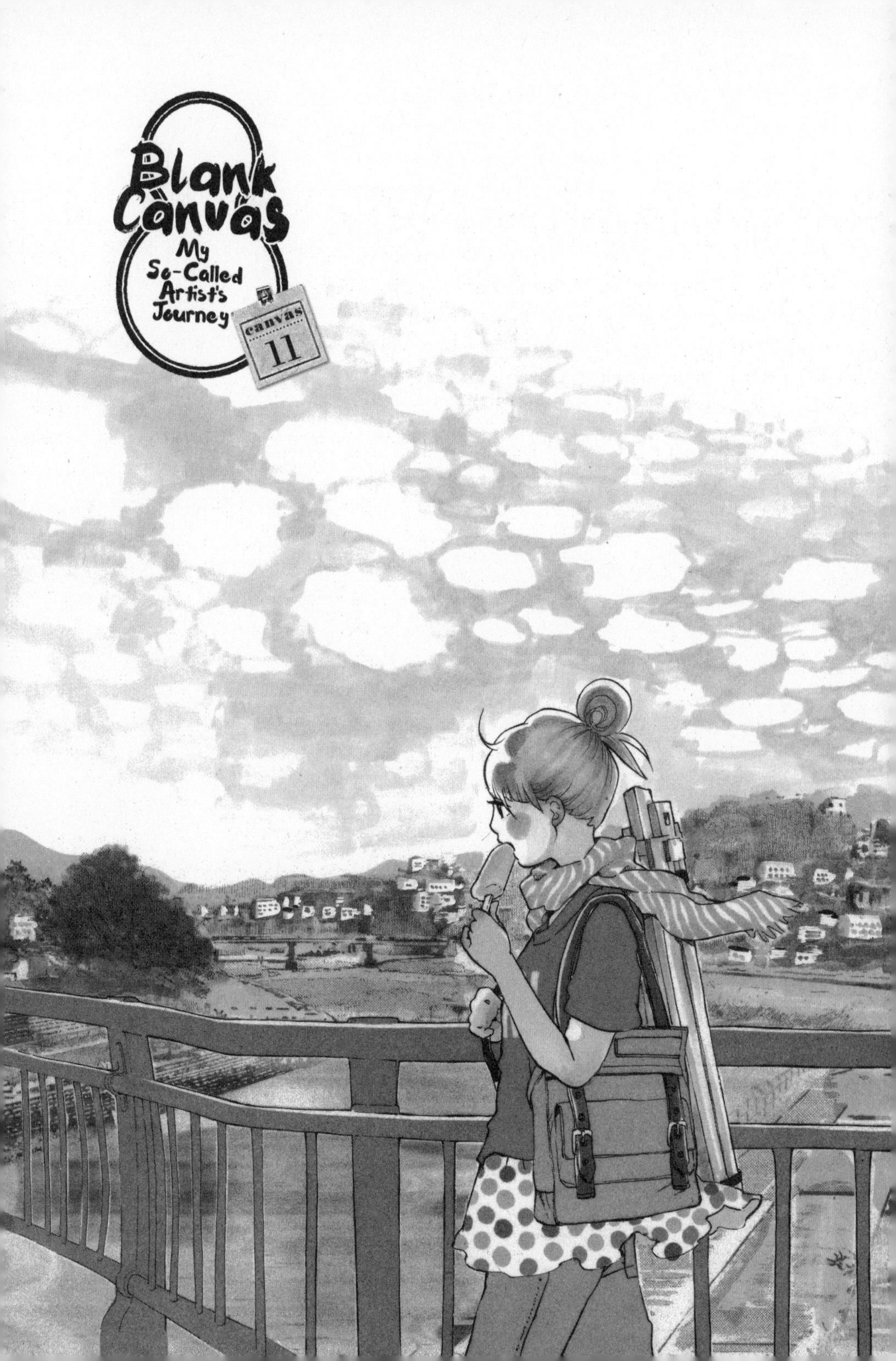
Blank Canvas
My So-Called Artist's Journey
canvas
11

Blank Canvas
My So-Called
Artist's Journey

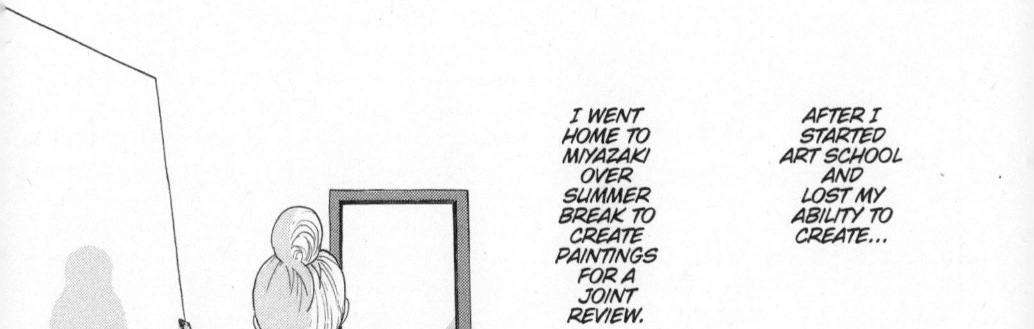

AFTER I STARTED ART SCHOOL AND LOST MY ABILITY TO CREATE...
I WENT HOME TO MIYAZAKI OVER SUMMER BREAK TO CREATE PAINTINGS FOR A JOINT REVIEW.

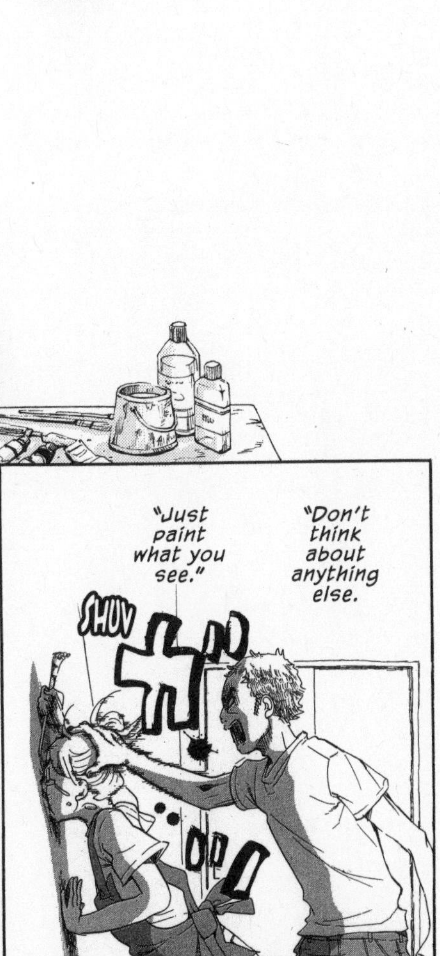

"Don't think about anything else.
"Just paint what you see."
SHUV

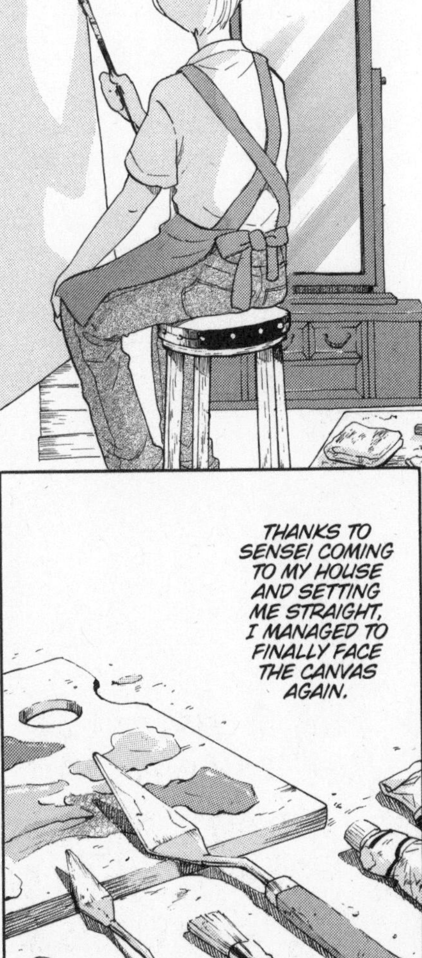

THANKS TO SENSEI COMING TO MY HOUSE AND SETTING ME STRAIGHT, I MANAGED TO FINALLY FACE THE CANVAS AGAIN.

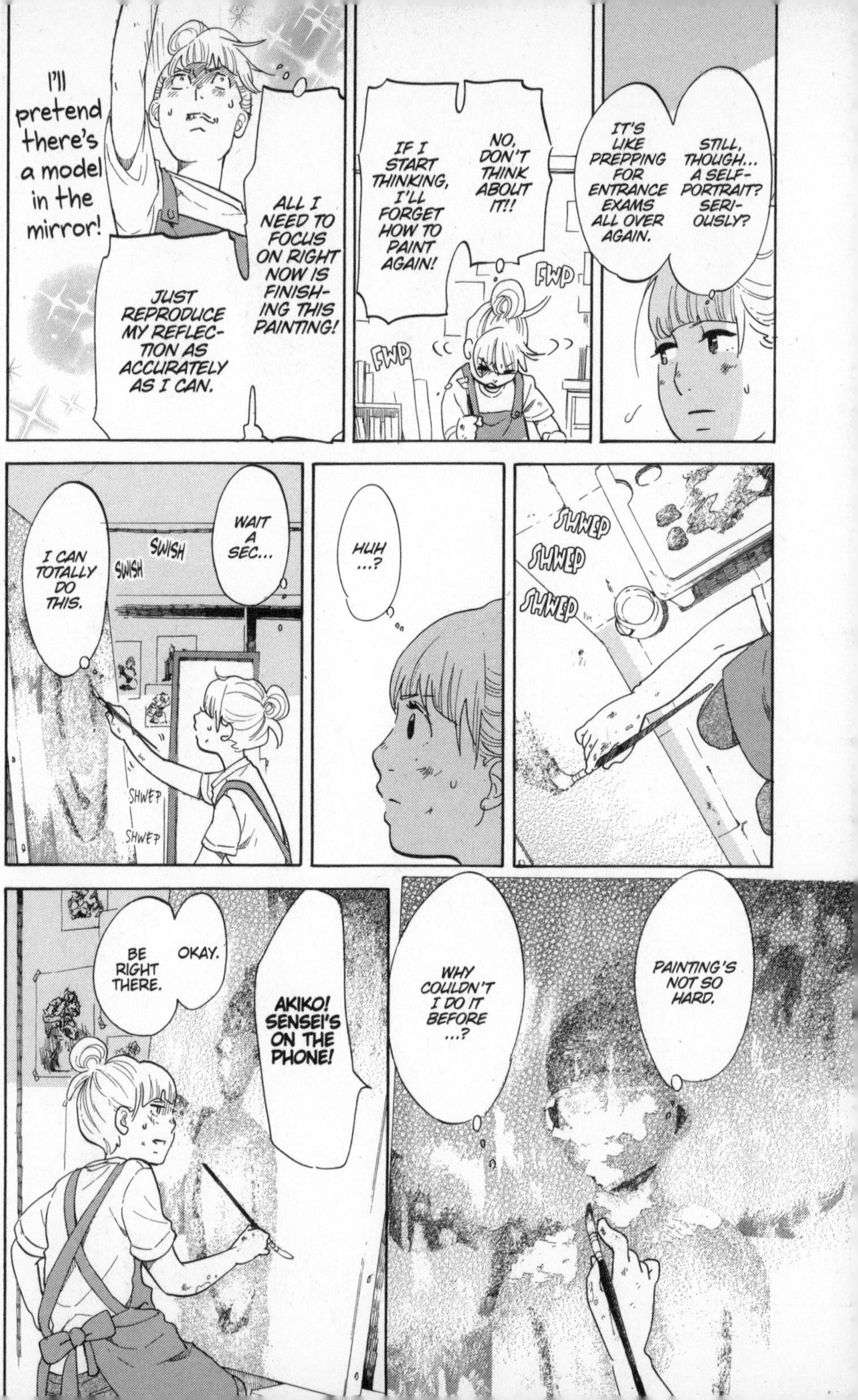
STILL, THOUGH... A SELF-PORTRAIT? SERIOUSLY?
IT'S LIKE PREPPING FOR ENTRANCE EXAMS ALL OVER AGAIN.
NO, DON'T THINK ABOUT IT!!
IF I START THINKING, I'LL FORGET HOW TO PAINT AGAIN!
FWP
FWP
ALL I NEED TO FOCUS ON RIGHT NOW IS FINISHING THIS PAINTING!
I'll pretend there's a model in the mirror!
JUST REPRODUCE MY REFLECTION AS ACCURATELY AS I CAN.
SHWEP
SHWEP
SHWEP
HUH ...?
WAIT A SEC...
SWISH
SWISH
I CAN TOTALLY DO THIS.
SHWEP
SHWEP
PAINTING'S NOT SO HARD.
WHY COULDN'T I DO IT BEFORE ...?
AKIKO! SENSEI'S ON THE PHONE!
OKAY.
BE RIGHT THERE.

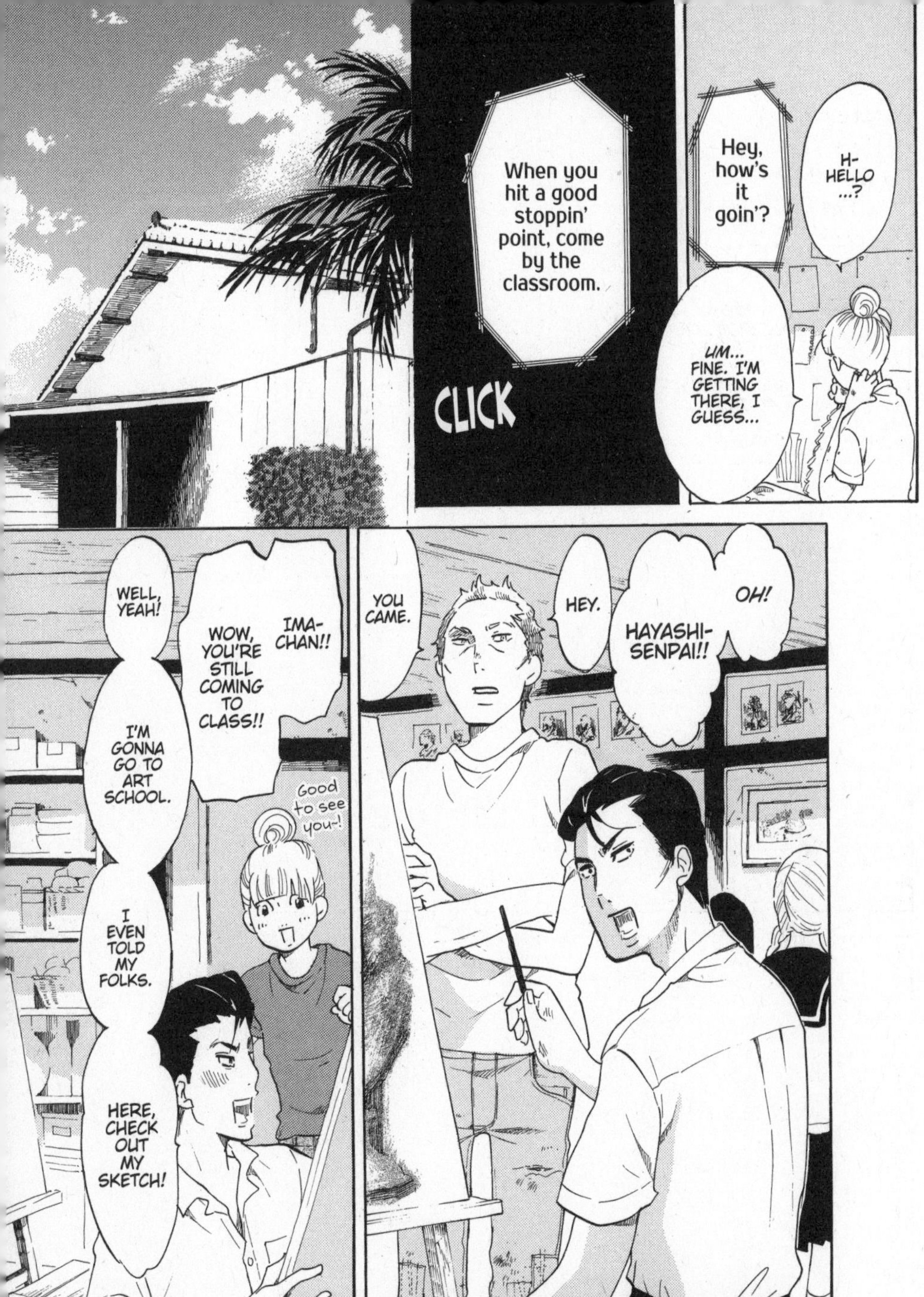
H-HELLO ...?
Hey, how's it goin'?
UM... FINE. I'M GETTING THERE, I GUESS...
When you hit a good stoppin' point, come by the classroom.
CLICK
OH! HAYASHI-SENPAI!!
HEY.
YOU CAME.
IMA-CHAN!!
WOW, YOU'RE STILL COMING TO CLASS!!
WELL, YEAH!
I'M GONNA GO TO ART SCHOOL.
Good to see you-!
I EVEN TOLD MY FOLKS.
HERE, CHECK OUT MY SKETCH!

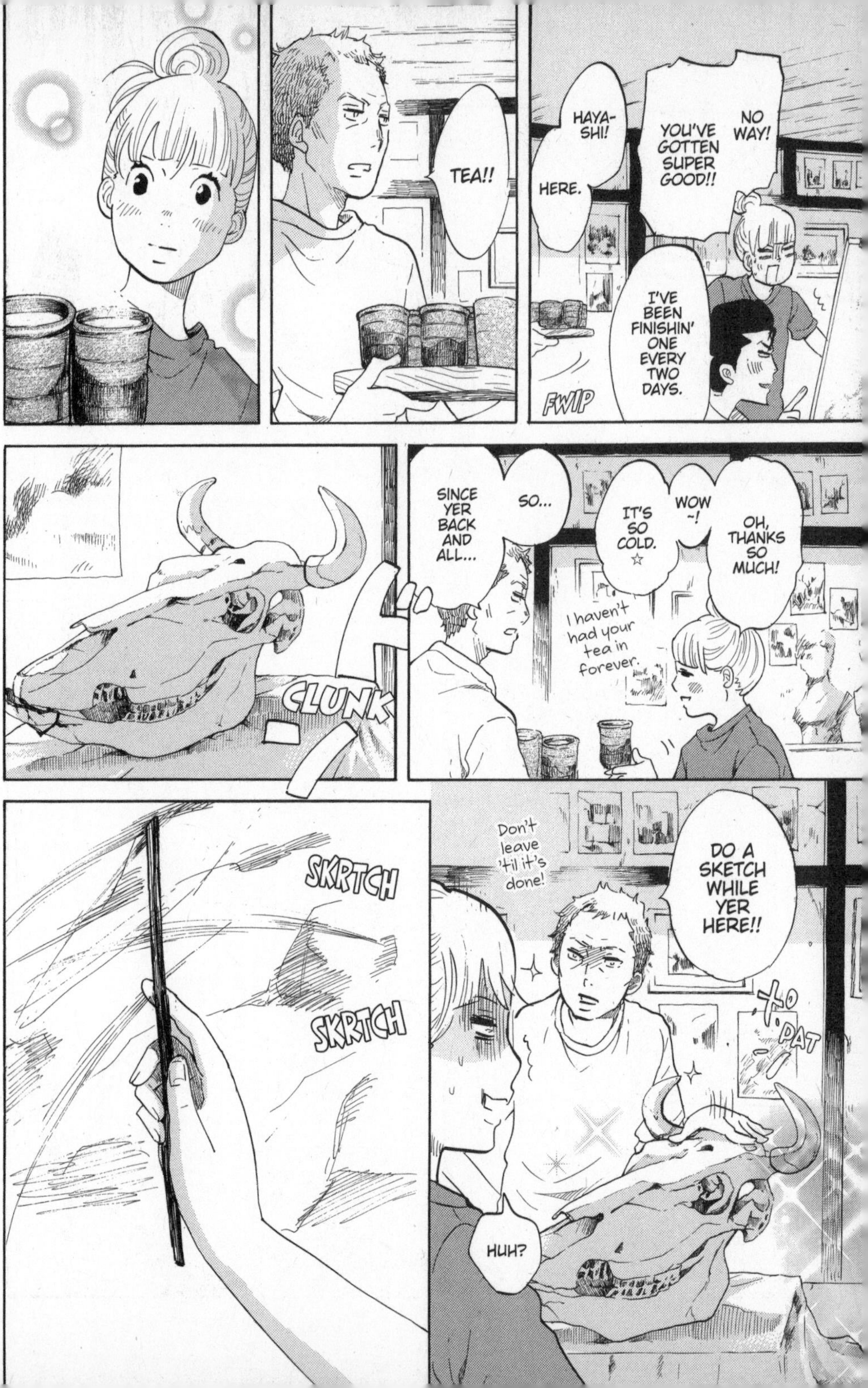
NO WAY!
YOU'VE GOTTEN SUPER GOOD!!
HAYA-SHI!
HERE.
I'VE BEEN FINISHIN' ONE EVERY TWO DAYS.
FWIP
TEA!!
OH, THANKS SO MUCH!
WOW~!
IT'S SO COLD. ☆
SO...
SINCE YER BACK AND ALL...
I haven't had your tea in forever.
CLUNK
DO A SKETCH WHILE YER HERE!!
Don't leave 'til it's done!
PAT
HUH?
SKRTCH
SKRTCH

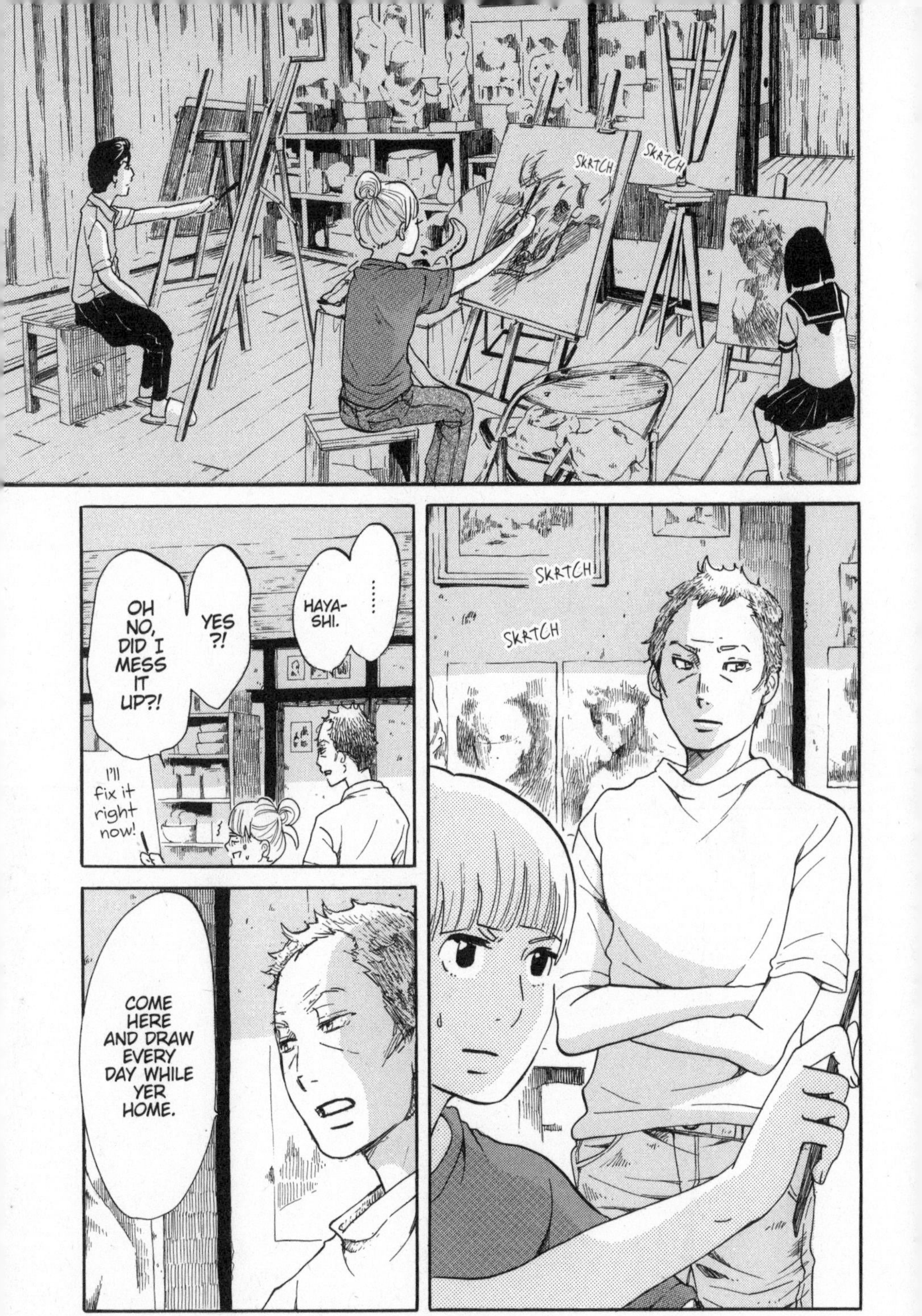
SKRTCH
SKRTCH
SKRTCH!
SKRTCH
......
HAYA-SHI.
YES?!
OH NO, DID I MESS IT UP?!
I'll fix it right now!
COME HERE AND DRAW EVERY DAY WHILE YER HOME.

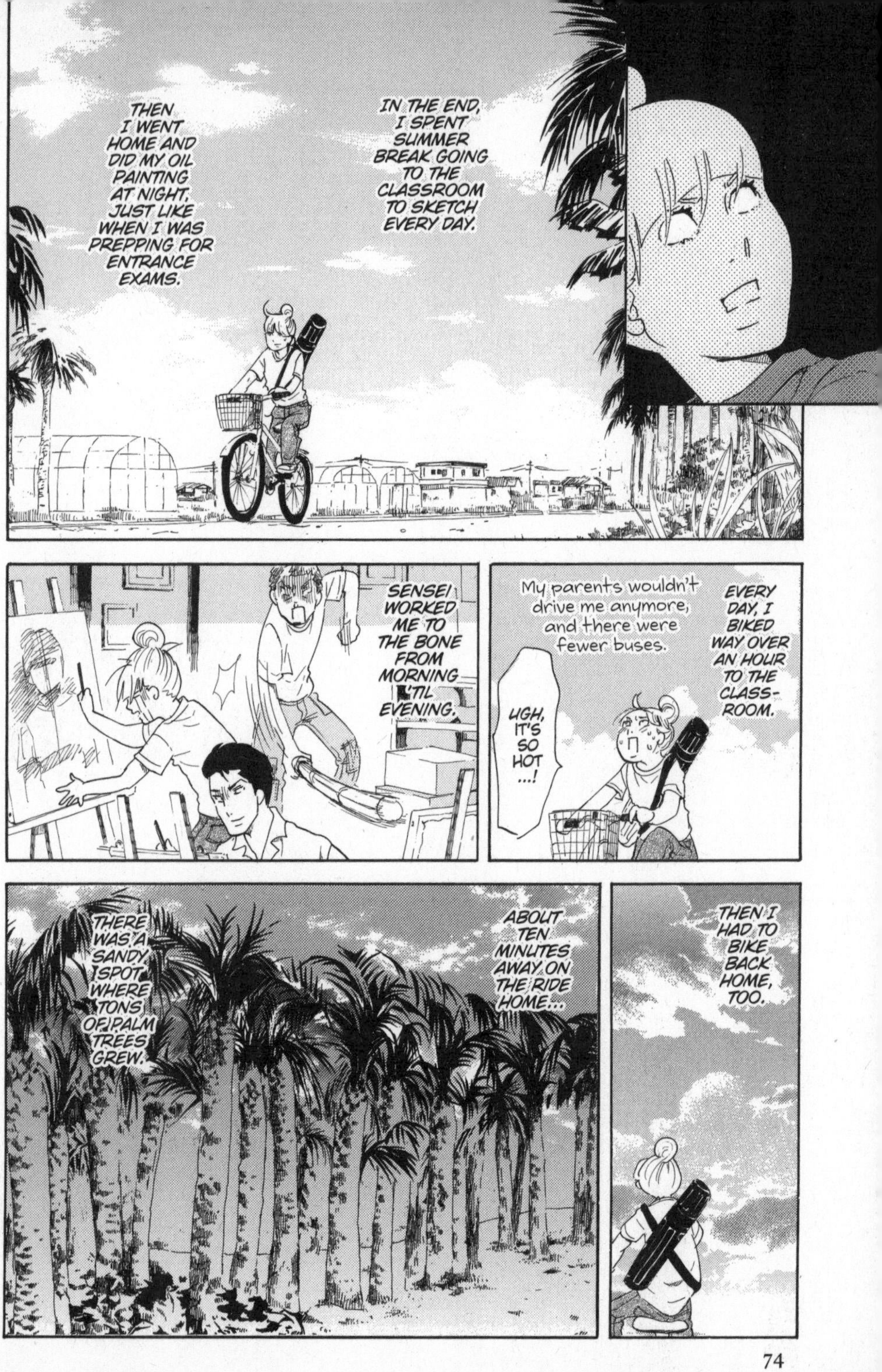
IN THE END, I SPENT SUMMER BREAK GOING TO THE CLASSROOM TO SKETCH EVERY DAY.
THEN I WENT HOME AND DID MY OIL PAINTING AT NIGHT, JUST LIKE WHEN I WAS PREPPING FOR ENTRANCE EXAMS.
EVERY DAY, I BIKED WAY OVER AN HOUR TO THE CLASS-ROOM.
My parents wouldn't drive me anymore, and there were fewer buses.
UGH, IT'S SO HOT ...!
SENSEI WORKED ME TO THE BONE FROM MORNING 'TIL EVENING.
THEN I HAD TO BIKE BACK HOME, TOO.
ABOUT TEN MINUTES AWAY ON THE RIDE HOME...
THERE WAS A SANDY SPOT WHERE TONS OF PALM TREES GREW.

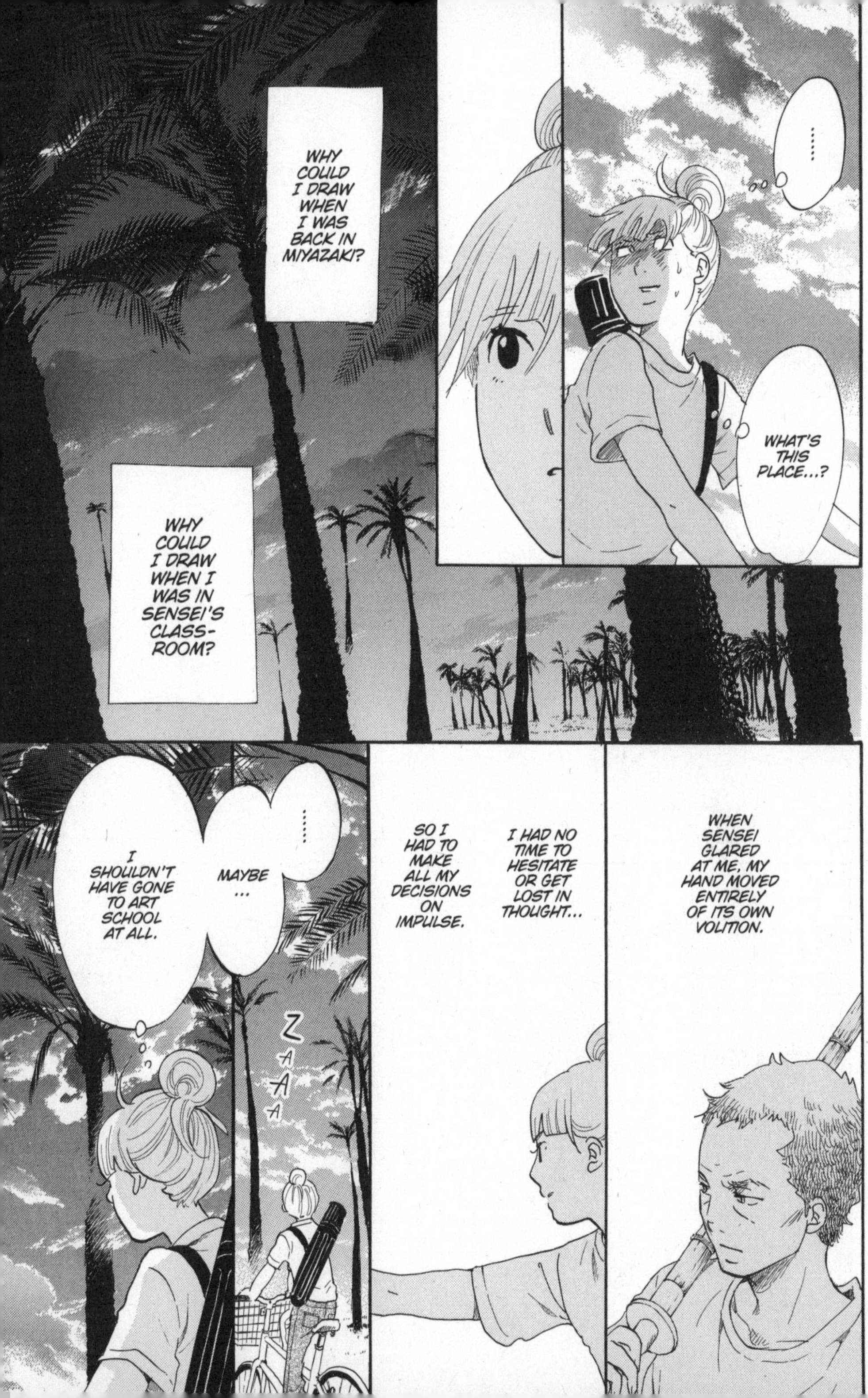
......
WHAT'S THIS PLACE...?
WHY COULD I DRAW WHEN I WAS BACK IN MIYAZAKI?
WHY COULD I DRAW WHEN I WAS IN SENSEI'S CLASS-ROOM?
WHEN SENSEI GLARED AT ME, MY HAND MOVED ENTIRELY OF ITS OWN VOLITION.
I HAD NO TIME TO HESITATE OR GET LOST IN THOUGHT...
SO I HAD TO MAKE ALL MY DECISIONS ON IMPULSE.
......
MAYBE ...
ZAAAA
I SHOULDN'T HAVE GONE TO ART SCHOOL AT ALL.

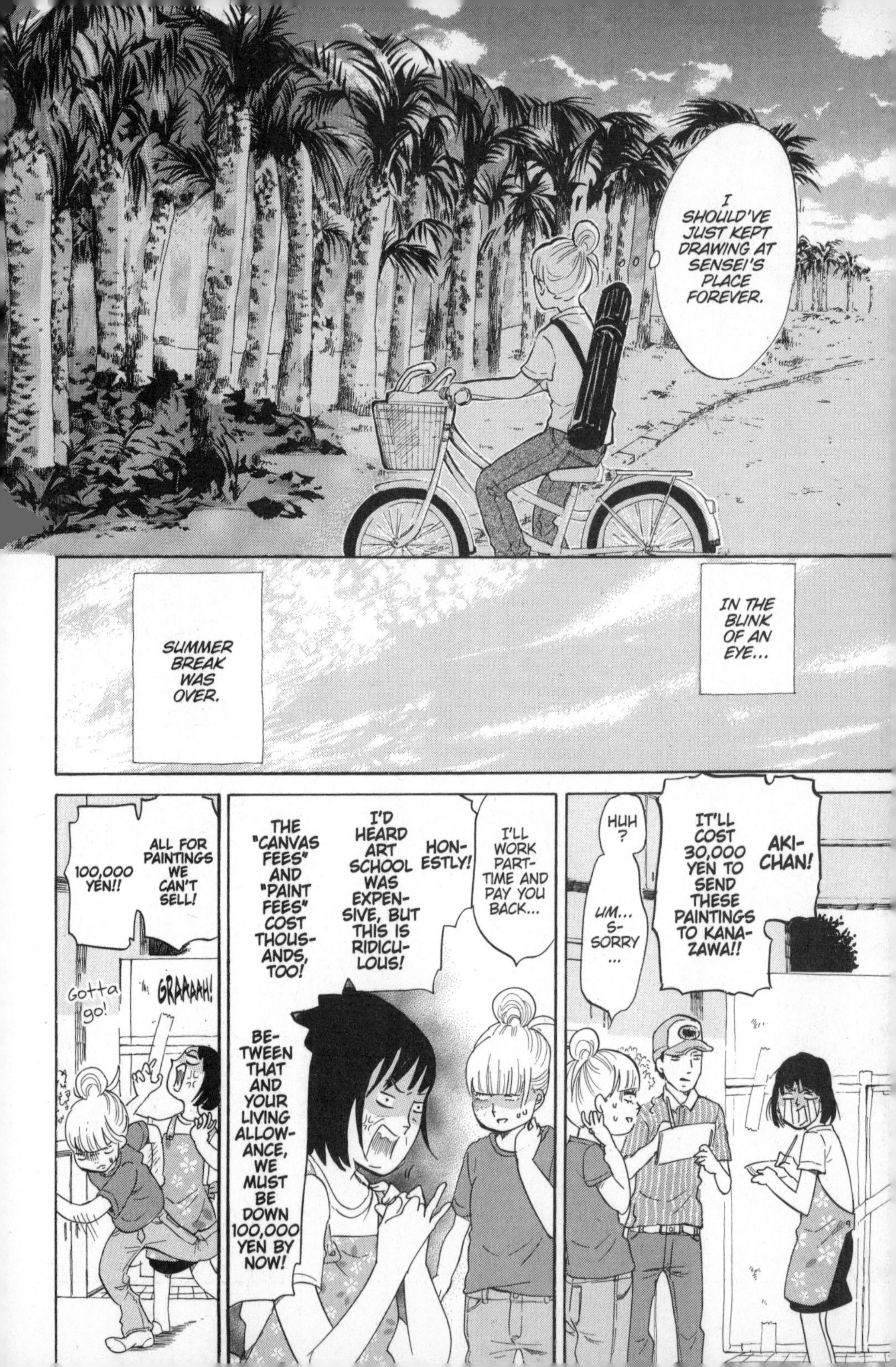

I SHOULD'VE JUST KEPT DRAWING AT SENSEI'S PLACE FOREVER.
IN THE BLINK OF AN EYE...
SUMMER BREAK WAS OVER.
AKI-CHAN!
IT'LL COST 30,000 YEN TO SEND THESE PAINTINGS TO KANAZAWA!!
HUH?
UM... S-SORRY...
I'LL WORK PART-TIME AND PAY YOU BACK...
HON-ESTLY!
I'D HEARD ART SCHOOL WAS EXPEN-SIVE, BUT THIS IS RIDICU-LOUS!
THE "CANVAS FEES" AND "PAINT FEES" COST THOUS-ANDS, TOO!
BE-TWEEN THAT AND YOUR LIVING ALLOW-ANCE, WE MUST BE DOWN 100,000 YEN BY NOW!
ALL FOR PAINTINGS WE CAN'T SELL!
100,000 YEN!!
GRAAAAH!
Gotta go!

BEFORE HEADING BACK TO KANAZAWA, I WENT TO THE CLASSROOM TO SAY GOODBYE.
HAYASHI.
KEEP DRAWIN' IN KANAZAWA, HEAR?
GULP!
ONCE YOU GOT ENOUGH FINISHED WORK, WE'LL DO A TWO-MAN SHOW.
DO AT LEAST TEN PIECES BY THE END OF THE YEAR, GOT IT?
ER...
DO TEN...?
UM...
I DON'T THINK...
I CAN...
GRAB
Guh!
JUST DRAW 'EM.
GOT IT?
OW OW OW!
LET GO!
WHAT'S IT GONNA BE?!!
ALL RIGHT, ALL RIGHT!
SEE YA, THEN.
COME BACK FOR WINTER BREAK.

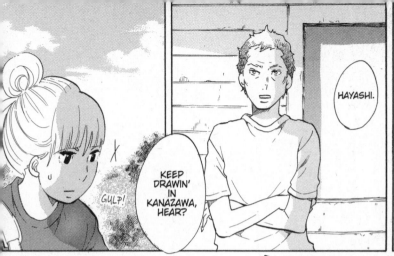

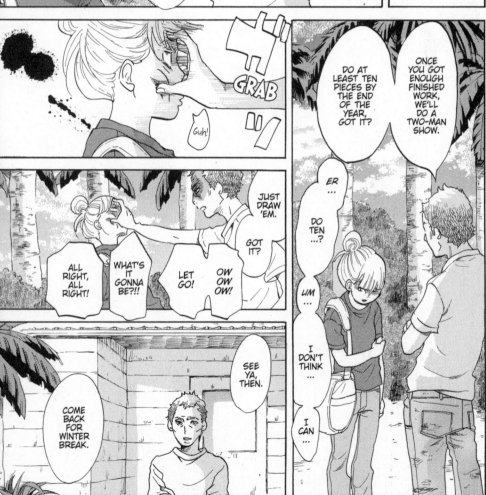

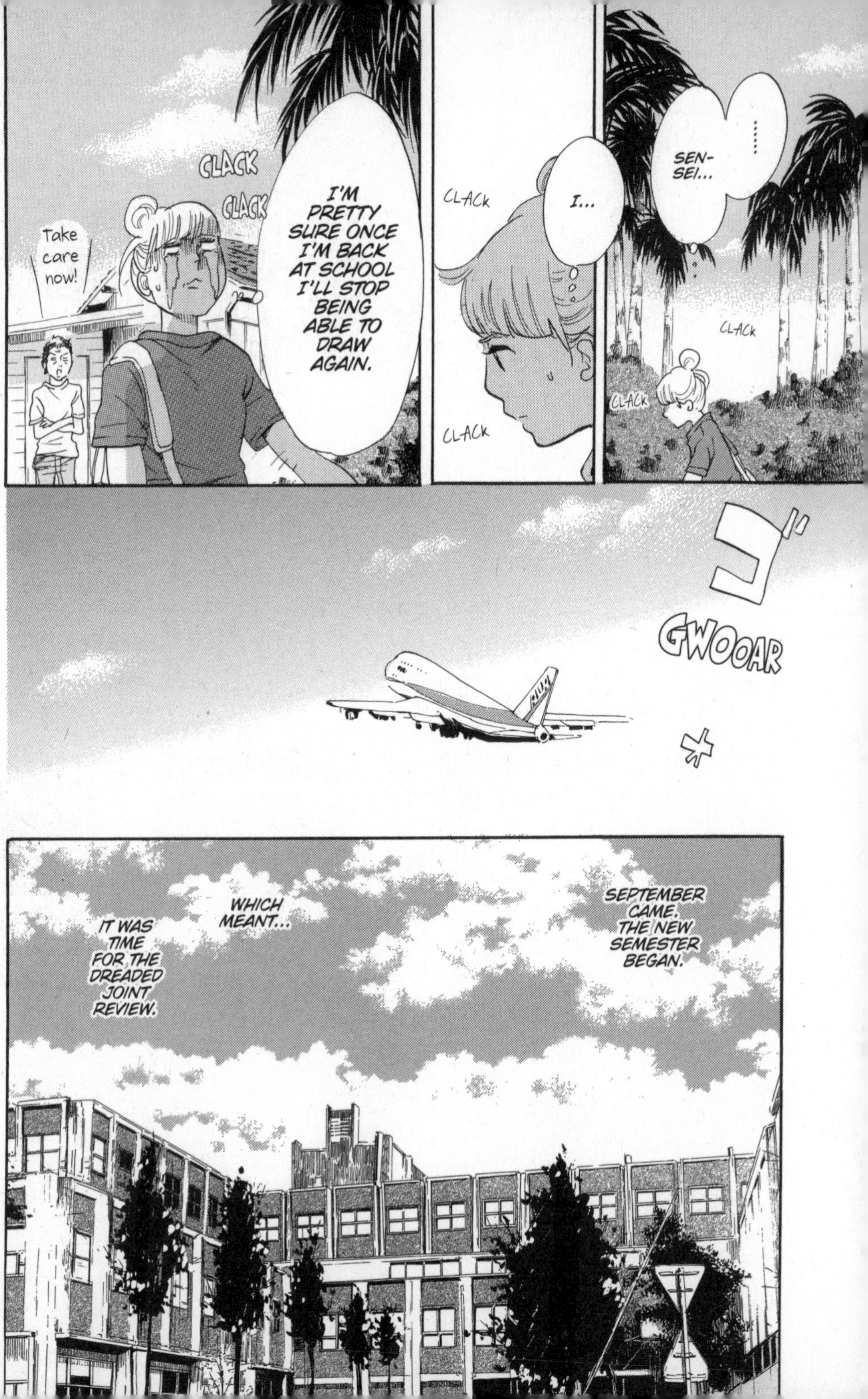
......
SEN-SEI...
CLACK
CLACK
I...
CLACK
CLACK
I'M PRETTY SURE ONCE I'M BACK AT SCHOOL I'LL STOP BEING ABLE TO DRAW AGAIN.
CLACK
CLACK
Take care now!
ゴ
GWOOAR
ォ
SEPTEMBER CAME. THE NEW SEMESTER BEGAN.
WHICH MEANT...
IT WAS TIME FOR THE DREADED JOINT REVIEW.

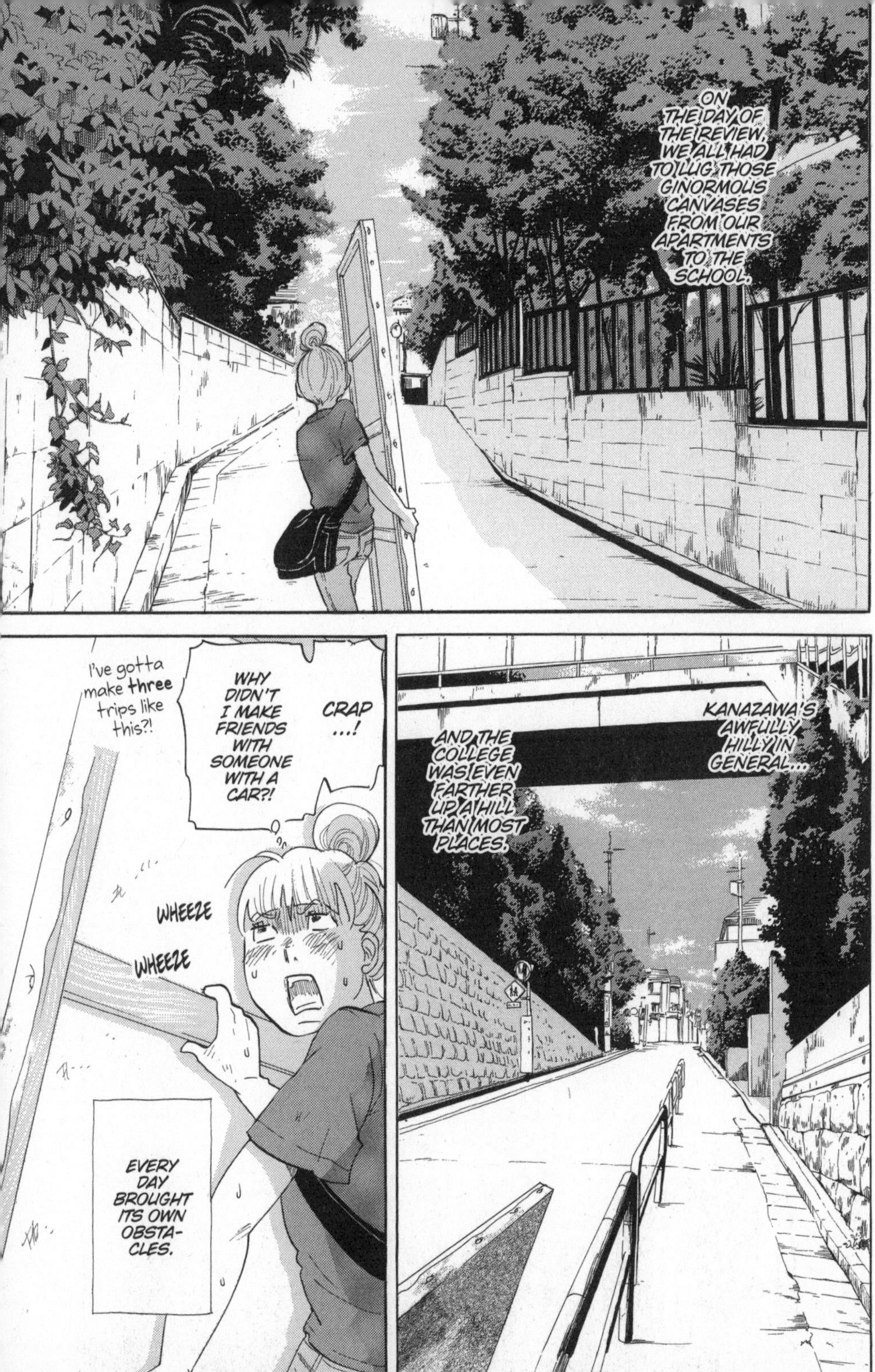

ON THE DAY OF THE REVIEW, WE ALL HAD TO LUG THOSE GINORMOUS CANVASES FROM OUR APARTMENTS TO THE SCHOOL.
KANAZAWA'S AWFULLY HILLY IN GENERAL...
AND THE COLLEGE WAS EVEN FARTHER UP A HILL THAN MOST PLACES.
CRAP ...!
WHY DIDN'T I MAKE FRIENDS WITH SOMEONE WITH A CAR?!
I've gotta make three trips like this?!
WHEEZE
WHEEZE
EVERY DAY BROUGHT ITS OWN OBSTACLES.

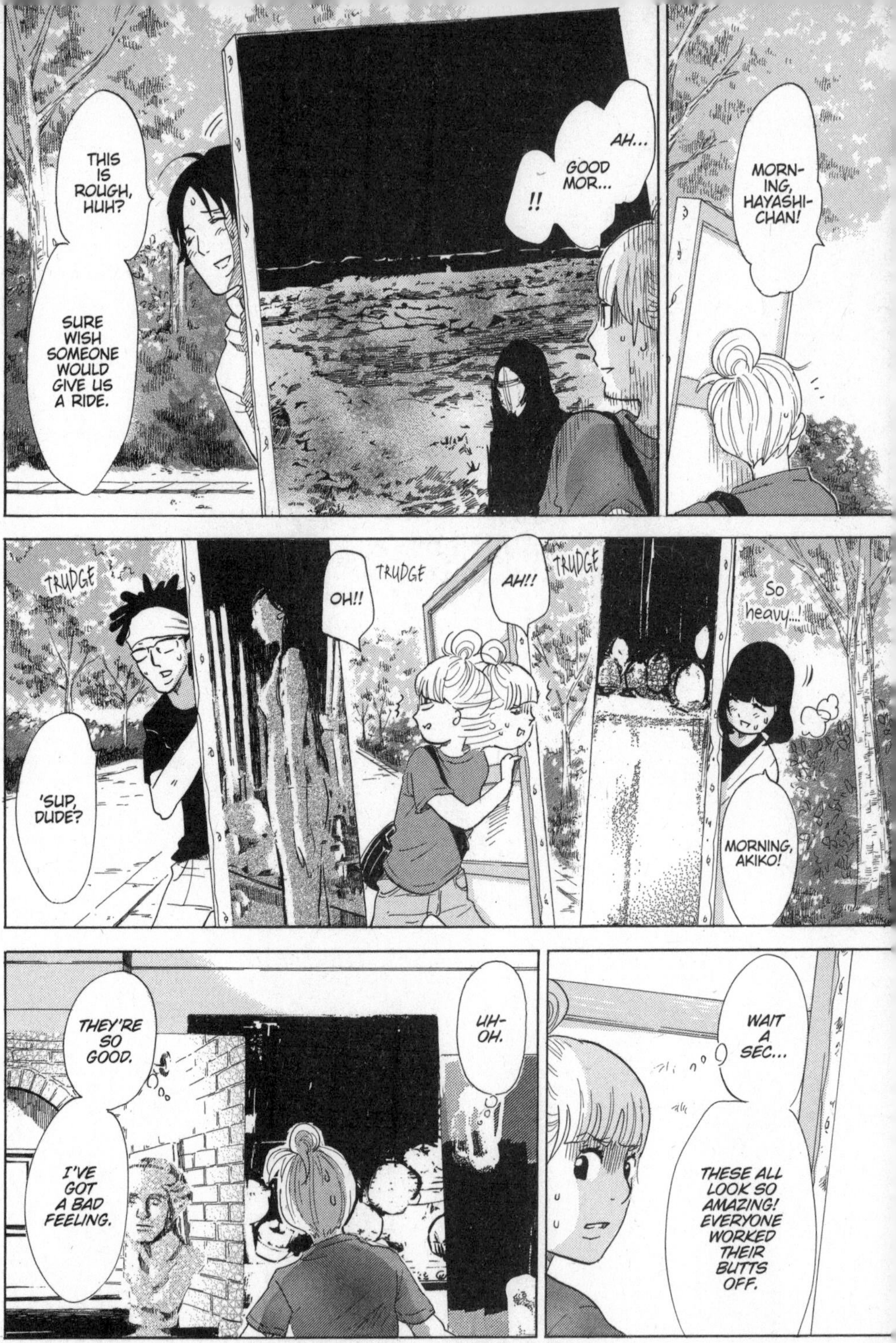
MORNING, HAYASHI-CHAN!
AH... GOOD MOR...
!!
THIS IS ROUGH, HUH?
SURE WISH SOMEONE WOULD GIVE US A RIDE.
So heavy...!
MORNING, AKIKO!
TRUDGE
AH!!
TRUDGE
OH!!
TRUDGE
'SUP, DUDE?
WAIT A SEC...
THESE ALL LOOK SO AMAZING! EVERYONE WORKED THEIR BUTTS OFF.
UH-OH.
THEY'RE SO GOOD.
I'VE GOT A BAD FEELING.

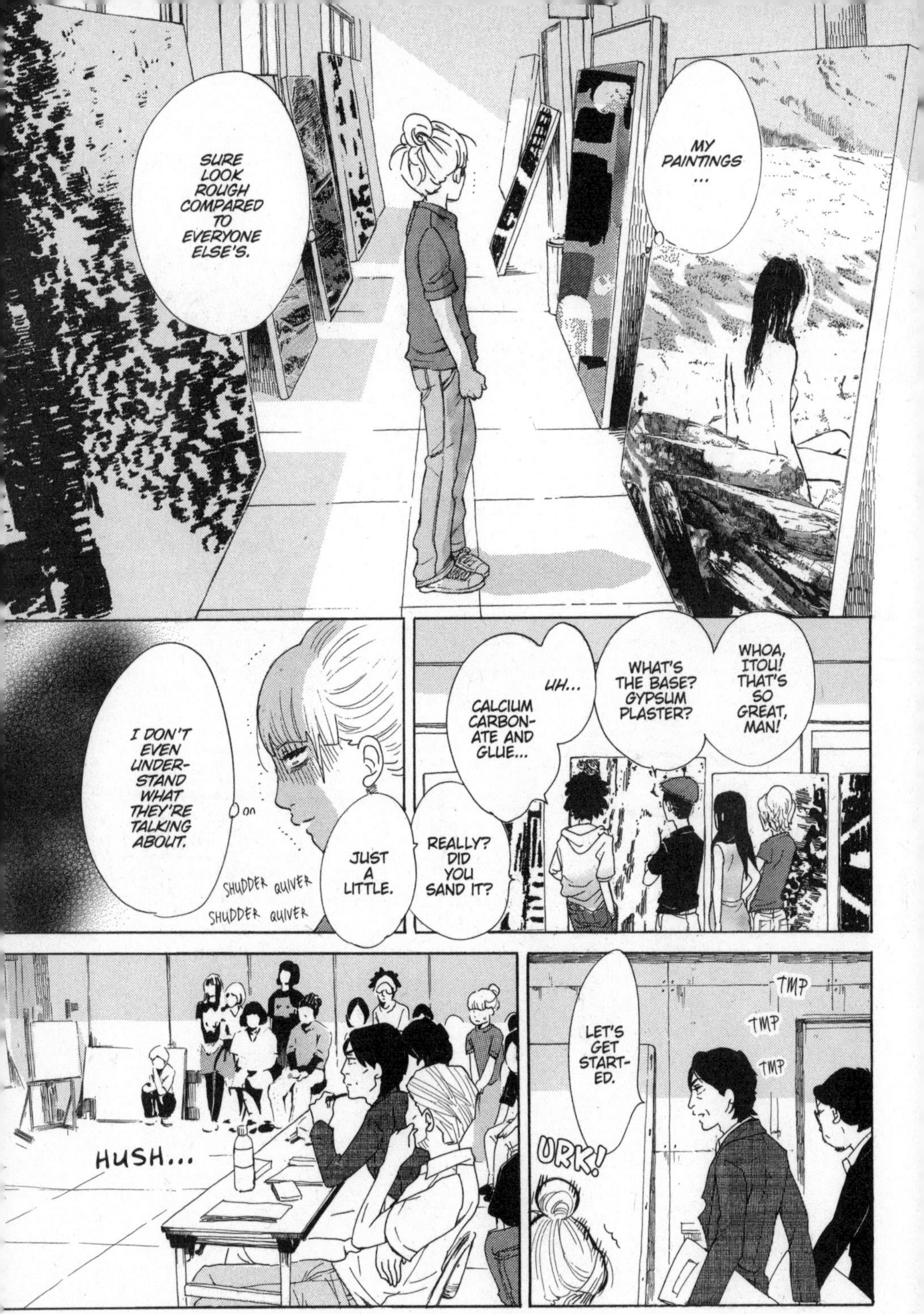
MY PAINTINGS ...
SURE LOOK ROUGH COMPARED TO EVERYONE ELSE'S.
WHOA, ITOU! THAT'S SO GREAT, MAN!
WHAT'S THE BASE? GYPSUM PLASTER?
UH...
CALCIUM CARBON-ATE AND GLUE...
REALLY? DID YOU SAND IT?
JUST A LITTLE.
I DON'T EVEN UNDER-STAND WHAT THEY'RE TALKING ABOUT.
SHUDDER QUIVER
SHUDDER QUIVER
TMP
TMP
TMP
LET'S GET START-ED.
URK!
HUSH...

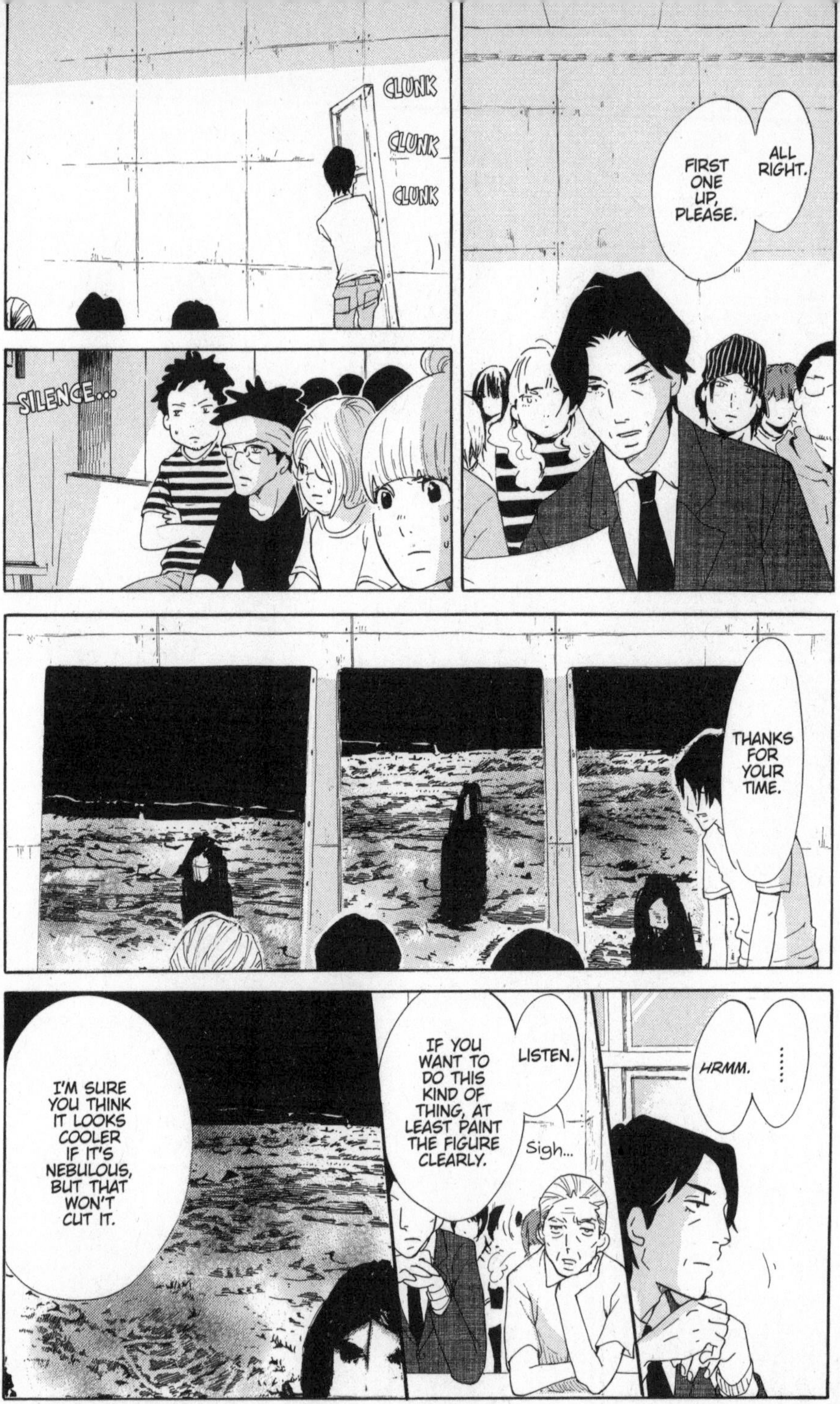
ALL RIGHT.
FIRST ONE UP, PLEASE.
CLUNK
CLUNK
CLUNK
SILENCE...
THANKS FOR YOUR TIME.
......
HRMM.
LISTEN.
IF YOU WANT TO DO THIS KIND OF THING, AT LEAST PAINT THE FIGURE CLEARLY.
Sigh...
I'M SURE YOU THINK IT LOOKS COOLER IF IT'S NEBULOUS, BUT THAT WON'T CUT IT.

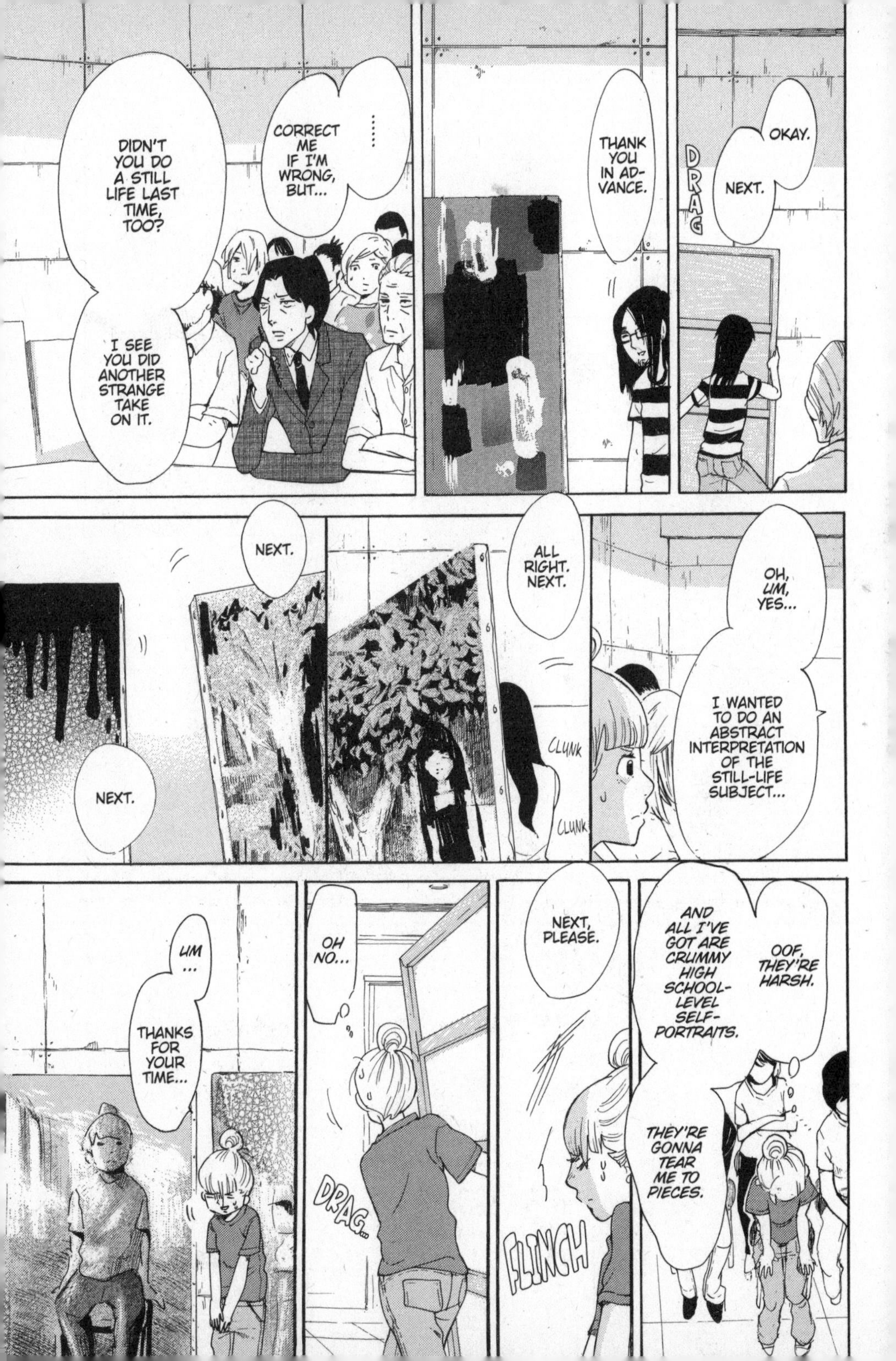
OKAY.
NEXT.
DRAG
THANK YOU IN AD-VANCE.
......
CORRECT ME IF I'M WRONG, BUT...
DIDN'T YOU DO A STILL LIFE LAST TIME, TOO?
I SEE YOU DID ANOTHER STRANGE TAKE ON IT.
OH, UM, YES...
I WANTED TO DO AN ABSTRACT INTERPRETATION OF THE STILL-LIFE SUBJECT...
ALL RIGHT. NEXT.
CLUNK
CLUNK
NEXT.
NEXT.
OOF, THEY'RE HARSH.
AND ALL I'VE GOT ARE CRUMMY HIGH SCHOOL-LEVEL SELF-PORTRAITS.
THEY'RE GONNA TEAR ME TO PIECES.
NEXT, PLEASE.
FLINCH
OH NO...
DRAG...
UM ...
THANKS FOR YOUR TIME...

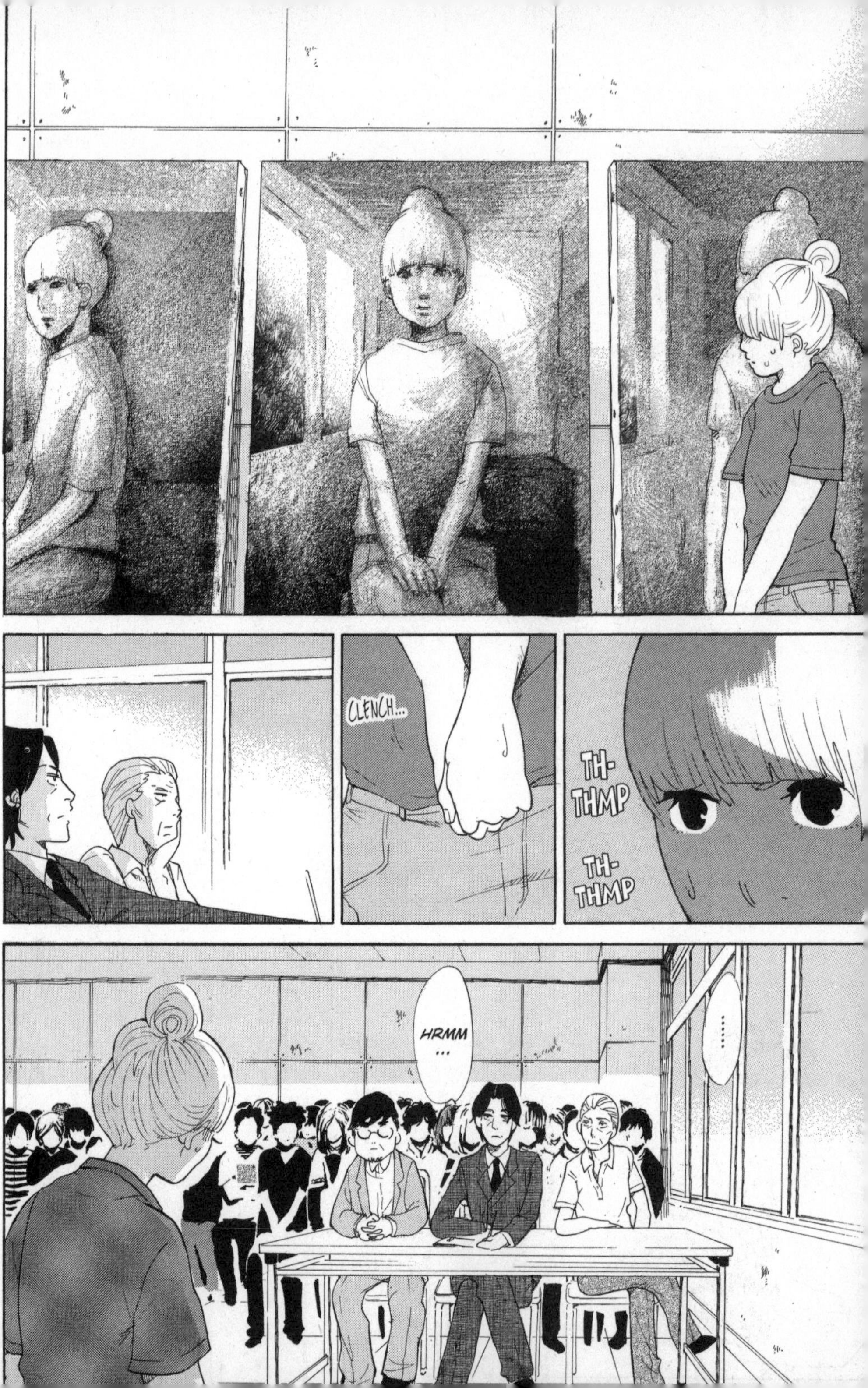
TH-
THMP
TH-
THMP
CLENCH...
......
HRMM
...

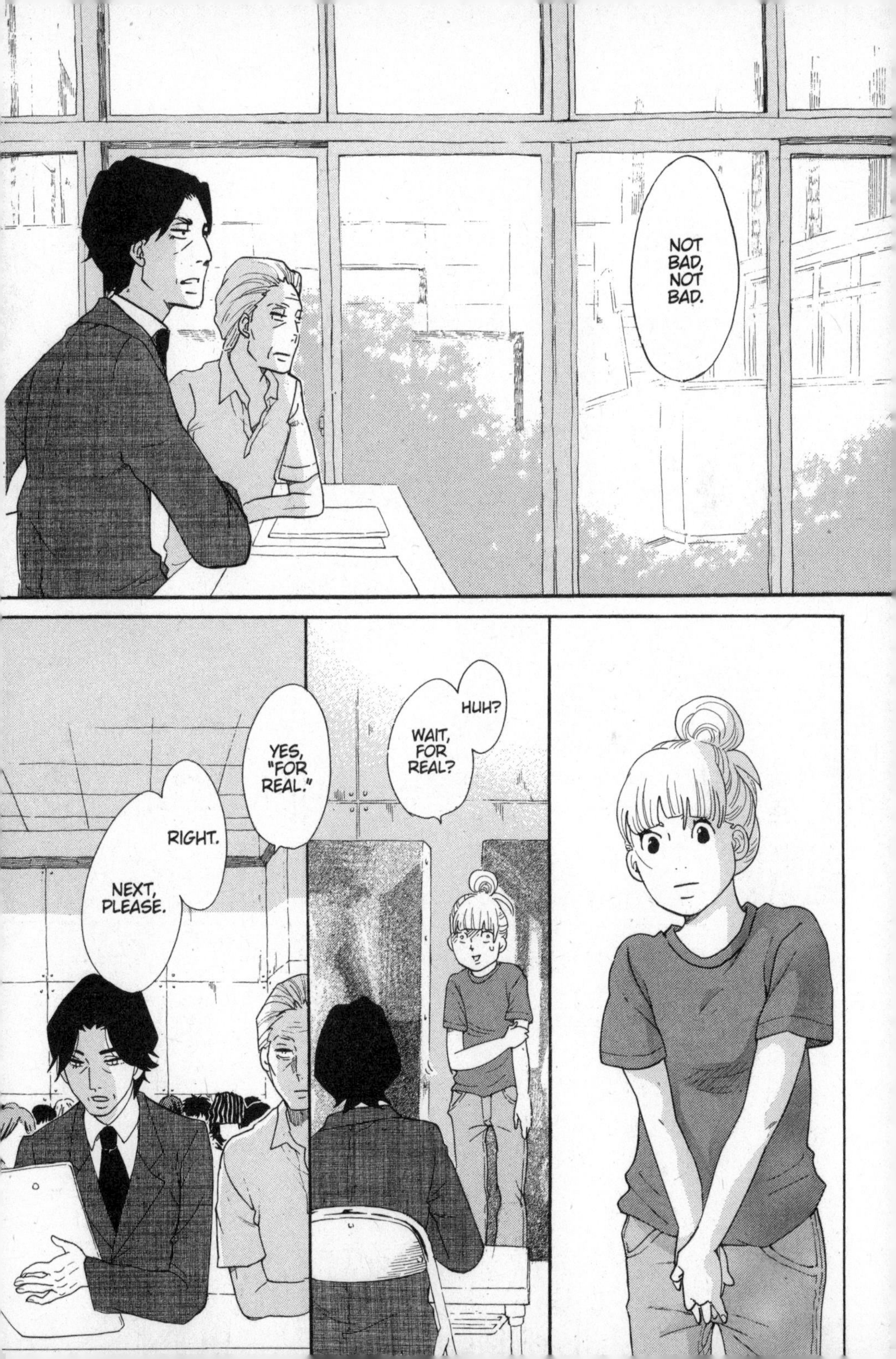
NOT BAD, NOT BAD.
HUH?
WAIT, FOR REAL?
YES, "FOR REAL."
RIGHT.
NEXT, PLEASE.

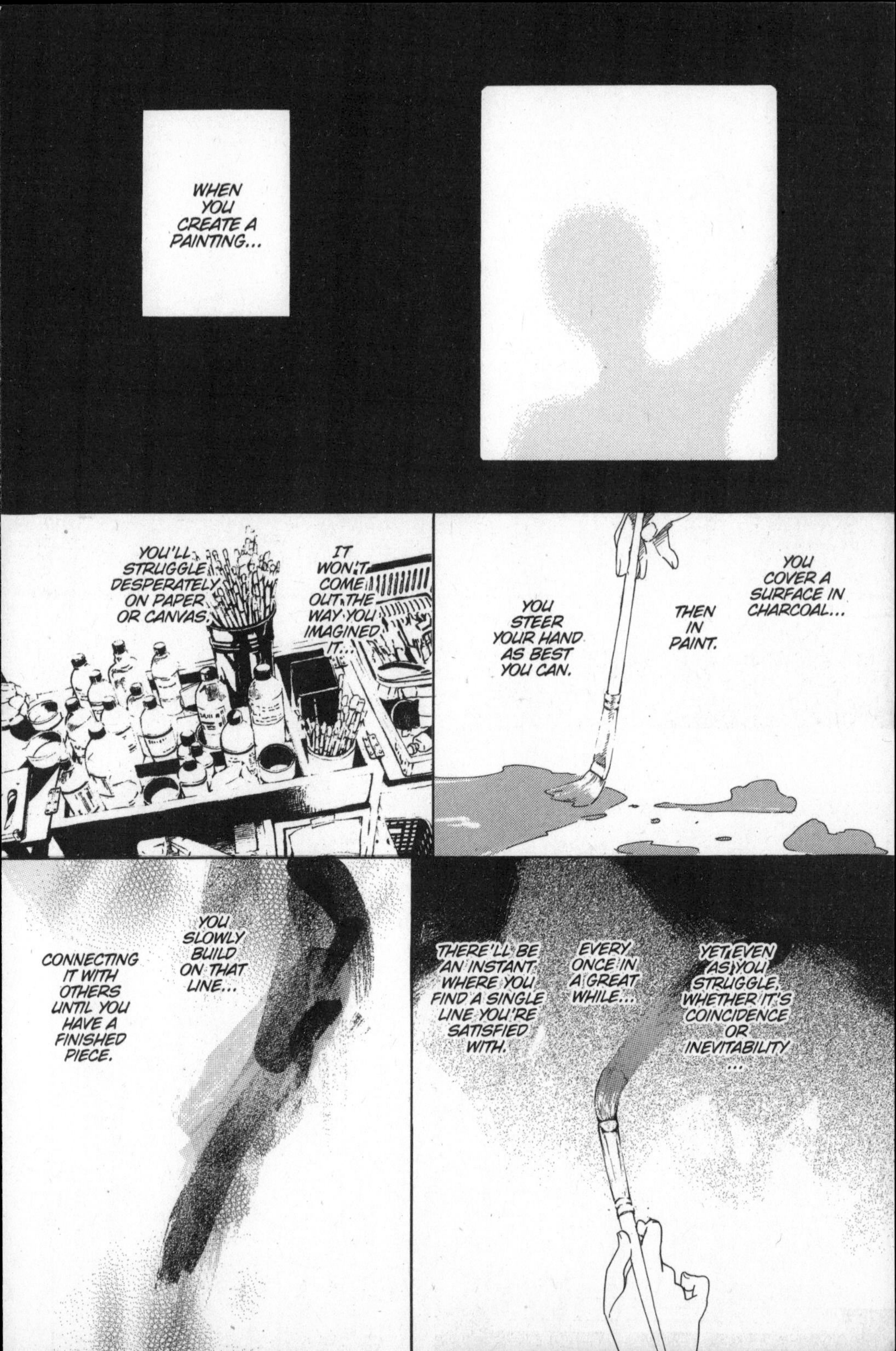
WHEN YOU CREATE A PAINTING...
YOU COVER A SURFACE IN CHARCOAL...
THEN IN PAINT.
YOU STEER YOUR HAND AS BEST YOU CAN.
IT WON'T COME OUT THE WAY YOU IMAGINED IT...
YOU'LL STRUGGLE DESPERATELY ON PAPER OR CANVAS.
YET EVEN AS YOU STRUGGLE, WHETHER IT'S COINCIDENCE OR INEVITABILITY...
EVERY ONCE IN A GREAT WHILE...
THERE'LL BE AN INSTANT WHERE YOU FIND A SINGLE LINE YOU'RE SATISFIED WITH.
YOU SLOWLY BUILD ON THAT LINE...
CONNECTING IT WITH OTHERS UNTIL YOU HAVE A FINISHED PIECE.

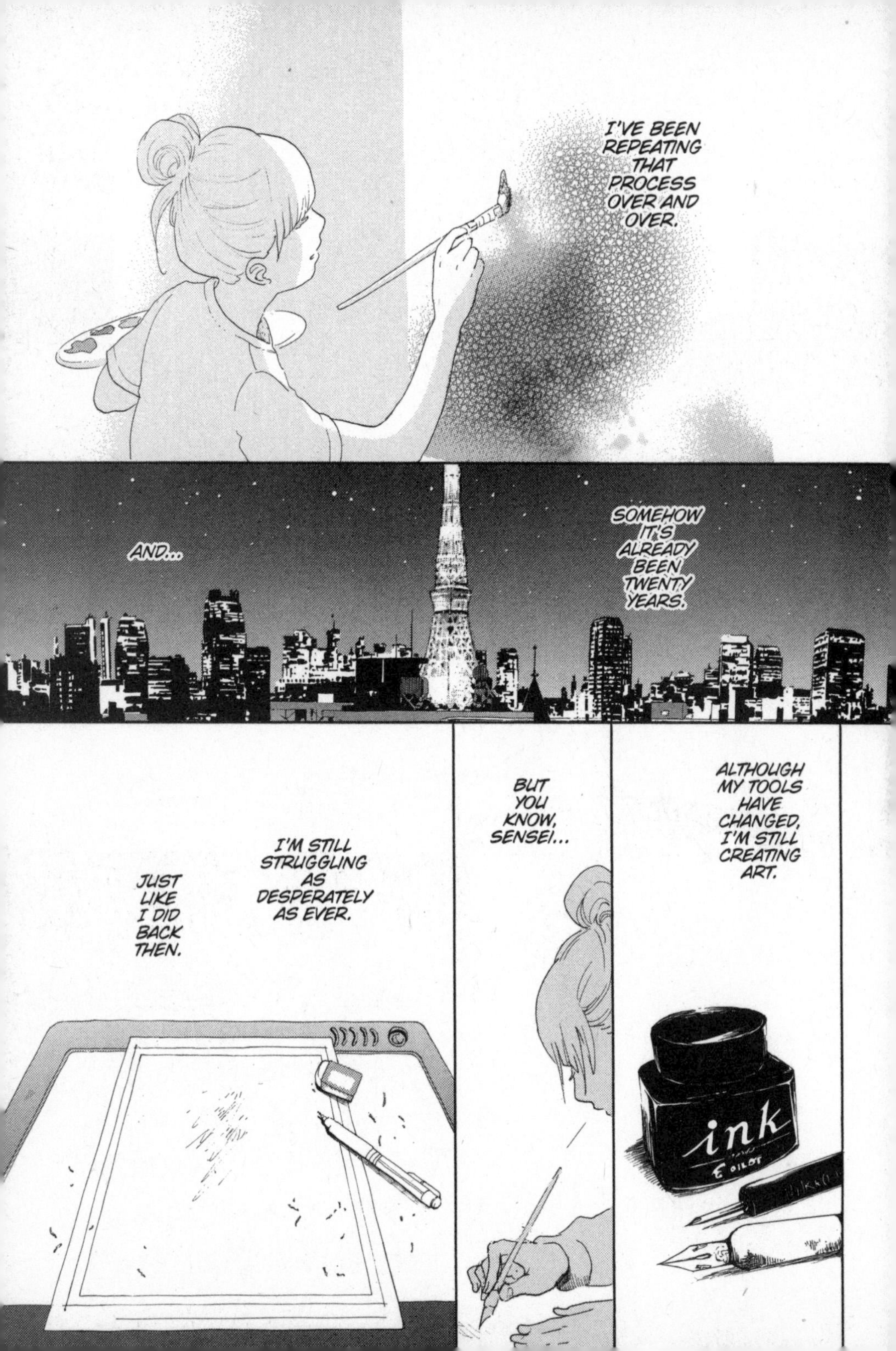
I'VE BEEN REPEATING THAT PROCESS OVER AND OVER.
SOMEHOW IT'S ALREADY BEEN TWENTY YEARS.
AND...
ALTHOUGH MY TOOLS HAVE CHANGED, I'M STILL CREATING ART.
ink
BUT YOU KNOW, SENSEI...
I'M STILL STRUGGLING AS DESPERATELY AS EVER.
JUST LIKE I DID BACK THEN.

Blank Canvas
My So-Called Artist's Journey

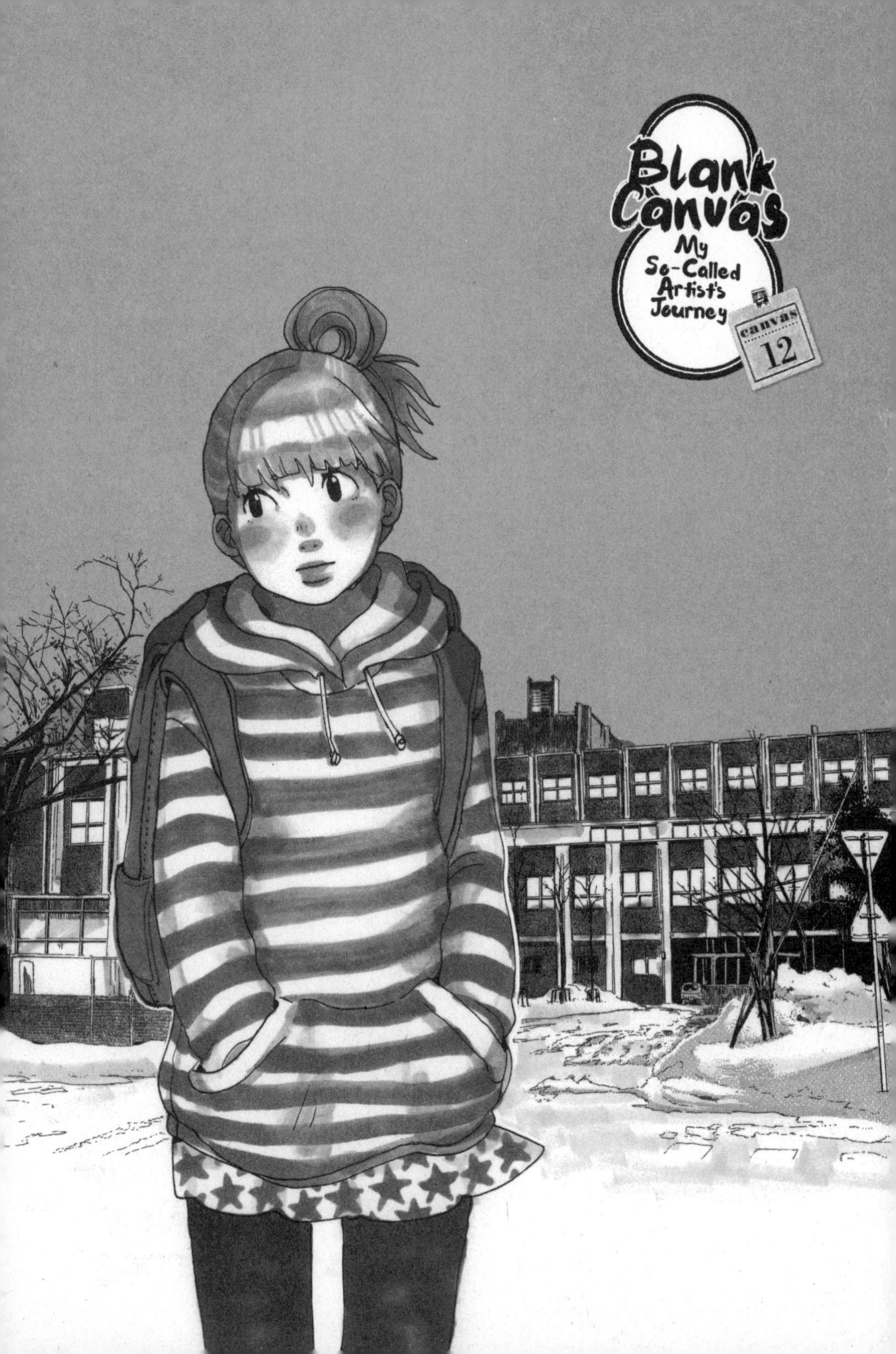
Blank Canvas
My So-Called Artist's Journey
canvas
12

Blank Canvas
My So-Called Artist's Journey

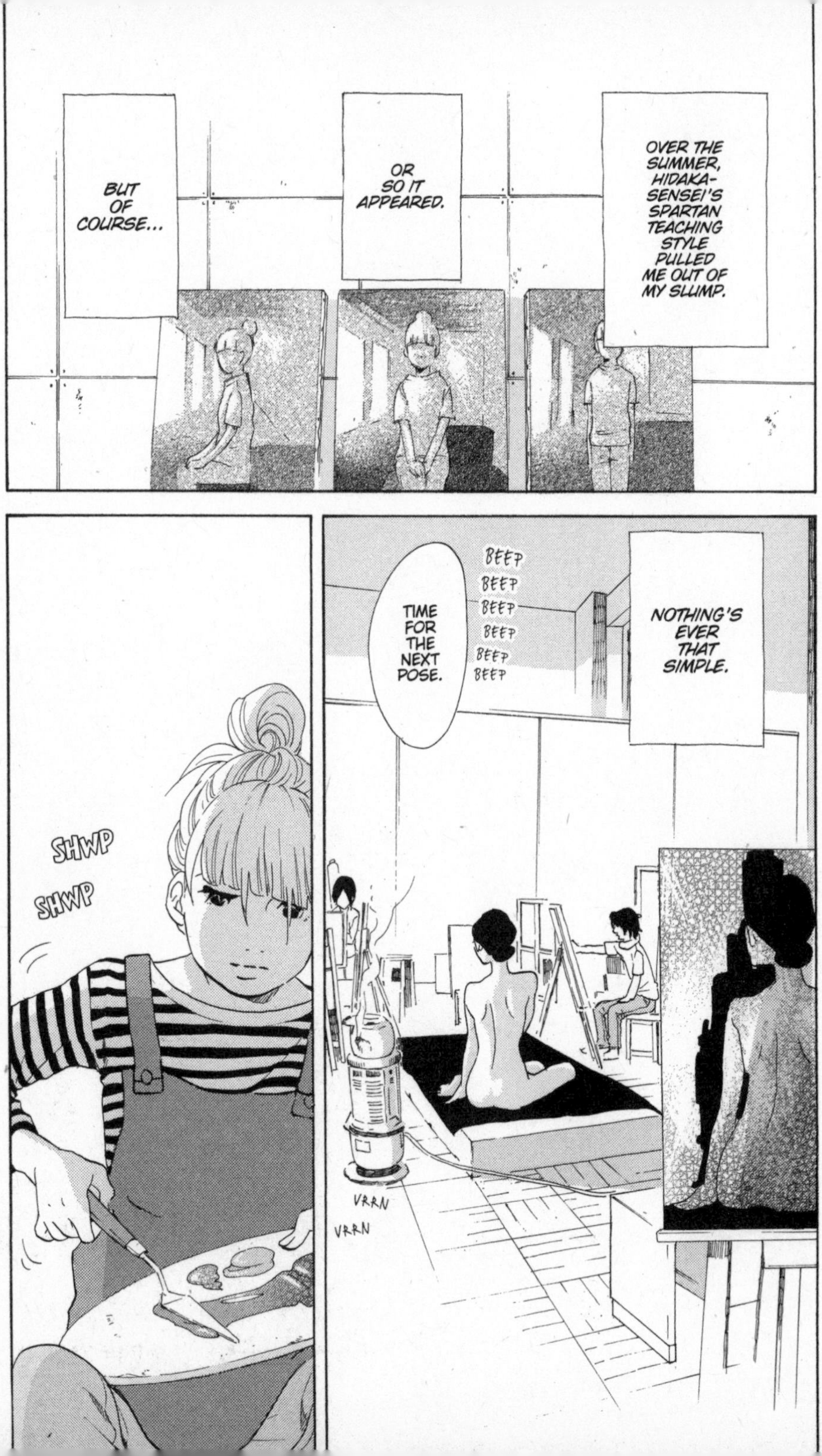
OVER THE SUMMER, HIDAKA-SENSEI'S SPARTAN TEACHING STYLE PULLED ME OUT OF MY SLUMP.
OR SO IT APPEARED.
BUT OF COURSE...
NOTHING'S EVER THAT SIMPLE.
BEEP BEEP BEEP BEEP BEEP BEEP
TIME FOR THE NEXT POSE.
VRRN VRRN
SHWP SHWP

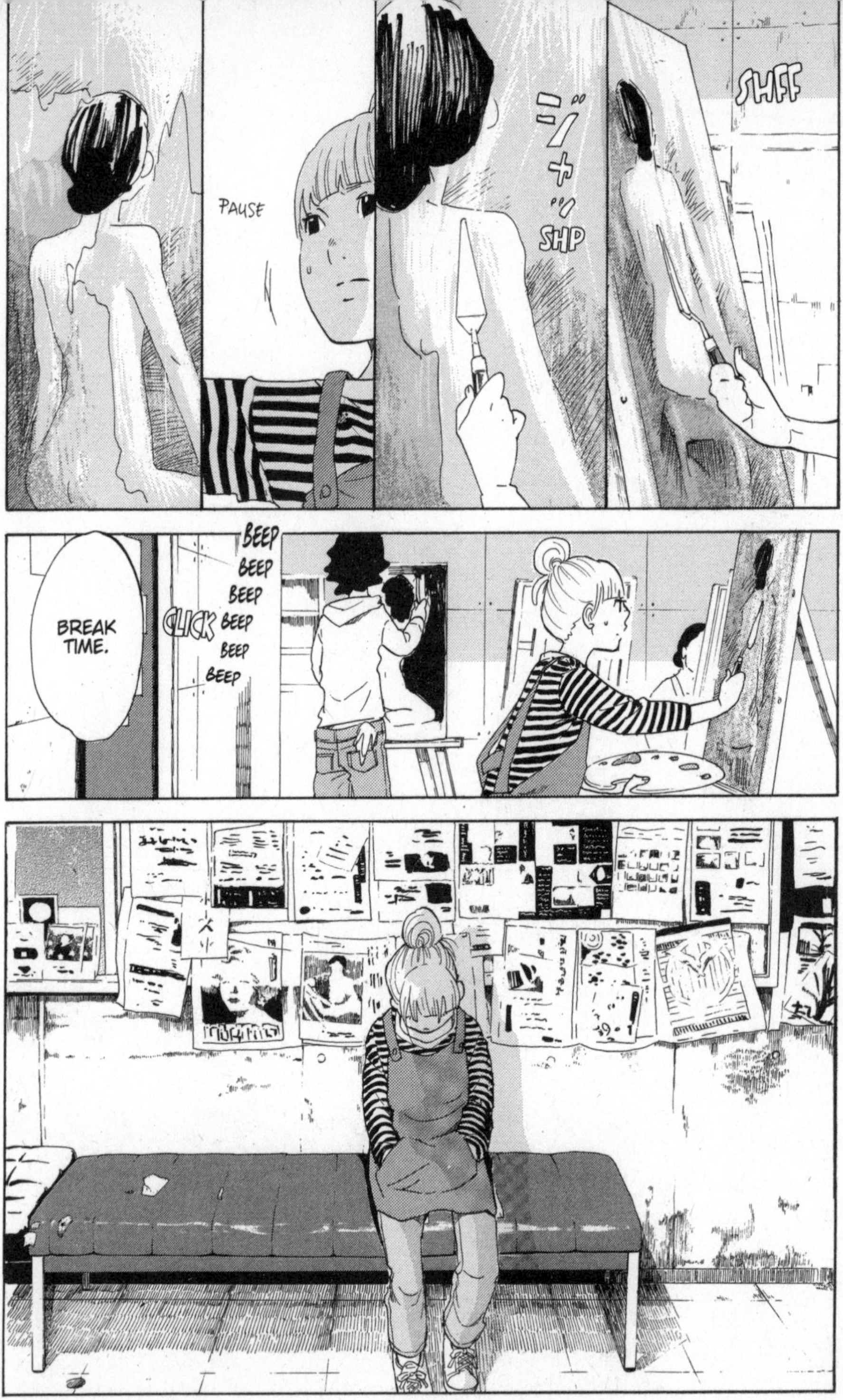
SHFF
ジャッ
SHP
PAUSE
BEEP
BEEP
BEEP
BEEP
BEEP
BEEP
CLICK
BREAK TIME.

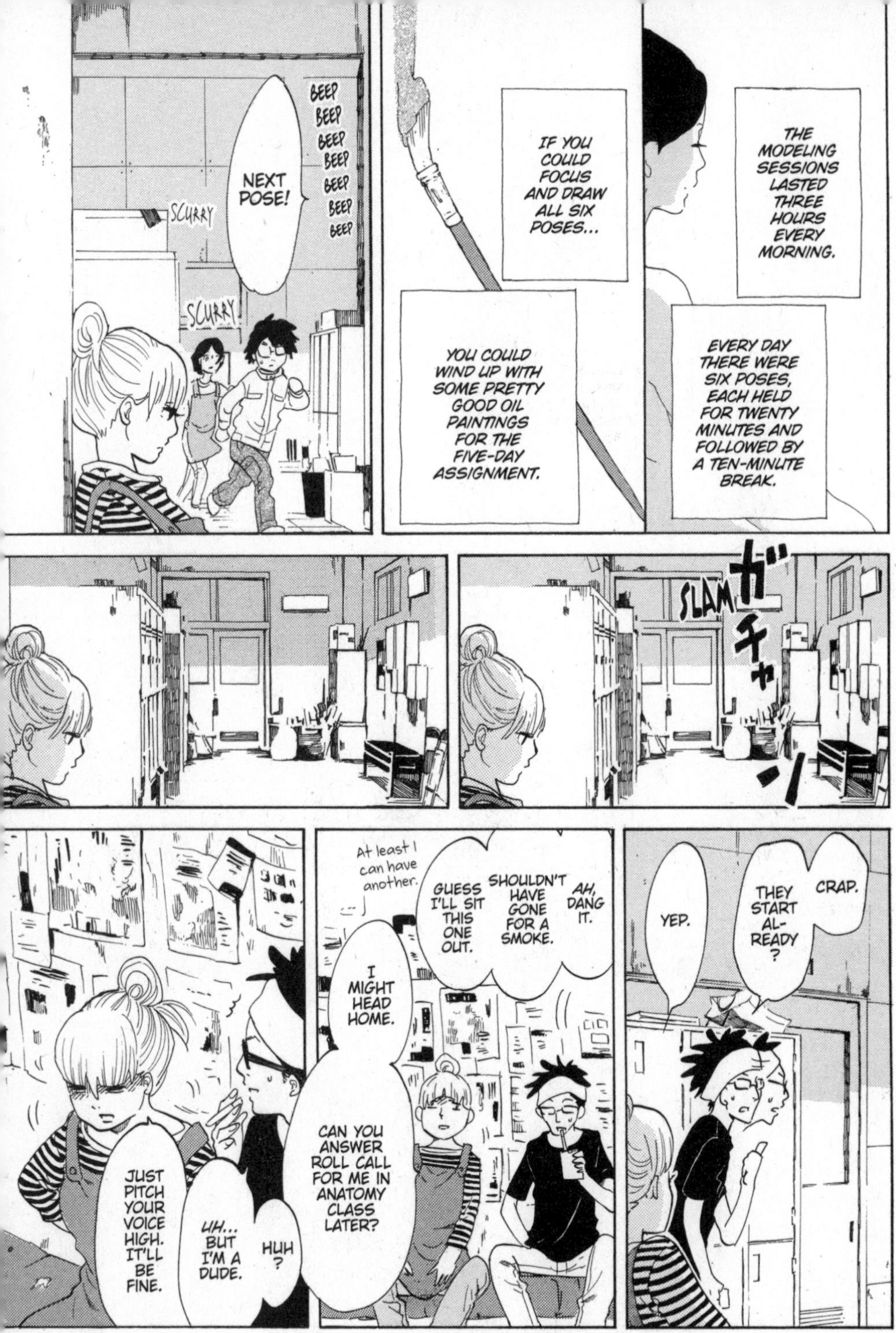
THE MODELING SESSIONS LASTED THREE HOURS EVERY MORNING.
EVERY DAY THERE WERE SIX POSES, EACH HELD FOR TWENTY MINUTES AND FOLLOWED BY A TEN-MINUTE BREAK.
IF YOU COULD FOCUS AND DRAW ALL SIX POSES...
YOU COULD WIND UP WITH SOME PRETTY GOOD OIL PAINTINGS FOR THE FIVE-DAY ASSIGNMENT.
BEEP BEEP BEEP BEEP BEEP BEEP BEEP
NEXT POSE!
SCURRY
SCURRY
SLAM
ガチャン
CRAP.
THEY START AL-READY?
YEP.
AH, DANG IT.
SHOULDN'T HAVE GONE FOR A SMOKE.
GUESS I'LL SIT THIS ONE OUT.
At least I can have another.
I MIGHT HEAD HOME.
CAN YOU ANSWER ROLL CALL FOR ME IN ANATOMY CLASS LATER?
HUH?
UH... BUT I'M A DUDE.
JUST PITCH YOUR VOICE HIGH. IT'LL BE FINE.

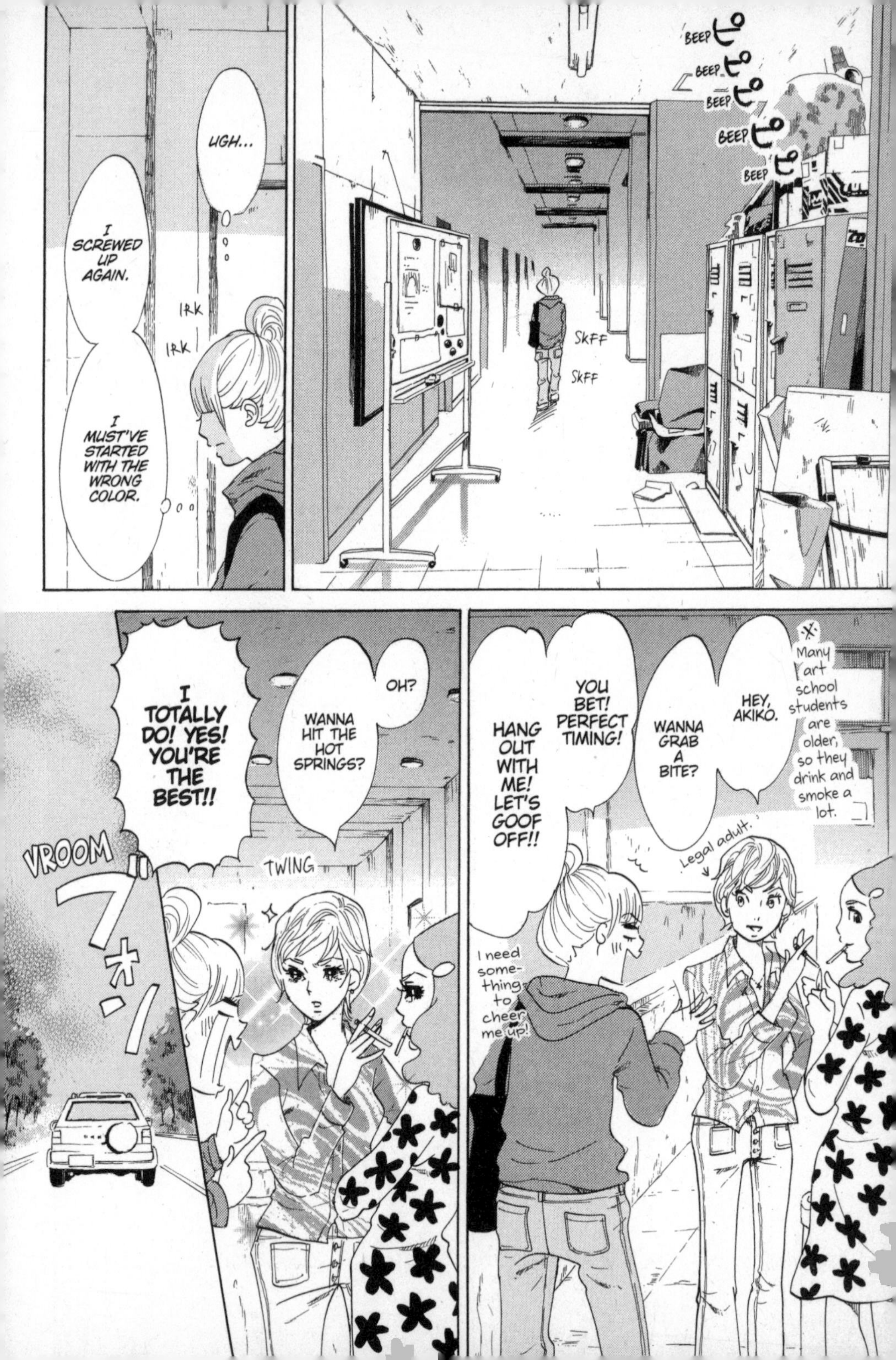
BEEP ピ
BEEP ピ
BEEP ピ
BEEP ピ
BEEP ピ
SKFF
SKFF
UGH...
I SCREWED UP AGAIN.
IRK
IRK
I MUST'VE STARTED WITH THE WRONG COLOR.
HEY, AKIKO.
WANNA GRAB A BITE?
※ Many art school students are older, so they drink and smoke a lot.
YOU BET! PERFECT TIMING!
HANG OUT WITH ME! LET'S GOOF OFF!!
Legal adult.
I need something to cheer me up!
OH?
WANNA HIT THE HOT SPRINGS?
I TOTALLY DO! YES! YOU'RE THE BEST!!
TWING
VROOM
ブォーン

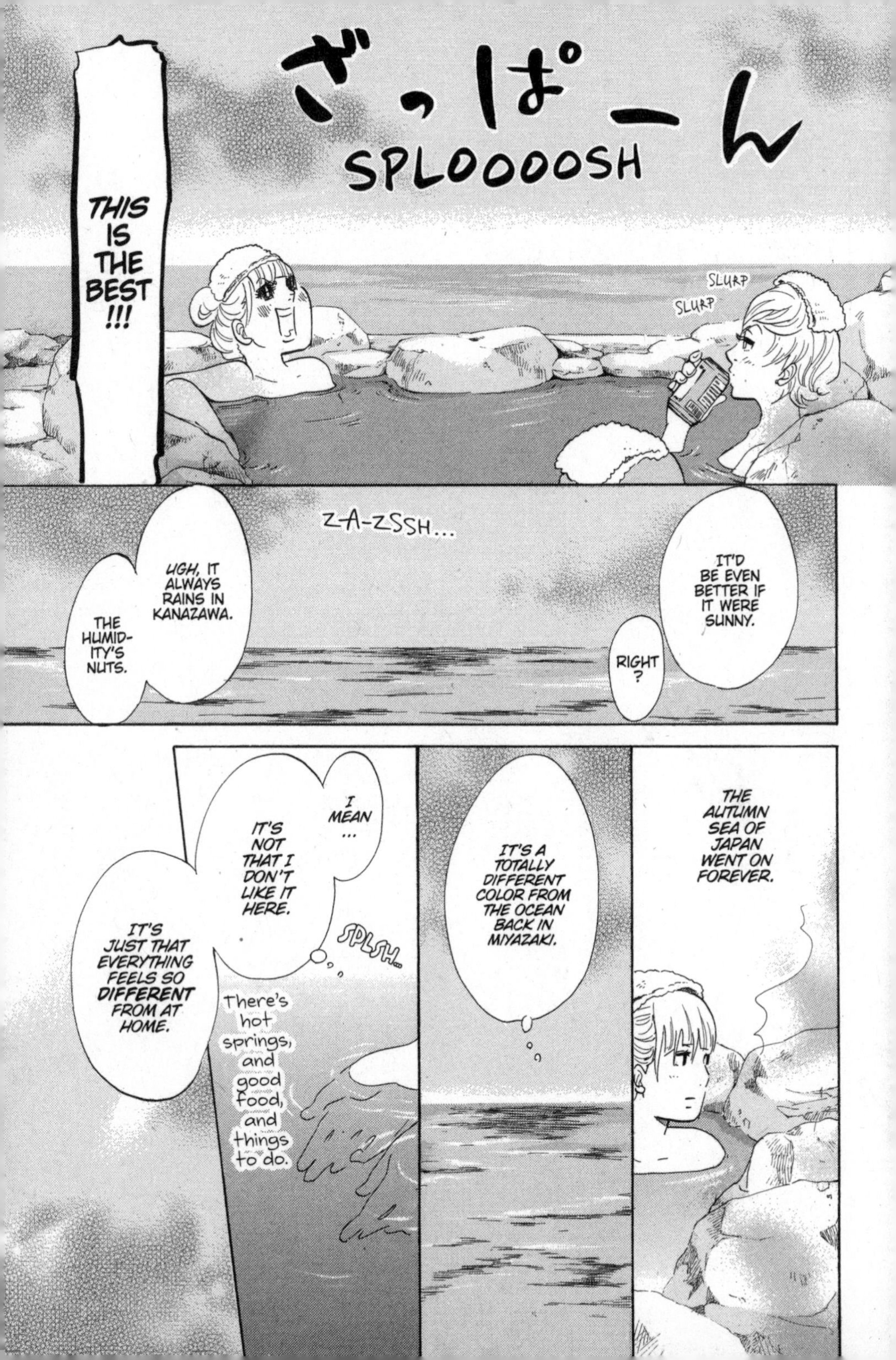
ざっぱーん
SPLOOOOSH
SLURP
SLURP
THIS IS THE BEST!!!
IT'D BE EVEN BETTER IF IT WERE SUNNY.
RIGHT?
Z-A-ZSSH...
UGH, IT ALWAYS RAINS IN KANAZAWA.
THE HUMIDITY'S NUTS.
THE AUTUMN SEA OF JAPAN WENT ON FOREVER.
IT'S A TOTALLY DIFFERENT COLOR FROM THE OCEAN BACK IN MIYAZAKI.
I MEAN...
IT'S NOT THAT I DON'T LIKE IT HERE.
IT'S JUST THAT EVERYTHING FEELS SO DIFFERENT FROM AT HOME.
SPLSH...
There's hot springs, and good food, and things to do.

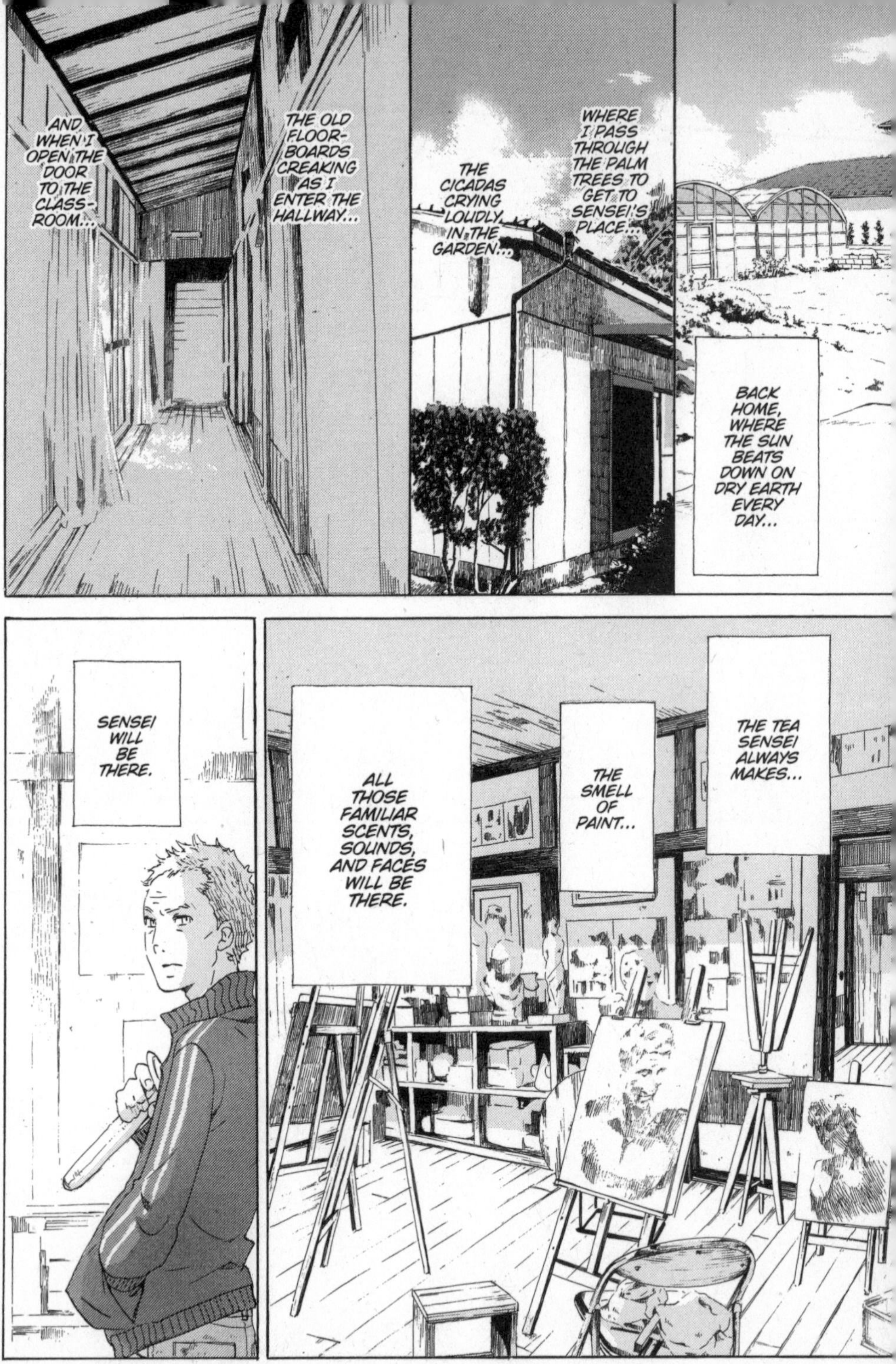
BACK HOME, WHERE THE SUN BEATS DOWN ON DRY EARTH EVERY DAY...
WHERE I PASS THROUGH THE PALM TREES TO GET TO SENSEI'S PLACE...
THE CICADAS CRYING LOUDLY IN THE GARDEN...
THE OLD FLOOR-BOARDS CREAKING AS I ENTER THE HALLWAY...
AND WHEN I OPEN THE DOOR TO THE CLASS-ROOM...
THE TEA SENSEI ALWAYS MAKES...
THE SMELL OF PAINT...
ALL THOSE FAMILIAR SCENTS, SOUNDS, AND FACES WILL BE THERE.
SENSEI WILL BE THERE.

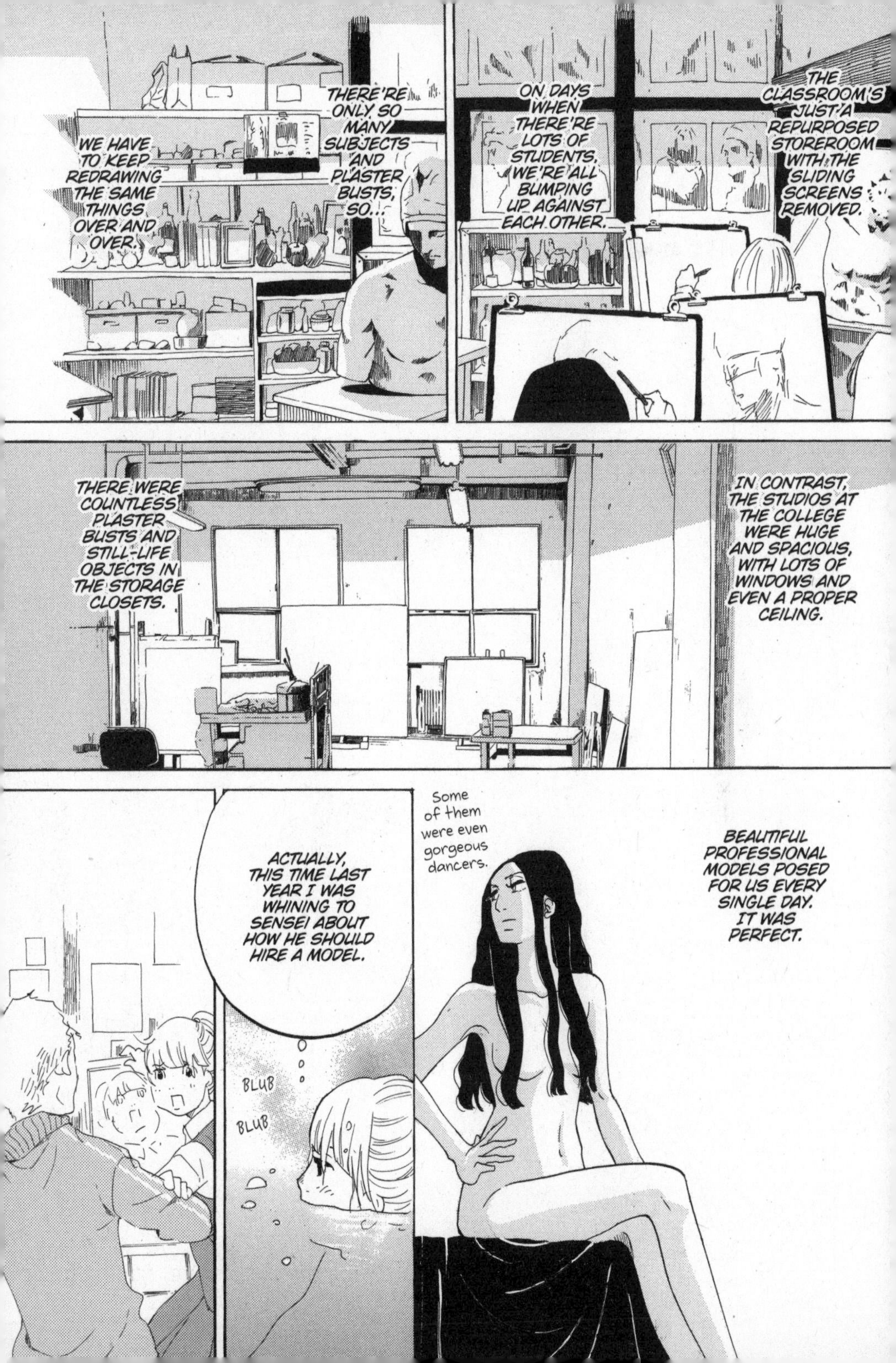
THE CLASSROOM'S JUST A REPURPOSED STOREROOM WITH THE SLIDING SCREENS REMOVED.
ON DAYS WHEN THERE'RE LOTS OF STUDENTS, WE'RE ALL BUMPING UP AGAINST EACH OTHER.
THERE'RE ONLY SO MANY SUBJECTS AND PLASTER BUSTS, SO...
WE HAVE TO KEEP REDRAWING THE SAME THINGS OVER AND OVER.
IN CONTRAST, THE STUDIOS AT THE COLLEGE WERE HUGE AND SPACIOUS, WITH LOTS OF WINDOWS AND EVEN A PROPER CEILING.
THERE WERE COUNTLESS PLASTER BUSTS AND STILL-LIFE OBJECTS IN THE STORAGE CLOSETS.
BEAUTIFUL PROFESSIONAL MODELS POSED FOR US EVERY SINGLE DAY. IT WAS PERFECT.
Some of them were even gorgeous dancers.
ACTUALLY, THIS TIME LAST YEAR I WAS WHINING TO SENSEI ABOUT HOW HE SHOULD HIRE A MODEL.
BLUB
BLUB

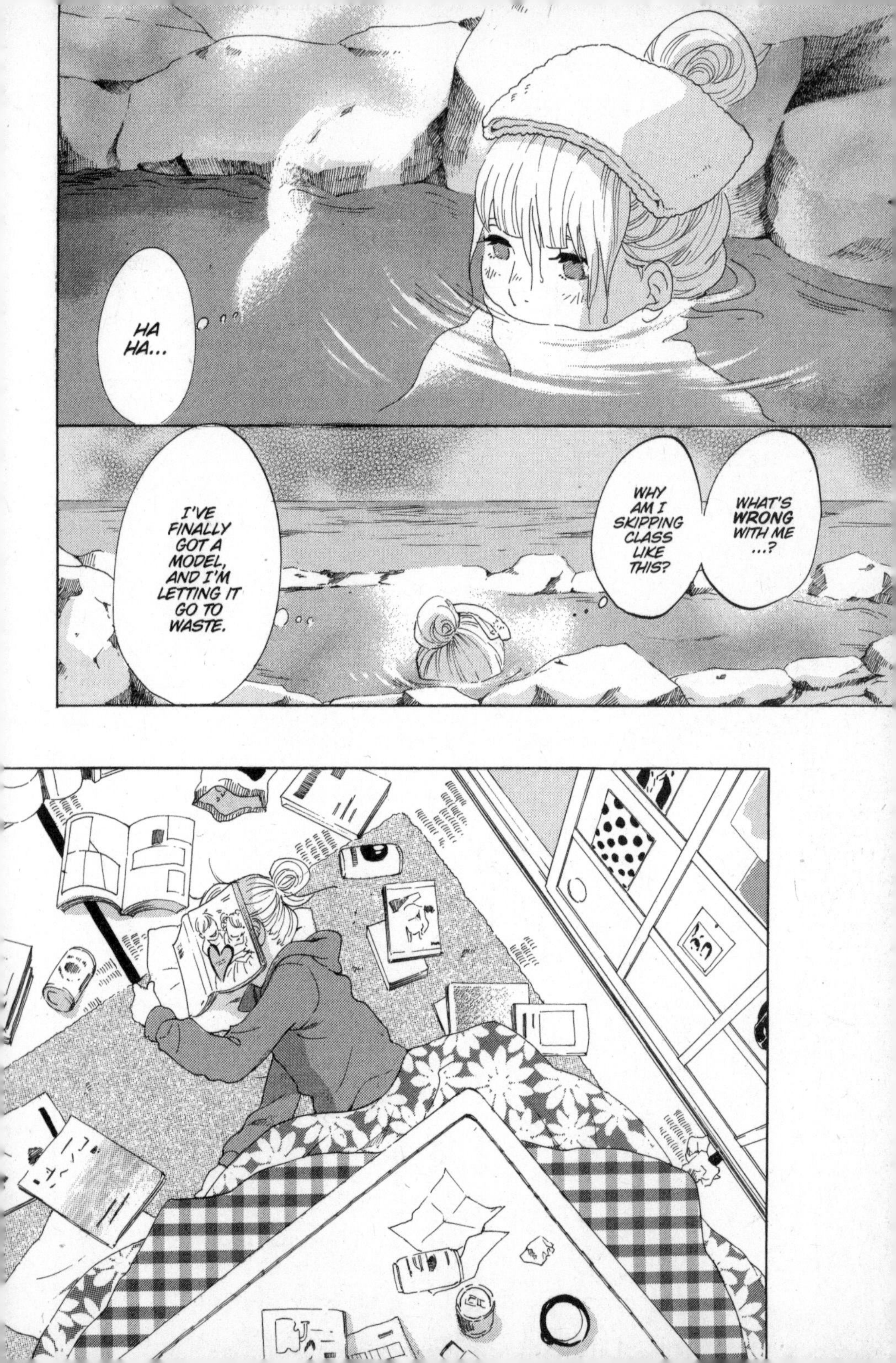
HA HA...
WHAT'S WRONG WITH ME ...?
WHY AM I SKIPPING CLASS LIKE THIS?
I'VE FINALLY GOT A MODEL, AND I'M LETTING IT GO TO WASTE.

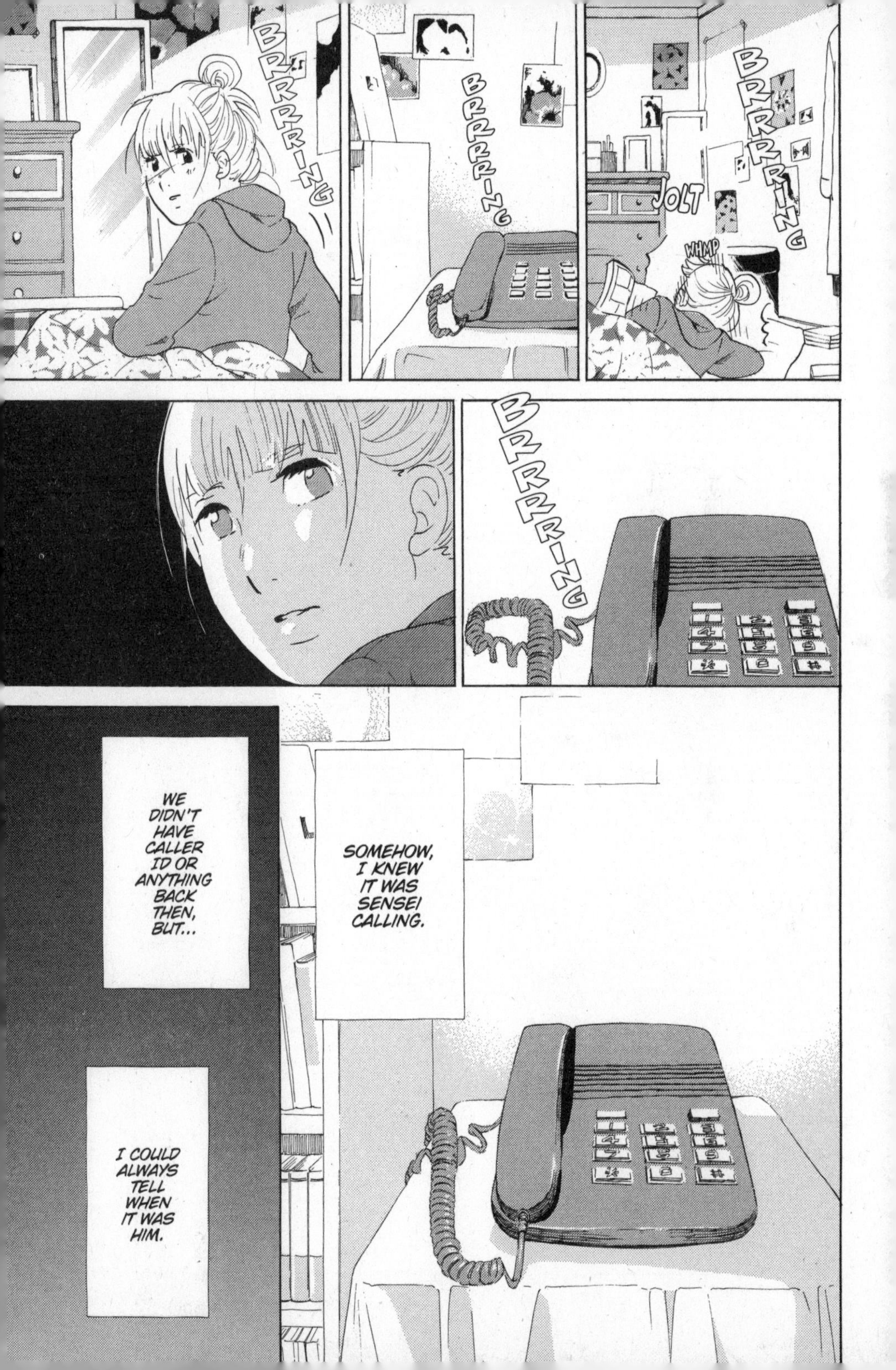
BRRRRING
JOLT
WHMP
BRRRRING
BRRRRING
BRRRRING
SOMEHOW, I KNEW IT WAS SENSEI CALLING.
WE DIDN'T HAVE CALLER ID OR ANYTHING BACK THEN, BUT...
I COULD ALWAYS TELL WHEN IT WAS HIM.

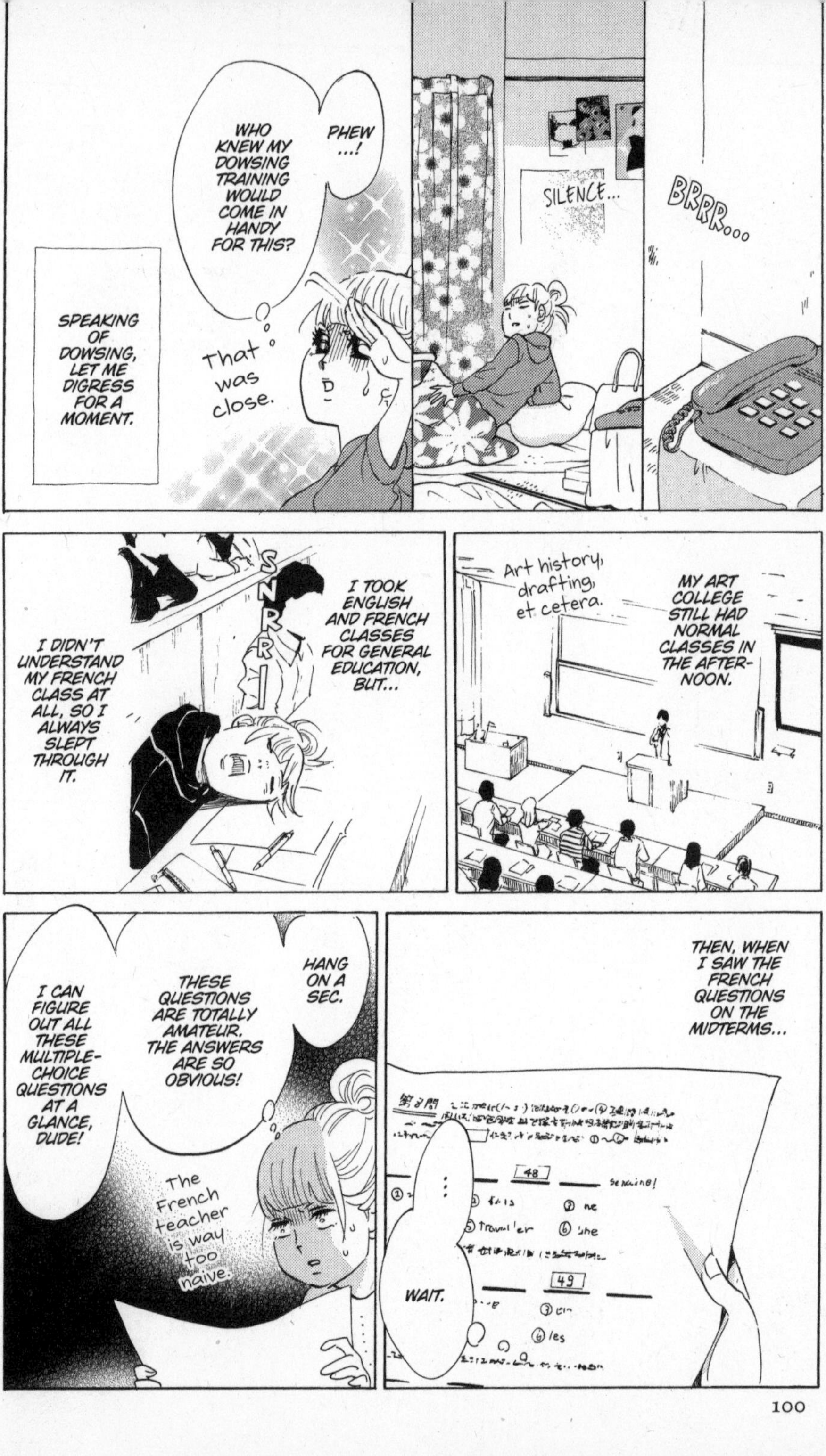
BRRR...
SILENCE...
PHEW ...!
WHO KNEW MY DOWSING TRAINING WOULD COME IN HANDY FOR THIS?
That was close.
SPEAKING OF DOWSING, LET ME DIGRESS FOR A MOMENT.
MY ART COLLEGE STILL HAD NORMAL CLASSES IN THE AFTERNOON.
Art history, drafting, et cetera.
I TOOK ENGLISH AND FRENCH CLASSES FOR GENERAL EDUCATION, BUT...
SNRRI
I DIDN'T UNDERSTAND MY FRENCH CLASS AT ALL, SO I ALWAYS SLEPT THROUGH IT.
THEN, WHEN I SAW THE FRENCH QUESTIONS ON THE MIDTERMS...
...
WAIT.
HANG ON A SEC.
THESE QUESTIONS ARE TOTALLY AMATEUR. THE ANSWERS ARE SO OBVIOUS!
I CAN FIGURE OUT ALL THESE MULTIPLE-CHOICE QUESTIONS AT A GLANCE, DUDE!
The French teacher is way too naive.

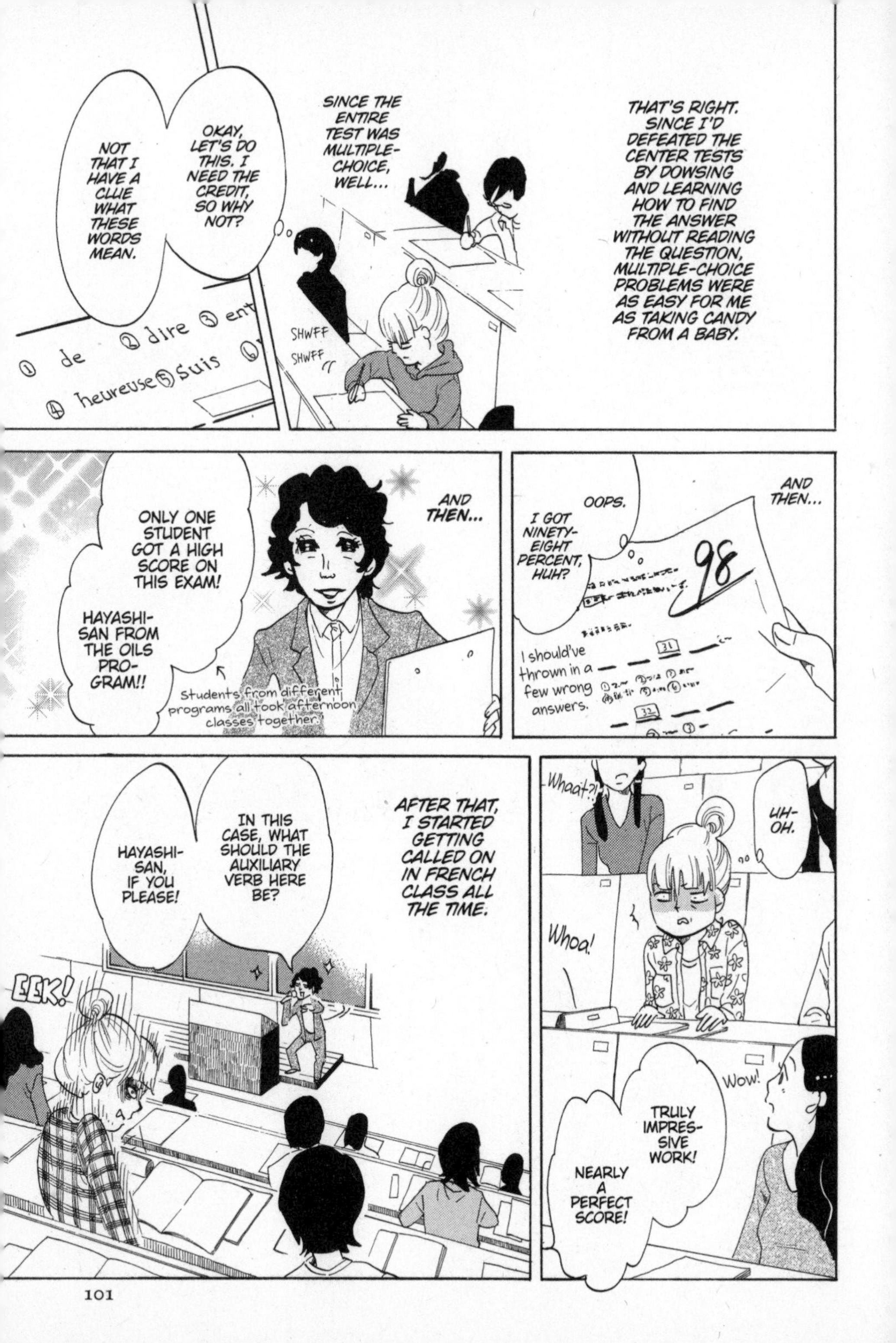

THAT'S RIGHT. SINCE I'D DEFEATED THE CENTER TESTS BY DOWSING AND LEARNING HOW TO FIND THE ANSWER WITHOUT READING THE QUESTION, MULTIPLE-CHOICE PROBLEMS WERE AS EASY FOR ME AS TAKING CANDY FROM A BABY.
SINCE THE ENTIRE TEST WAS MULTIPLE-CHOICE, WELL...
OKAY, LET'S DO THIS. I NEED THE CREDIT, SO WHY NOT?
NOT THAT I HAVE A CLUE WHAT THESE WORDS MEAN.
① de ② dire ③ ent
④ heureuse ⑤ Suis
SHWFF
SHWFF
AND THEN...
OOPS.
I GOT NINETY-EIGHT PERCENT, HUH?
98
31
I should've thrown in a few wrong answers.
32
AND THEN...
ONLY ONE STUDENT GOT A HIGH SCORE ON THIS EXAM!
HAYASHI-SAN FROM THE OILS PROGRAM!!
Students from different programs all took afternoon classes together.
UH-OH.
Whaat?!
Whoa!
Wow!
TRULY IMPRESSIVE WORK!
NEARLY A PERFECT SCORE!
AFTER THAT, I STARTED GETTING CALLED ON IN FRENCH CLASS ALL THE TIME.
IN THIS CASE, WHAT SHOULD THE AUXILIARY VERB HERE BE?
HAYASHI-SAN, IF YOU PLEASE!
EEK!

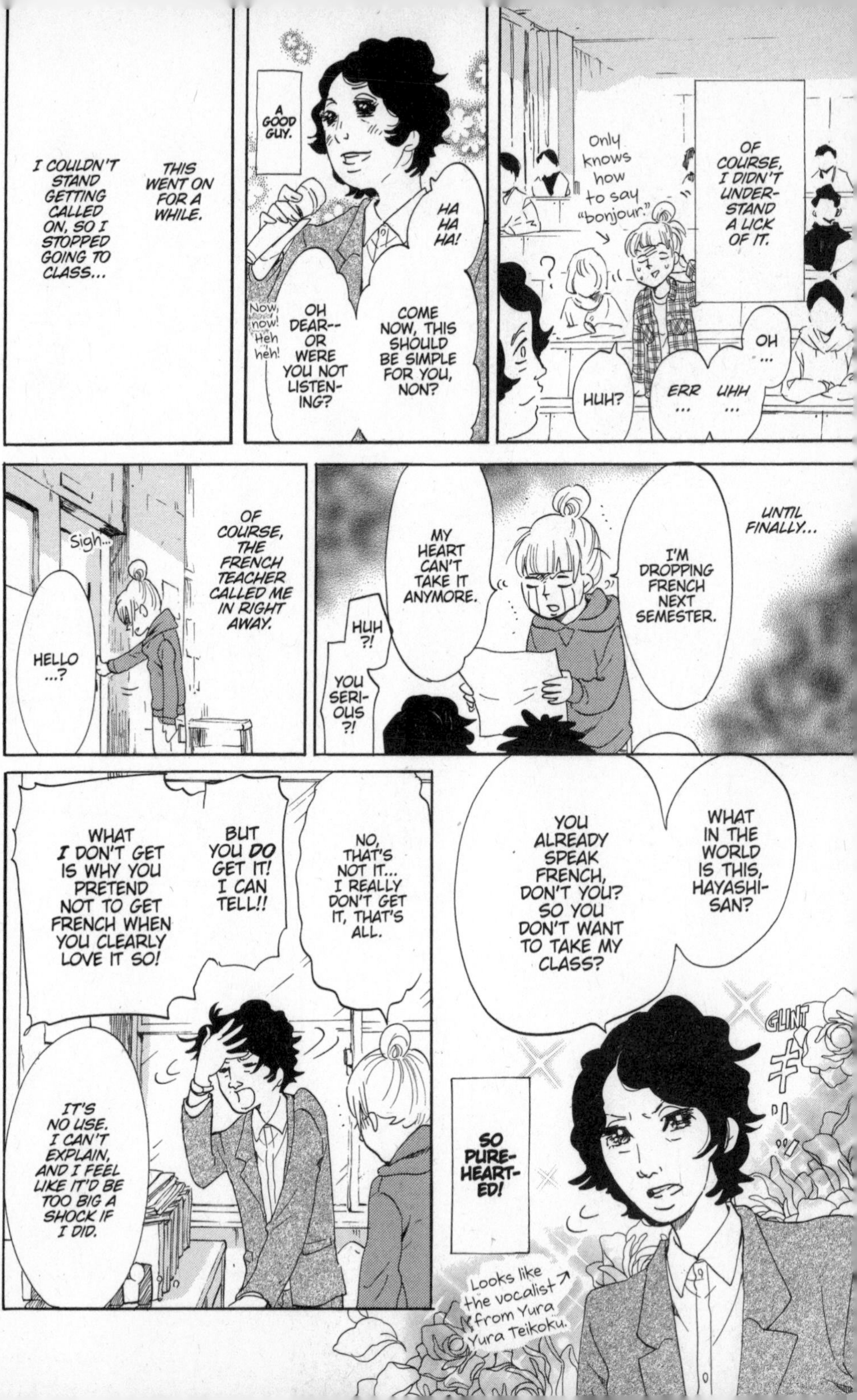
OF COURSE, I DIDN'T UNDERSTAND A LICK OF IT.
Only knows how to say "bonjour."
OH ...
UHH ...
ERR ...
HUH?
A GOOD GUY.
HA HA HA!
COME NOW, THIS SHOULD BE SIMPLE FOR YOU, NON?
OH DEAR-- OR WERE YOU NOT LISTENING?
Now, now! Heh heh!
THIS WENT ON FOR A WHILE.
I COULDN'T STAND GETTING CALLED ON, SO I STOPPED GOING TO CLASS...
UNTIL FINALLY...
I'M DROPPING FRENCH NEXT SEMESTER.
MY HEART CAN'T TAKE IT ANYMORE.
HUH ?!
YOU SERIOUS ?!
OF COURSE, THE FRENCH TEACHER CALLED ME IN RIGHT AWAY.
Sigh...
HELLO ...?
WHAT IN THE WORLD IS THIS, HAYASHI-SAN?
YOU ALREADY SPEAK FRENCH, DON'T YOU? SO YOU DON'T WANT TO TAKE MY CLASS?
GLINT
SO PURE-HEARTED!
Looks like the vocalist from Yura Yura Teikoku.
NO, THAT'S NOT IT... I REALLY DON'T GET IT, THAT'S ALL.
BUT YOU DO GET IT! I CAN TELL!!
WHAT I DON'T GET IS WHY YOU PRETEND NOT TO GET FRENCH WHEN YOU CLEARLY LOVE IT SO!
IT'S NO USE. I CAN'T EXPLAIN, AND I FEEL LIKE IT'D BE TOO BIG A SHOCK IF I DID.

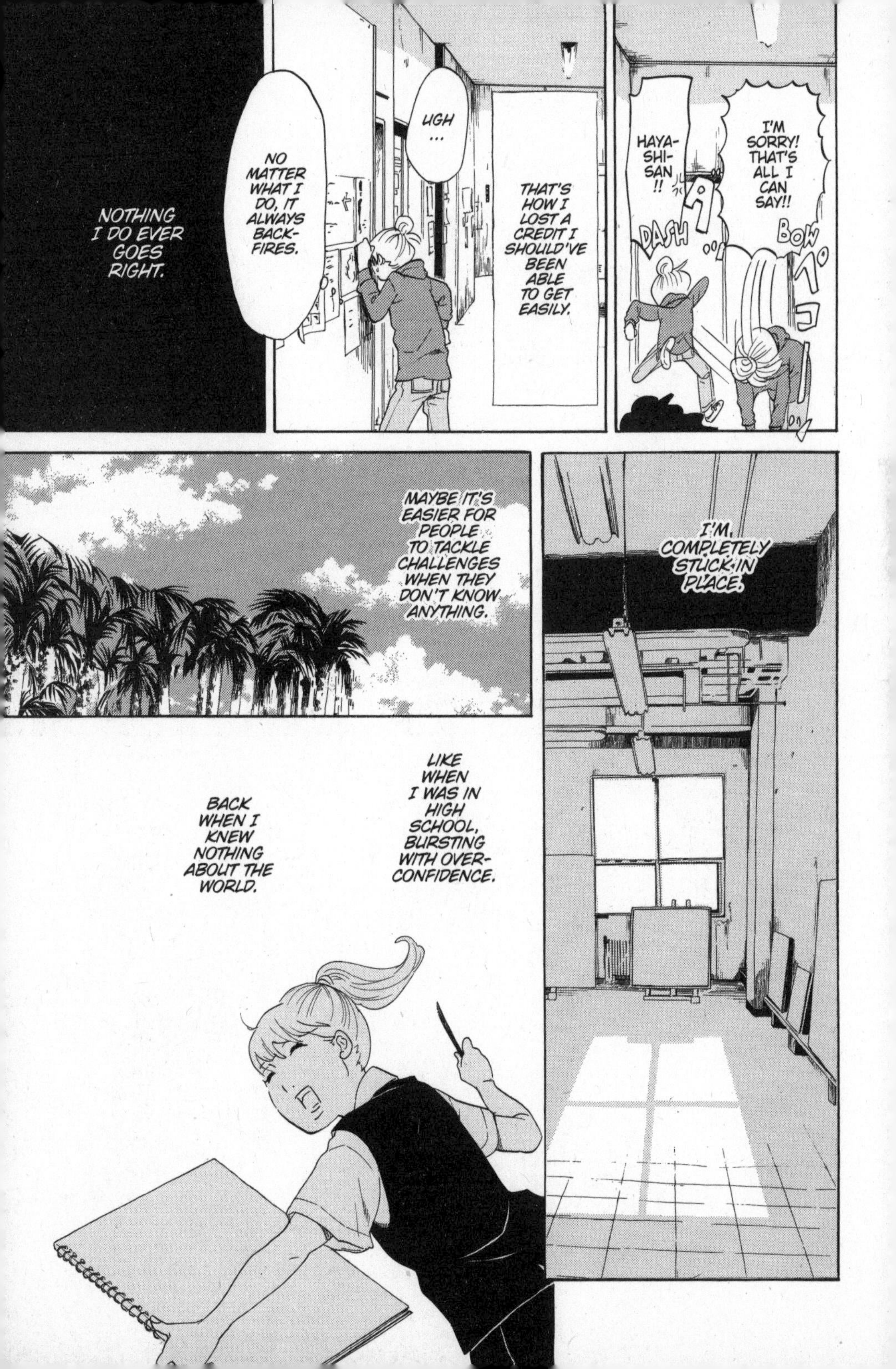
I'M SORRY! THAT'S ALL I CAN SAY!!
HAYA-SHI-SAN!!
BOW
DASH
THAT'S HOW I LOST A CREDIT I SHOULD'VE BEEN ABLE TO GET EASILY.
UGH ...
NO MATTER WHAT I DO, IT ALWAYS BACK-FIRES.
NOTHING I DO EVER GOES RIGHT.
I'M COMPLETELY STUCK IN PLACE.
MAYBE IT'S EASIER FOR PEOPLE TO TACKLE CHALLENGES WHEN THEY DON'T KNOW ANYTHING.
LIKE WHEN I WAS IN HIGH SCHOOL, BURSTING WITH OVER-CONFIDENCE.
BACK WHEN I KNEW NOTHING ABOUT THE WORLD.

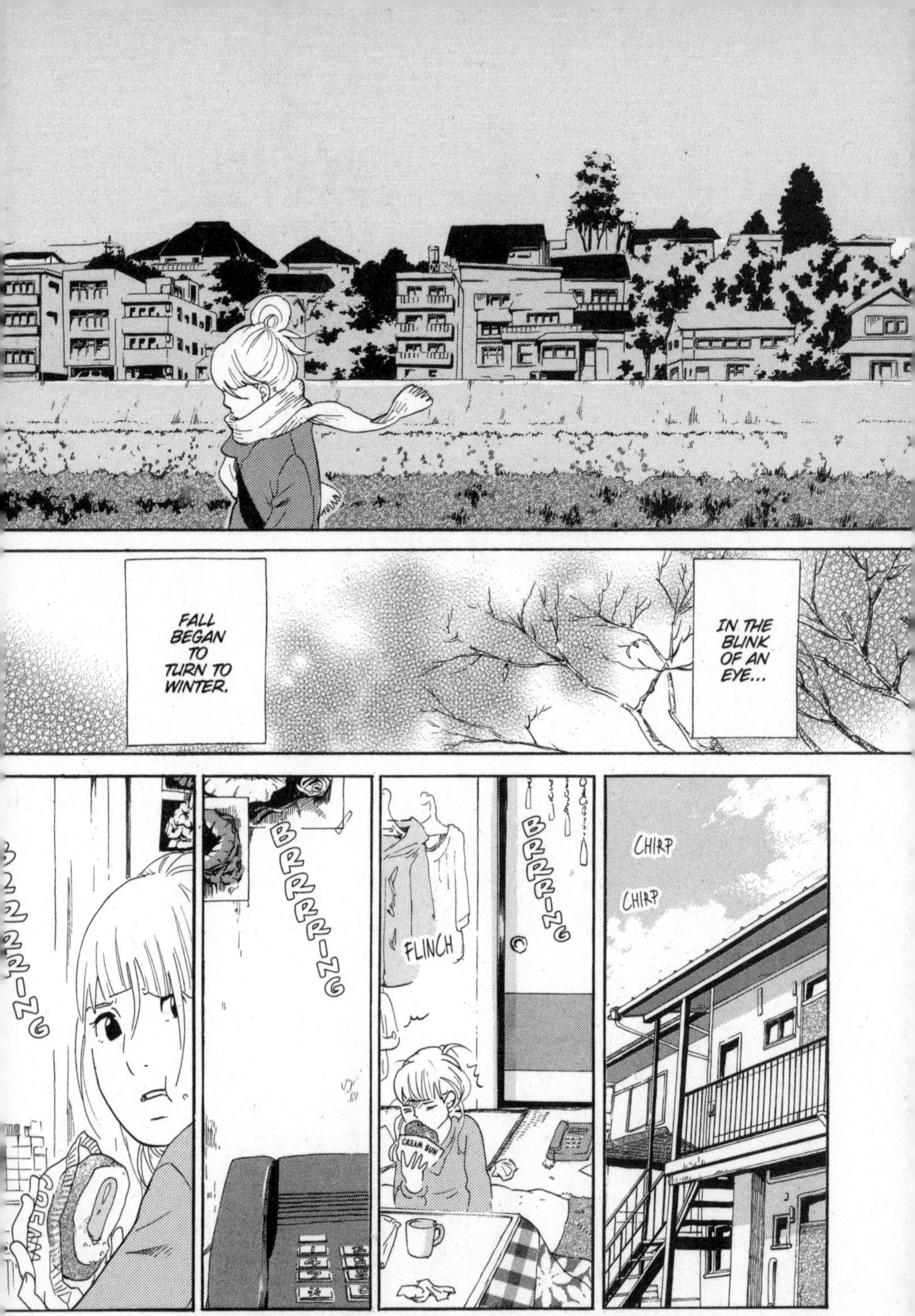
IN THE BLINK OF AN EYE...
FALL BEGAN TO TURN TO WINTER.
CHIRP
CHIRP
BRRRR-ING
FLINCH
CREAM BUN
BRRRR-ING

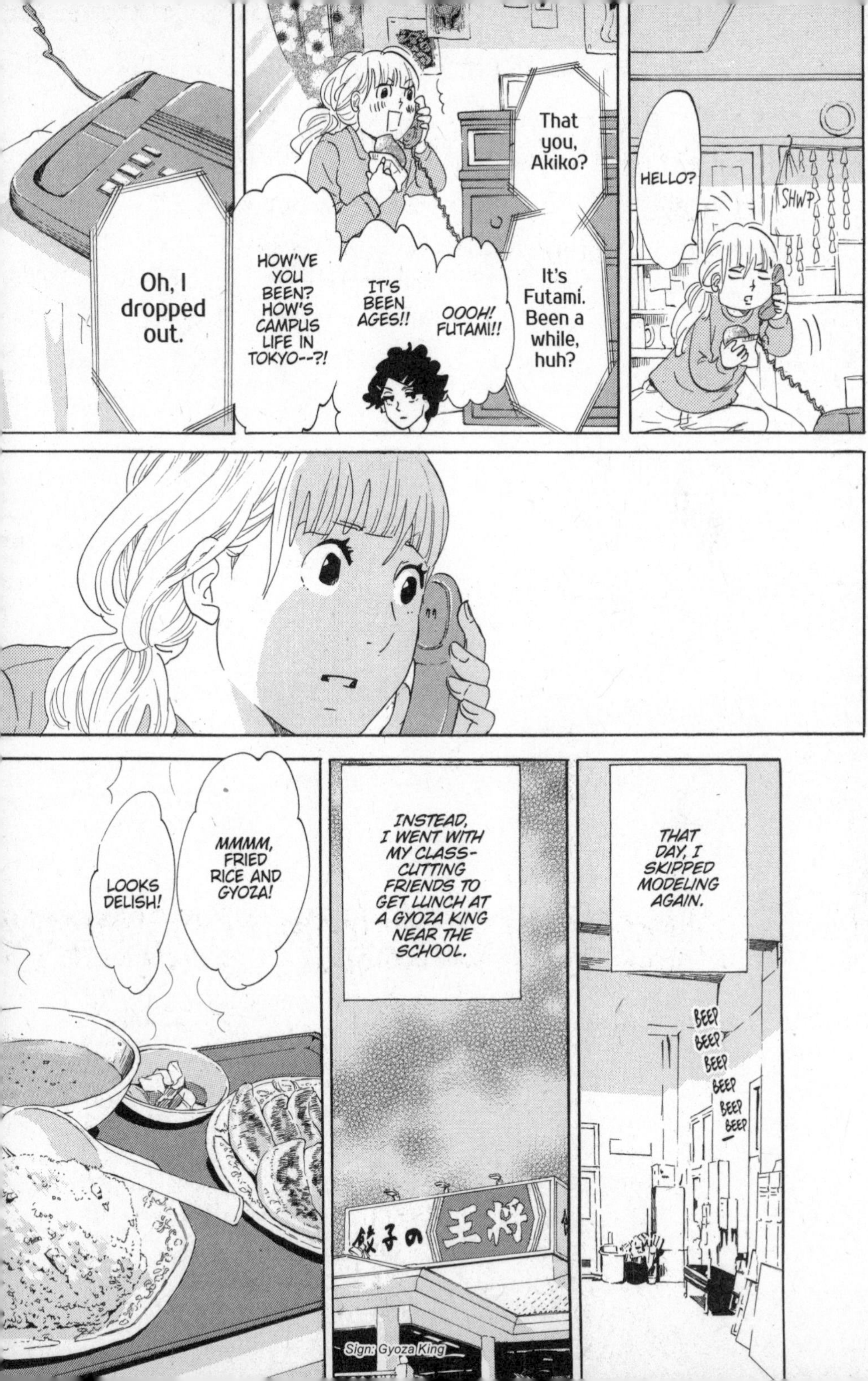
HELLO?
SHWP
That you, Akiko?
It's Futami. Been a while, huh?
OOOH! FUTAMI!!
IT'S BEEN AGES!!
HOW'VE YOU BEEN? HOW'S CAMPUS LIFE IN TOKYO--?!
Oh, I dropped out.
THAT DAY, I SKIPPED MODELING AGAIN.
BEEP BEEP BEEP BEEP BEEP BEEP
INSTEAD, I WENT WITH MY CLASS-CUTTING FRIENDS TO GET LUNCH AT A GYOZA KING NEAR THE SCHOOL.
餃子の王将
Sign: Gyoza King
MMMM, FRIED RICE AND GYOZA!
LOOKS DELISH!

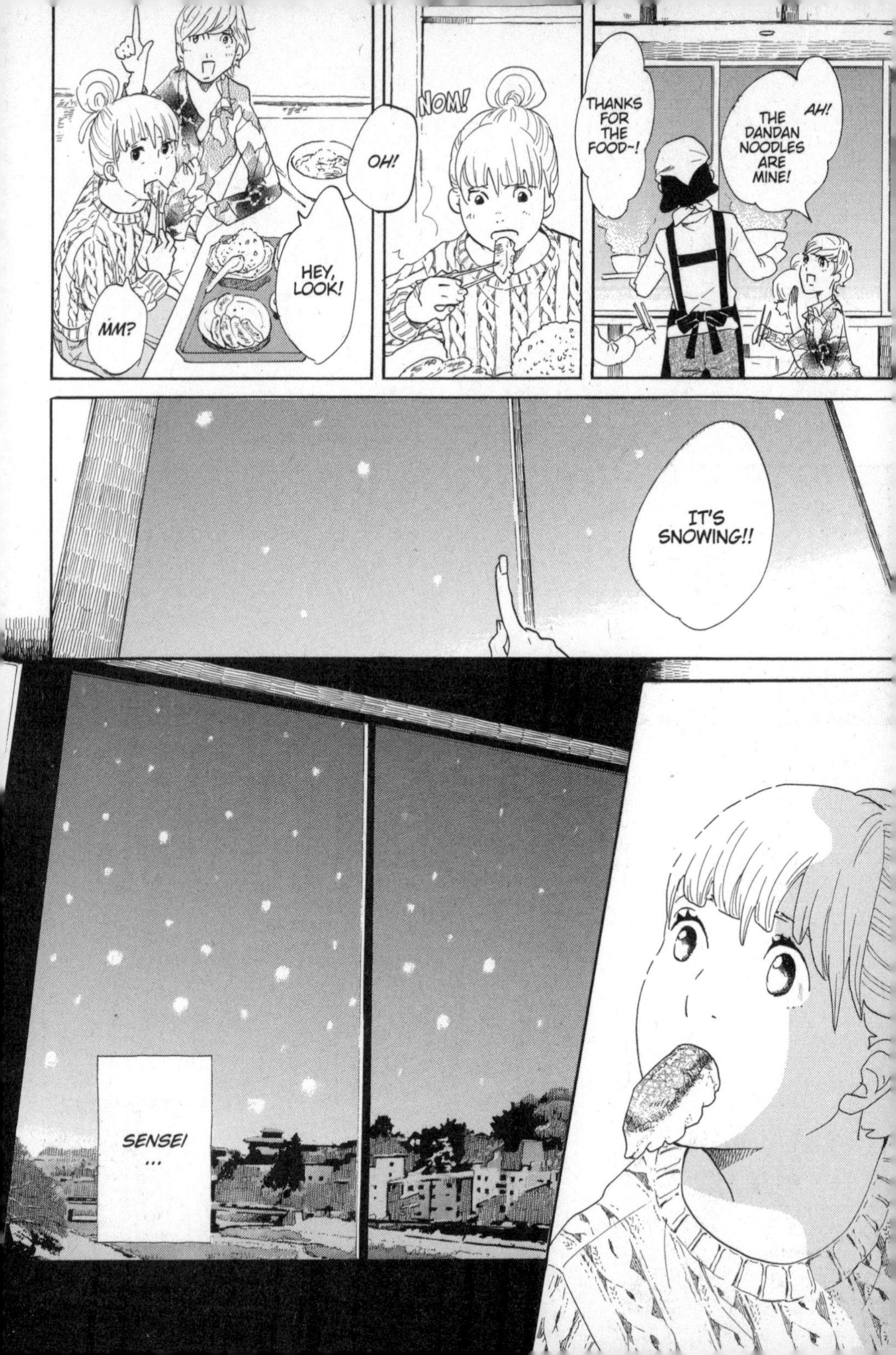
AH! THE DANDAN NOODLES ARE MINE!
THANKS FOR THE FOOD~!
NOM!
OH!
HEY, LOOK!
MM?
IT'S SNOWING!!
SENSEI ...

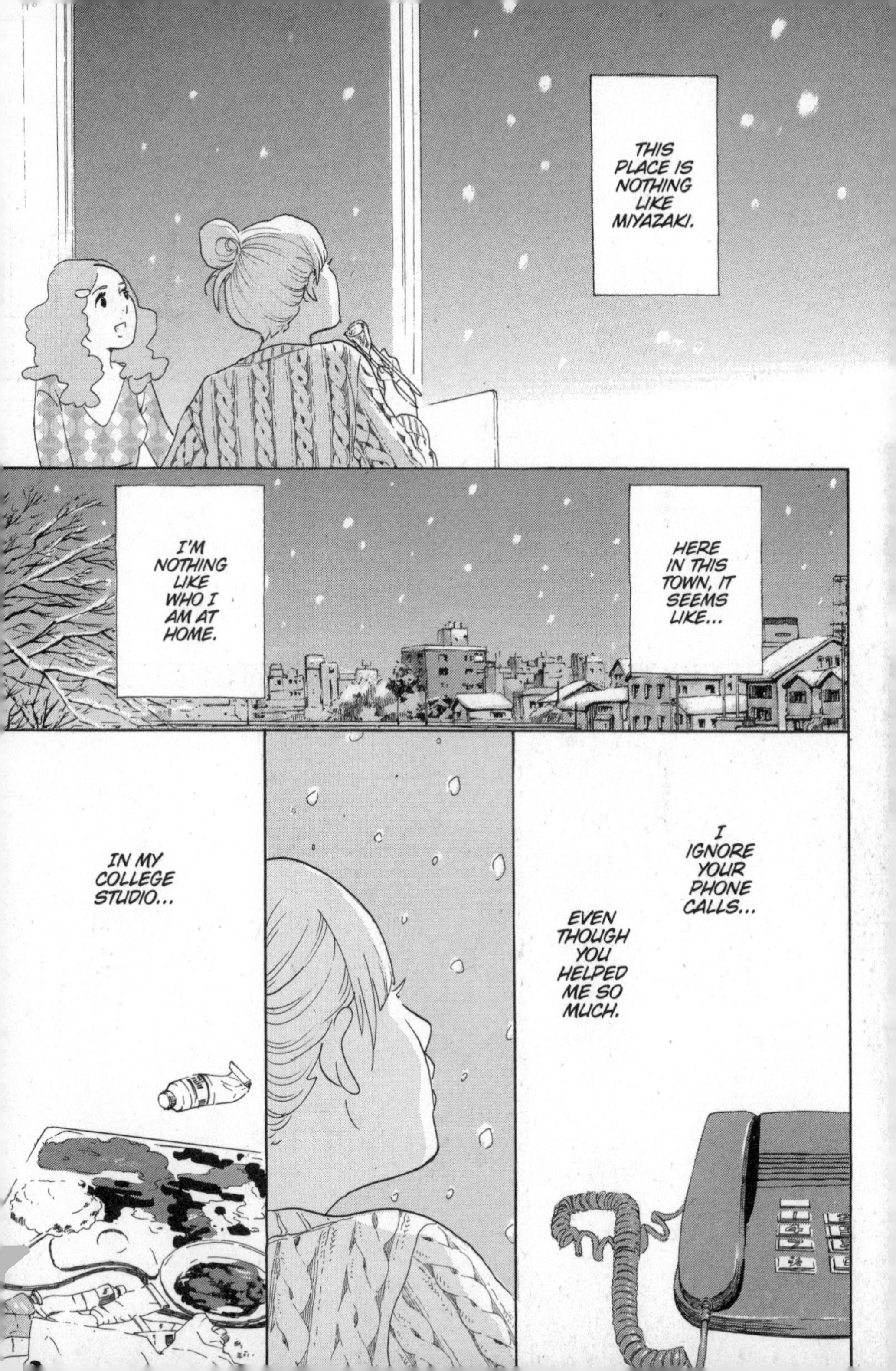
THIS PLACE IS NOTHING LIKE MIYAZAKI.
HERE IN THIS TOWN, IT SEEMS LIKE...
I'M NOTHING LIKE WHO I AM AT HOME.
I IGNORE YOUR PHONE CALLS...
EVEN THOUGH YOU HELPED ME SO MUCH.
IN MY COLLEGE STUDIO...

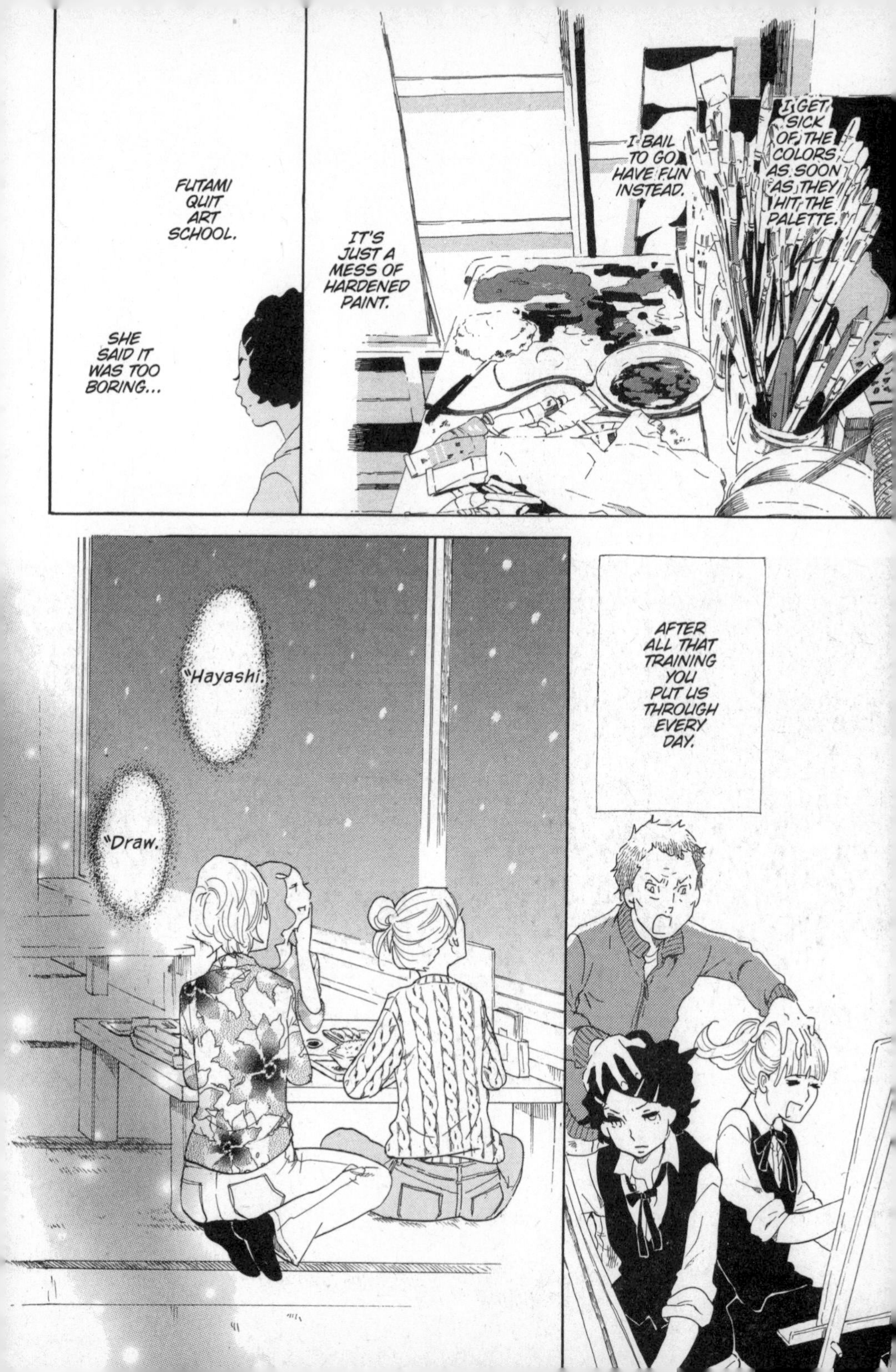
I GET SICK OF THE COLORS AS SOON AS THEY HIT THE PALETTE.
I BAIL TO GO HAVE FUN INSTEAD.
IT'S JUST A MESS OF HARDENED PAINT.
FUTAMI QUIT ART SCHOOL.
SHE SAID IT WAS TOO BORING...
AFTER ALL THAT TRAINING YOU PUT US THROUGH EVERY DAY.
"Hayashi.
"Draw.

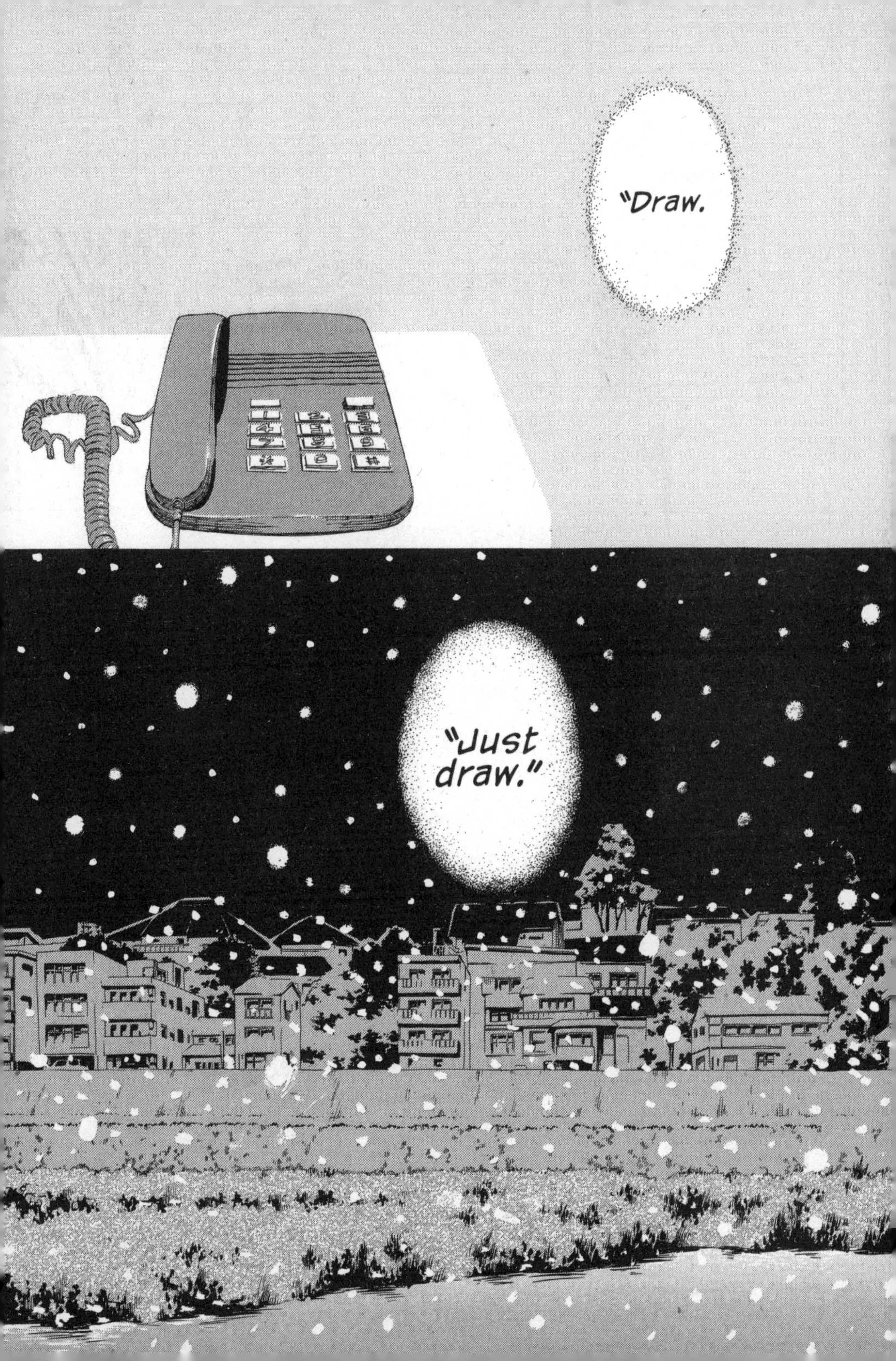
"Draw.
"Just draw."

Blank Canvas
My So-Called
Artist's Journey

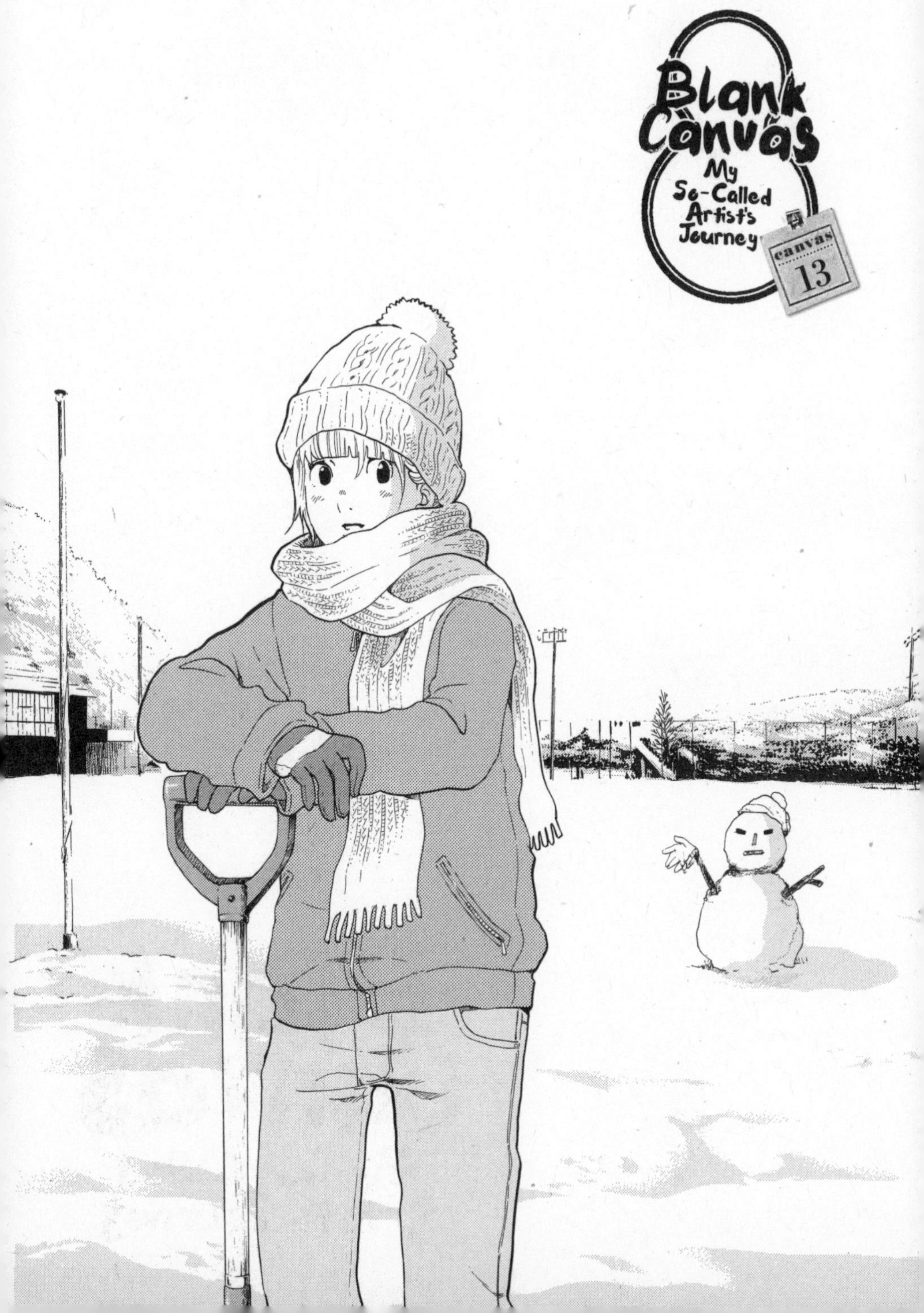

Blank Canvas
My So-Called Artist's Journey
canvas 13

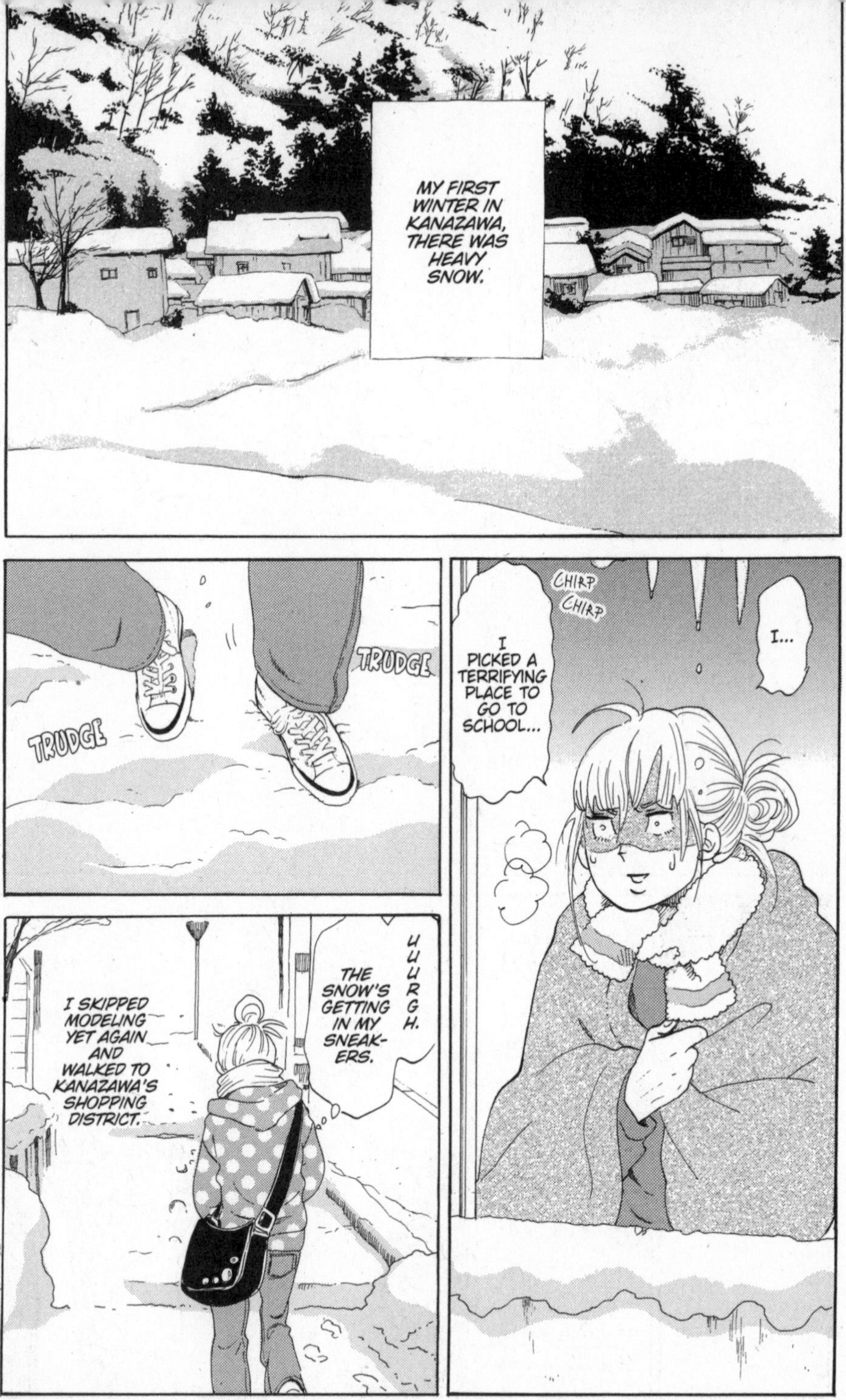
MY FIRST WINTER IN KANAZAWA, THERE WAS HEAVY SNOW.
I...
CHIRP CHIRP
I PICKED A TERRIFYING PLACE TO GO TO SCHOOL...
TRUDGE
TRUDGE
UUURGH.
THE SNOW'S GETTING IN MY SNEAKERS.
I SKIPPED MODELING YET AGAIN AND WALKED TO KANAZAWA'S SHOPPING DISTRICT.

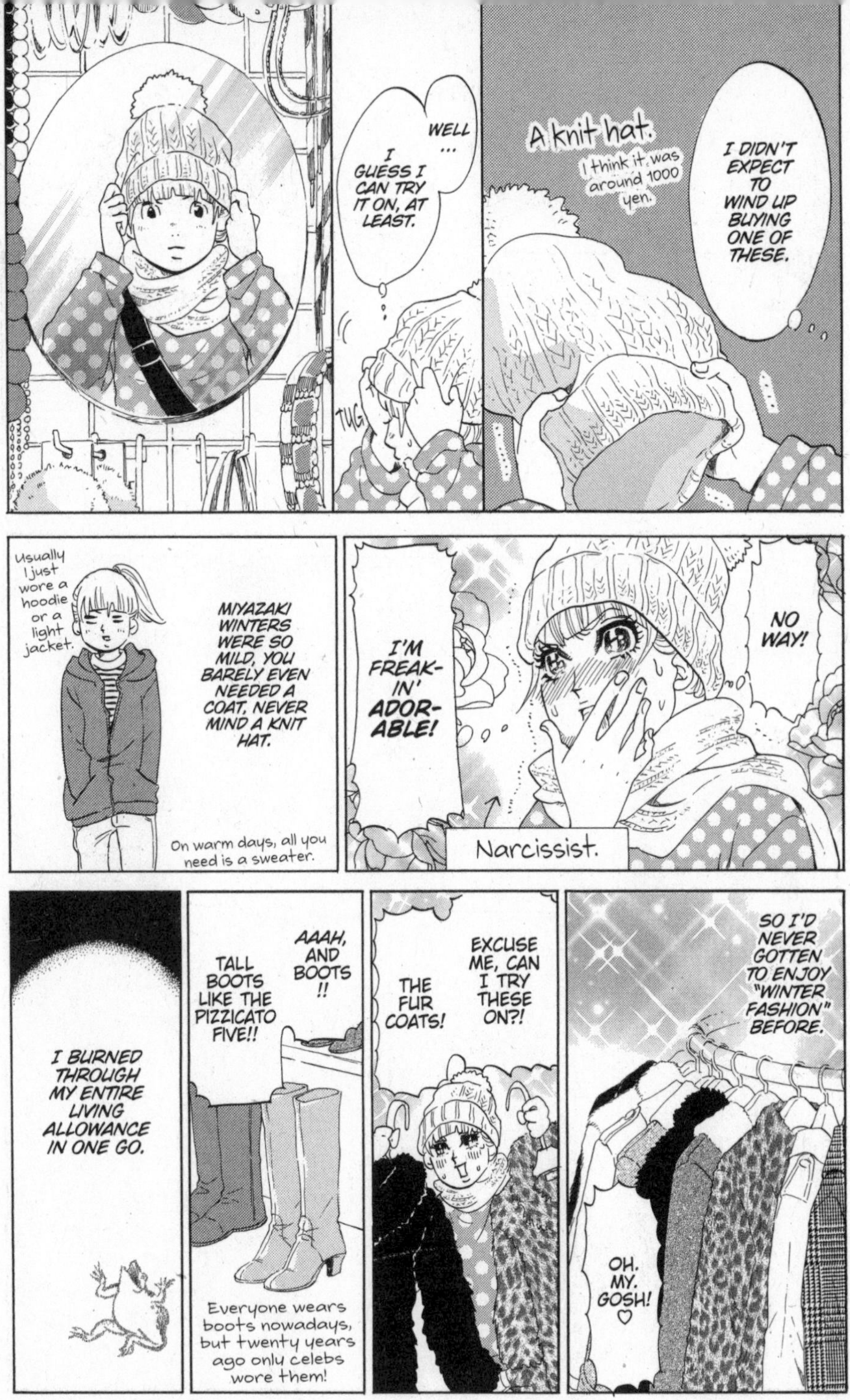
A knit hat.
I think it was around 1000 yen.
I DIDN'T EXPECT TO WIND UP BUYING ONE OF THESE.
WELL ... I GUESS I CAN TRY IT ON, AT LEAST.
TUG
NO WAY!
I'M FREAK-IN' ADORABLE!
Narcissist.
MIYAZAKI WINTERS WERE SO MILD, YOU BARELY EVEN NEEDED A COAT, NEVER MIND A KNIT HAT.
Usually I just wore a hoodie or a light jacket.
On warm days, all you need is a sweater.
SO I'D NEVER GOTTEN TO ENJOY "WINTER FASHION" BEFORE.
OH. MY. GOSH! ♡
EXCUSE ME, CAN I TRY THESE ON?!
THE FUR COATS!
AAAH, AND BOOTS!!
TALL BOOTS LIKE THE PIZZICATO FIVE!!
Everyone wears boots nowadays, but twenty years ago only celebs wore them!
I BURNED THROUGH MY ENTIRE LIVING ALLOWANCE IN ONE GO.

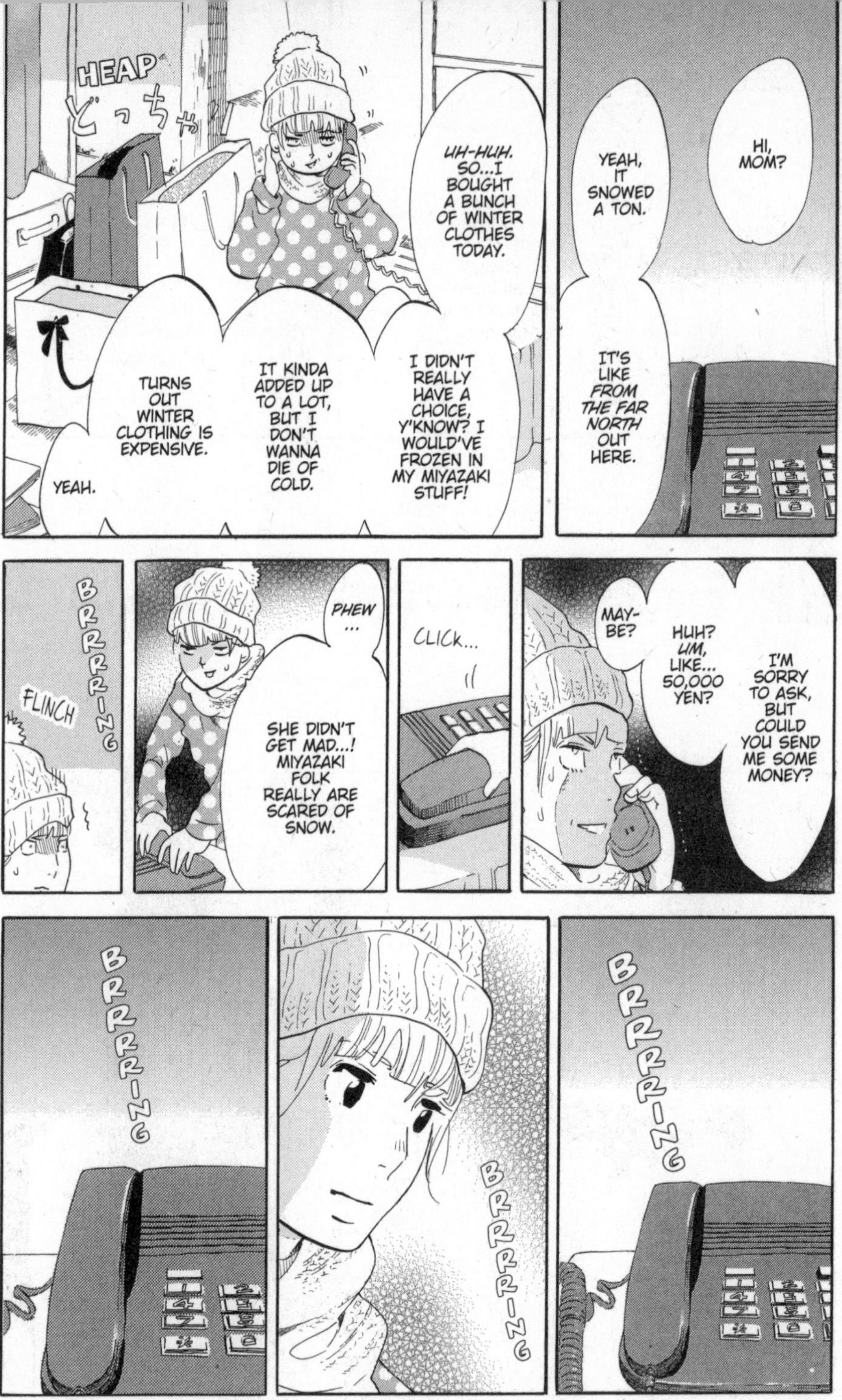
HI, MOM?
YEAH, IT SNOWED A TON.
IT'S LIKE FROM THE FAR NORTH OUT HERE.
HEAP
どっちゃ
UH-HUH. SO...I BOUGHT A BUNCH OF WINTER CLOTHES TODAY.
I DIDN'T REALLY HAVE A CHOICE, Y'KNOW? I WOULD'VE FROZEN IN MY MIYAZAKI STUFF!
IT KINDA ADDED UP TO A LOT, BUT I DON'T WANNA DIE OF COLD.
TURNS OUT WINTER CLOTHING IS EXPENSIVE.
YEAH.
I'M SORRY TO ASK, BUT COULD YOU SEND ME SOME MONEY?
HUH? UM, LIKE... 50,000 YEN?
MAY-BE?
CLICK...
PHEW...
SHE DIDN'T GET MAD...! MIYAZAKI FOLK REALLY ARE SCARED OF SNOW.
BRRRRING
FLINCH
BRRRRING
BRRRRING
BRRRRING

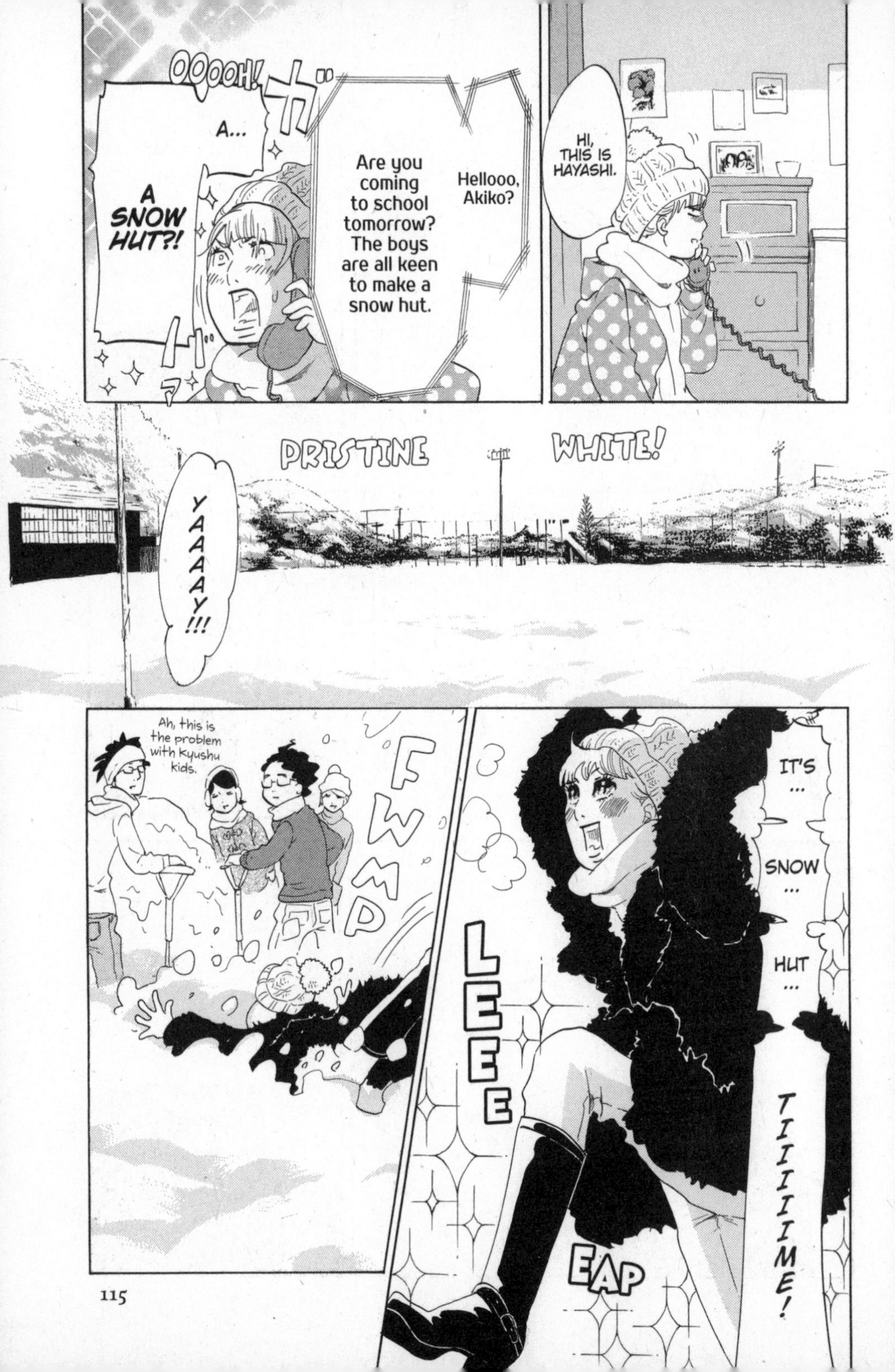
HI, THIS IS HAYASHI.
Hellooo, Akiko?
Are you coming to school tomorrow? The boys are all keen to make a snow hut.
OOOOH!
A...
A SNOW HUT?!
PRISTINE WHITE!
YAAAAAY!!!
IT'S ...
SNOW ...
HUT ...
TIIIIIME!
LEEEEAP
FWMP
Ah, this is the problem with Kyushu kids.

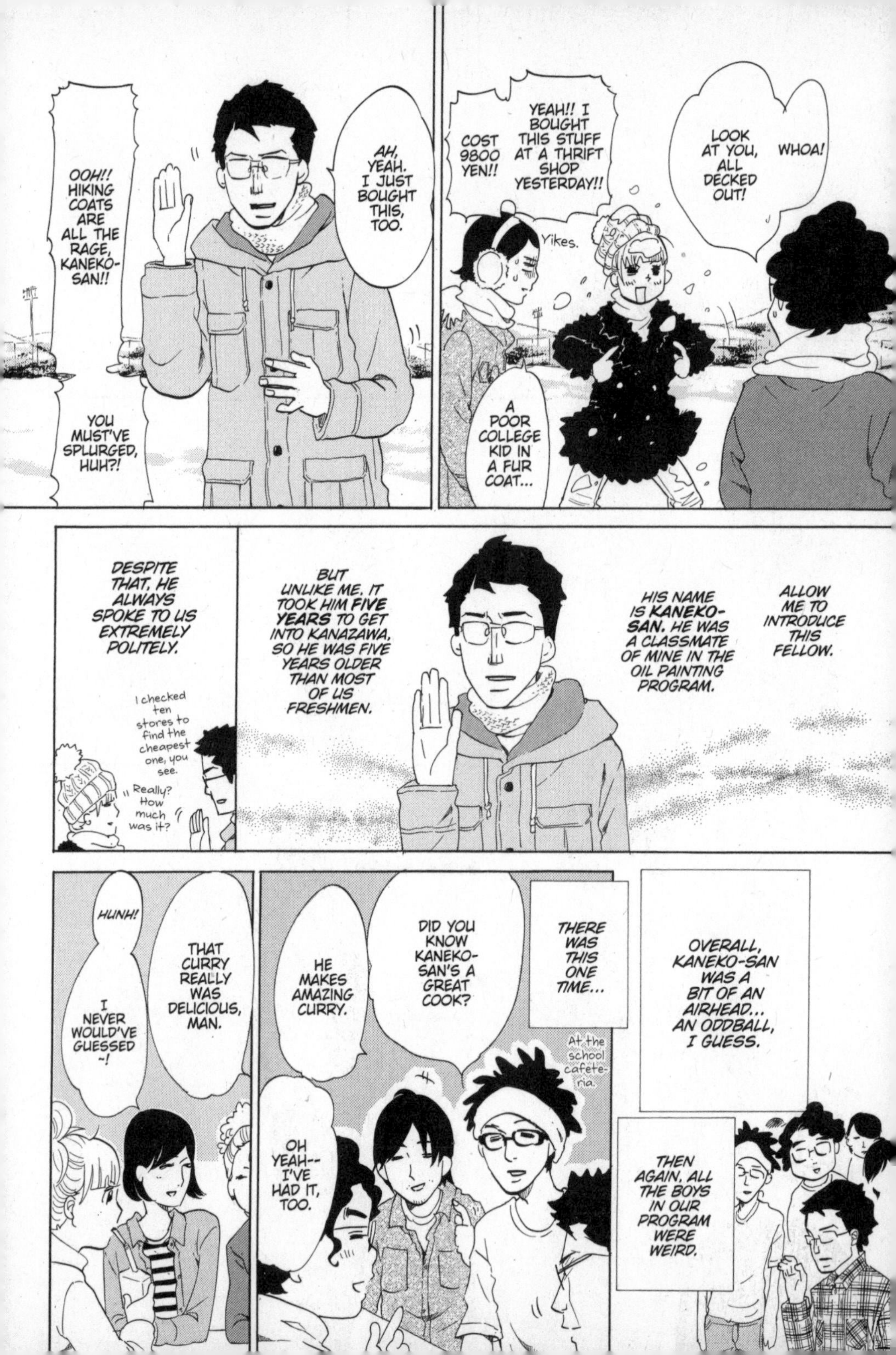
WHOA!
LOOK AT YOU, ALL DECKED OUT!
YEAH!! I BOUGHT THIS STUFF AT A THRIFT SHOP YESTERDAY!!
COST 9800 YEN!!
Yikes.
A POOR COLLEGE KID IN A FUR COAT...
AH, YEAH. I JUST BOUGHT THIS, TOO.
OOH!! HIKING COATS ARE ALL THE RAGE, KANEKO-SAN!!
YOU MUST'VE SPLURGED, HUH?!
ALLOW ME TO INTRODUCE THIS FELLOW.
HIS NAME IS **KANEKO-SAN.** HE WAS A CLASSMATE OF MINE IN THE OIL PAINTING PROGRAM.
BUT UNLIKE ME, IT TOOK HIM **FIVE YEARS** TO GET INTO KANAZAWA, SO HE WAS FIVE YEARS OLDER THAN MOST OF US FRESHMEN.
DESPITE THAT, HE ALWAYS SPOKE TO US EXTREMELY POLITELY.
I checked ten stores to find the cheapest one, you see.
Really? How much was it?
OVERALL, KANEKO-SAN WAS A BIT OF AN AIRHEAD... AN ODDBALL, I GUESS.
THEN AGAIN, ALL THE BOYS IN OUR PROGRAM WERE WEIRD.
THERE WAS THIS ONE TIME...
DID YOU KNOW KANEKO-SAN'S A GREAT COOK?
At the school cafeteria.
HE MAKES AMAZING CURRY.
OH YEAH-- I'VE HAD IT, TOO.
THAT CURRY REALLY WAS DELICIOUS, MAN.
HUNH!
I NEVER WOULD'VE GUESSED ~!

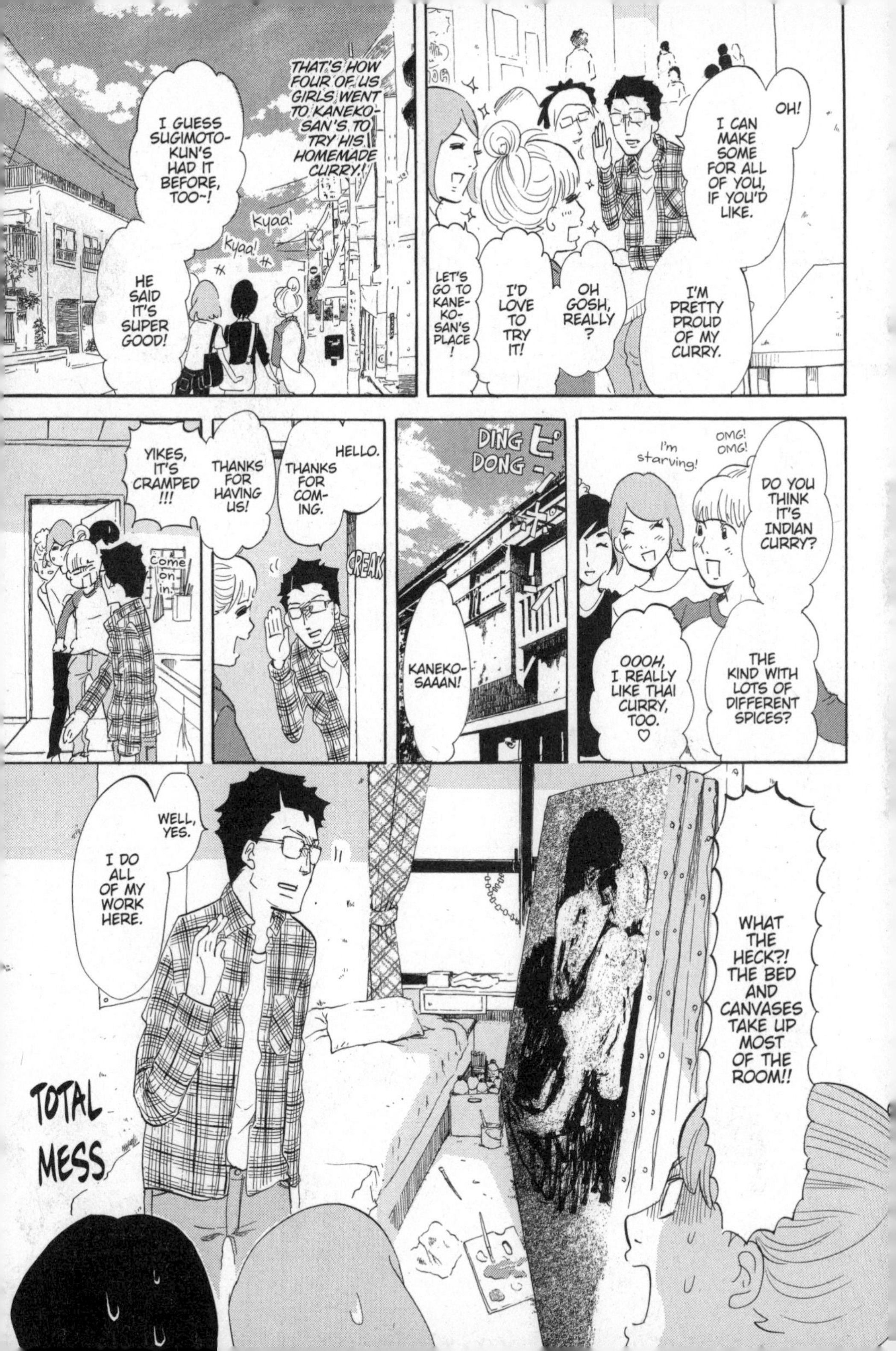
OH!
I CAN MAKE SOME FOR ALL OF YOU, IF YOU'D LIKE.
I'M PRETTY PROUD OF MY CURRY.
OH GOSH, REALLY?
I'D LOVE TO TRY IT!
LET'S GO TO KANEKO-SAN'S PLACE!
THAT'S HOW FOUR OF US GIRLS WENT TO KANEKO-SAN'S TO TRY HIS HOMEMADE CURRY!
I GUESS SUGIMOTO-KUN'S HAD IT BEFORE, TOO~!
Kyaa!
Kyaa!
HE SAID IT'S SUPER GOOD!
OMG! OMG!
I'm starving!
DO YOU THINK IT'S INDIAN CURRY?
THE KIND WITH LOTS OF DIFFERENT SPICES?
OOOH, I REALLY LIKE THAI CURRY, TOO. ♡
DING DONG
KANEKO-SAAAN!
HELLO.
THANKS FOR COMING.
CREAK
THANKS FOR HAVING US!
YIKES, IT'S CRAMPED!!!
Come on in.
WHAT THE HECK?! THE BED AND CANVASES TAKE UP MOST OF THE ROOM!!
WELL, YES.
I DO ALL OF MY WORK HERE.
TOTAL MESS

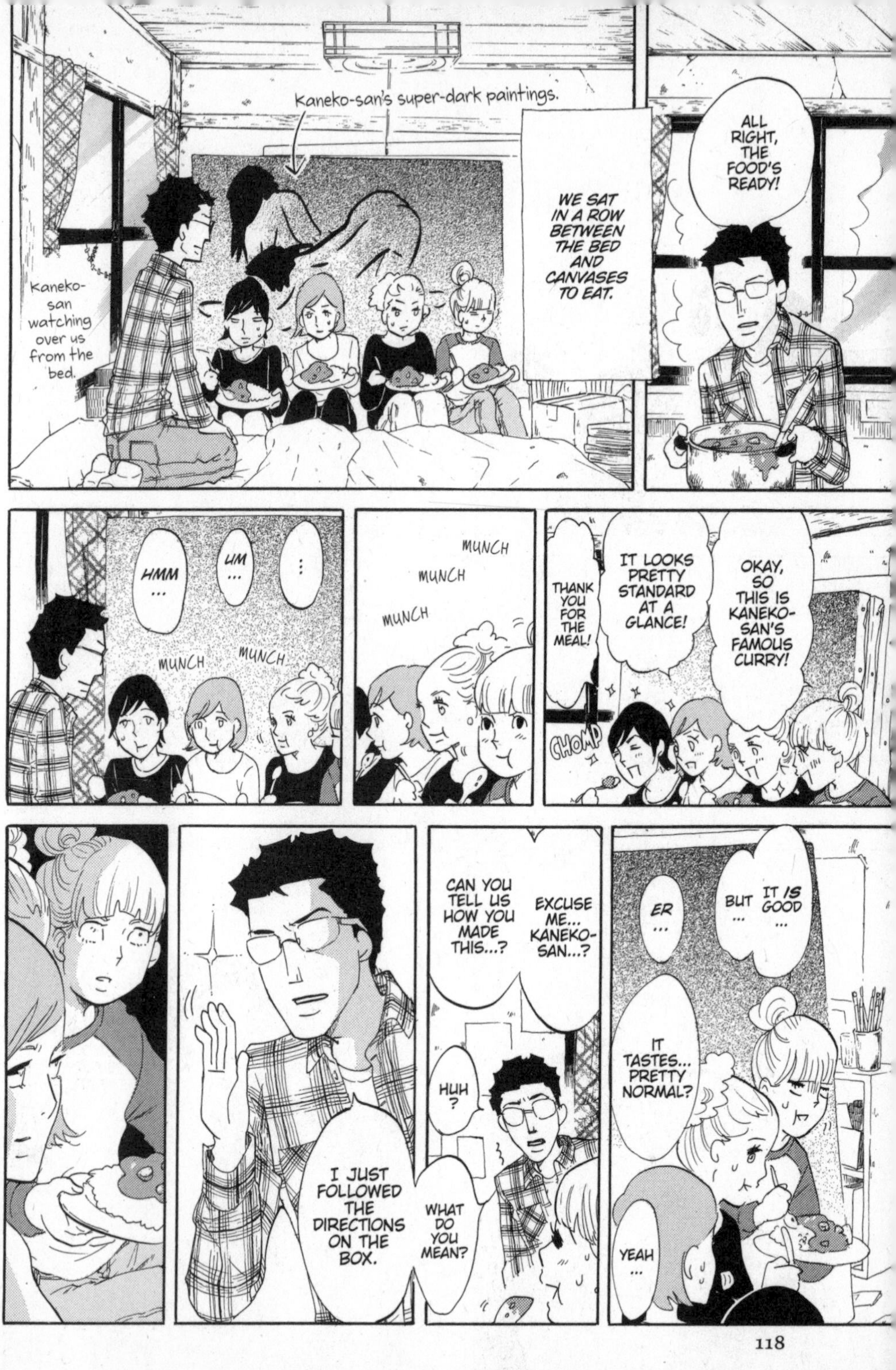
ALL RIGHT, THE FOOD'S READY!
WE SAT IN A ROW BETWEEN THE BED AND CANVASES TO EAT.
Kaneko-san's super-dark paintings.
Kaneko-san watching over us from the bed.
OKAY, SO THIS IS KANEKO-SAN'S FAMOUS CURRY!
IT LOOKS PRETTY STANDARD AT A GLANCE!
THANK YOU FOR THE MEAL!
CHOMP
MUNCH
MUNCH
MUNCH
...
UM ...
HMM ...
MUNCH
MUNCH
BUT ... IT *IS* GOOD ...
ER ...
IT TASTES... PRETTY NORMAL?
YEAH ...
EXCUSE ME... KANEKO-SAN...?
CAN YOU TELL US HOW YOU MADE THIS...?
HUH ?
WHAT DO YOU MEAN?
I JUST FOLLOWED THE DIRECTIONS ON THE BOX.

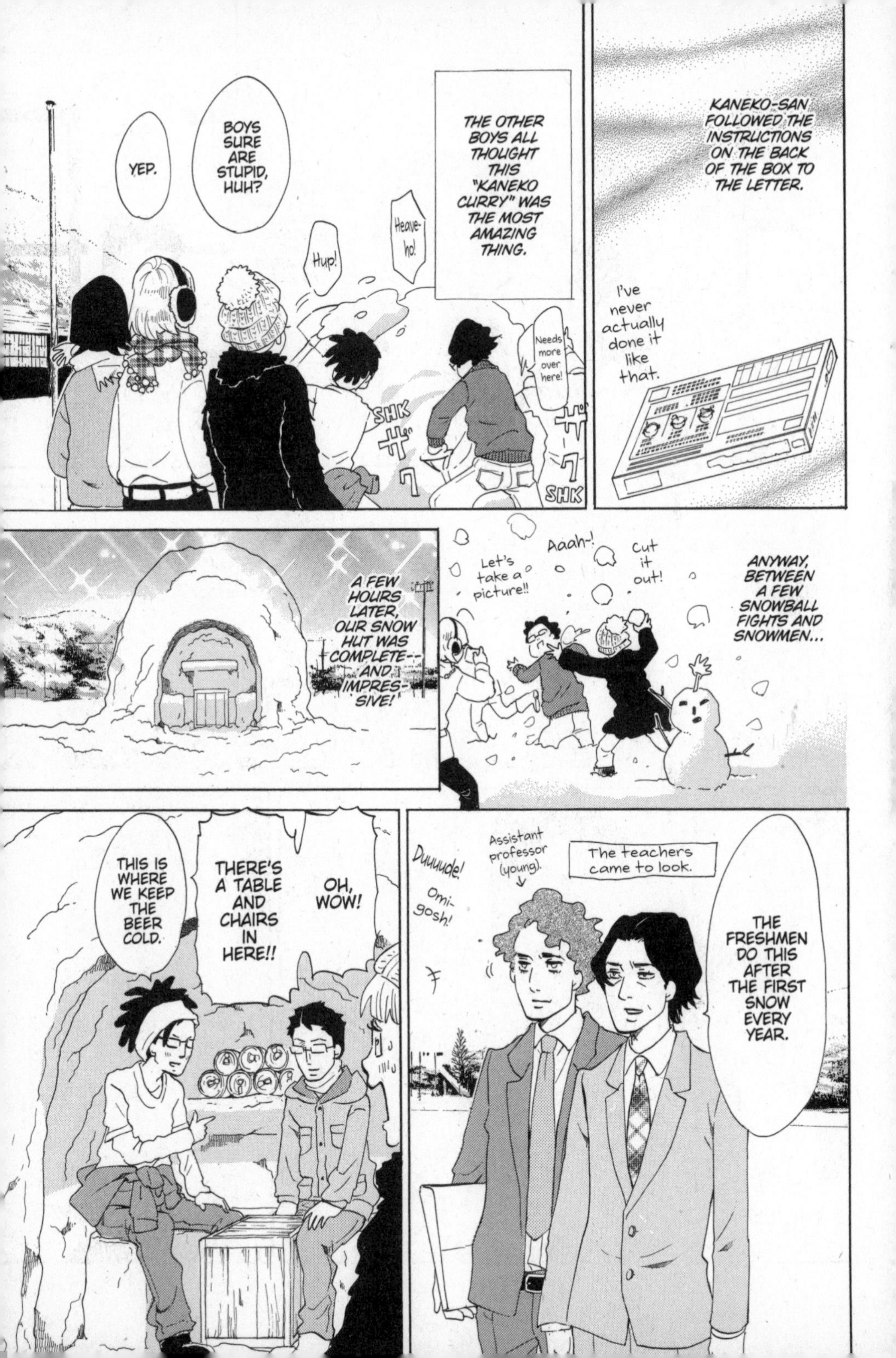
KANEKO-SAN FOLLOWED THE INSTRUCTIONS ON THE BACK OF THE BOX TO THE LETTER.
I've never actually done it like that.
THE OTHER BOYS ALL THOUGHT THIS "KANEKO CURRY" WAS THE MOST AMAZING THING.
Heave-ho!
Hup!
Needs more over here!
SHK
SHK
BOYS SURE ARE STUPID, HUH?
YEP.
ANYWAY, BETWEEN A FEW SNOWBALL FIGHTS AND SNOWMEN...
Cut it out!
Aaah~!
Let's take a picture!!
A FEW HOURS LATER, OUR SNOW HUT WAS COMPLETE--AND IMPRESSIVE!
THE FRESHMEN DO THIS AFTER THE FIRST SNOW EVERY YEAR.
The teachers came to look.
Assistant professor (young).
Duuuude!
Omigosh!
OH, WOW!
THERE'S A TABLE AND CHAIRS IN HERE!!
THIS IS WHERE WE KEEP THE BEER COLD.

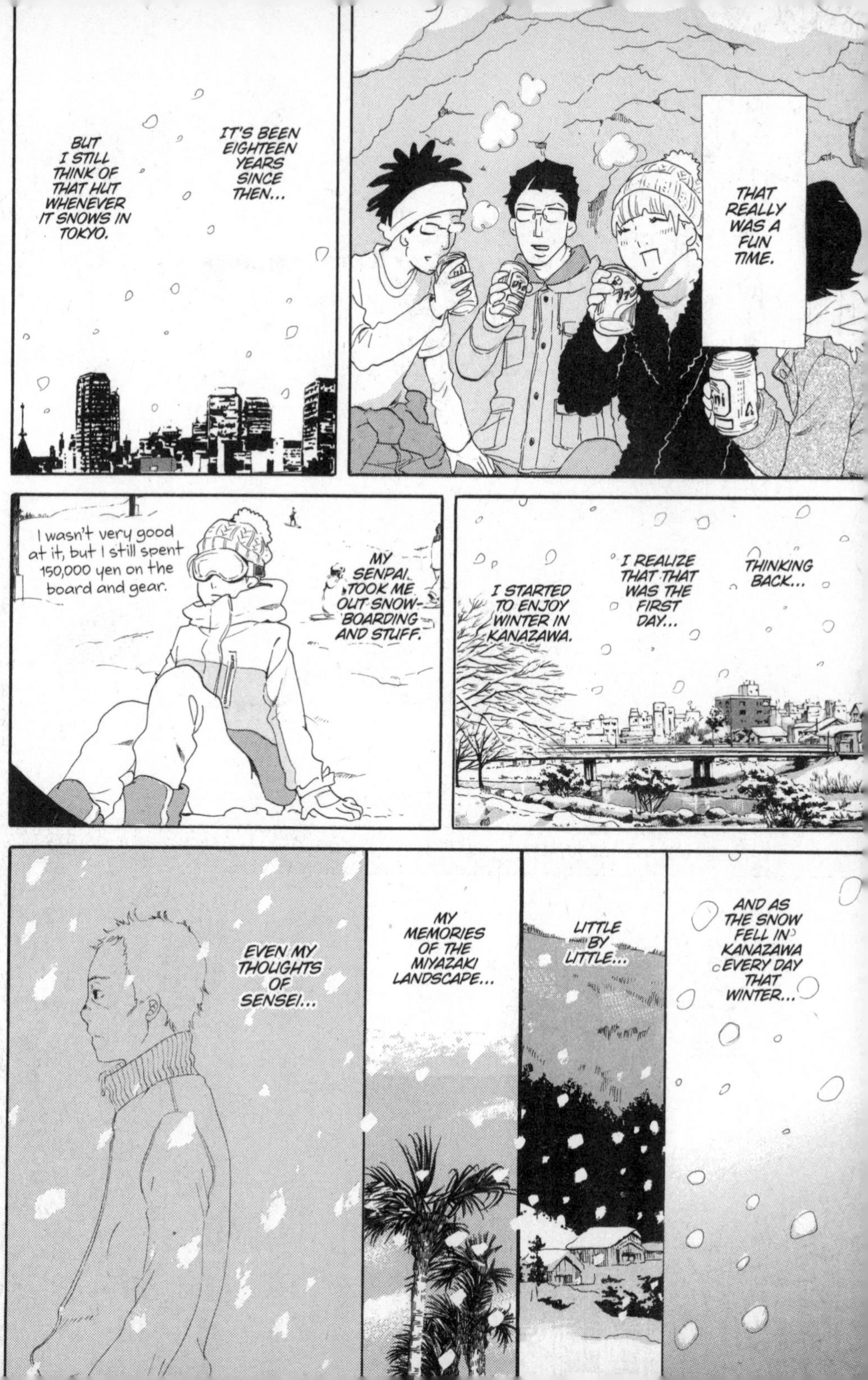
THAT REALLY WAS A FUN TIME.
IT'S BEEN EIGHTEEN YEARS SINCE THEN...
BUT I STILL THINK OF THAT HUT WHENEVER IT SNOWS IN TOKYO.
THINKING BACK...
I REALIZE THAT THAT WAS THE FIRST DAY...
I STARTED TO ENJOY WINTER IN KANAZAWA.
MY SENPAI TOOK ME OUT SNOW-BOARDING AND STUFF.
I wasn't very good at it, but I still spent 150,000 yen on the board and gear.
AND AS THE SNOW FELL IN KANAZAWA EVERY DAY THAT WINTER...
LITTLE BY LITTLE...
MY MEMORIES OF THE MIYAZAKI LANDSCAPE...
EVEN MY THOUGHTS OF SENSEI...

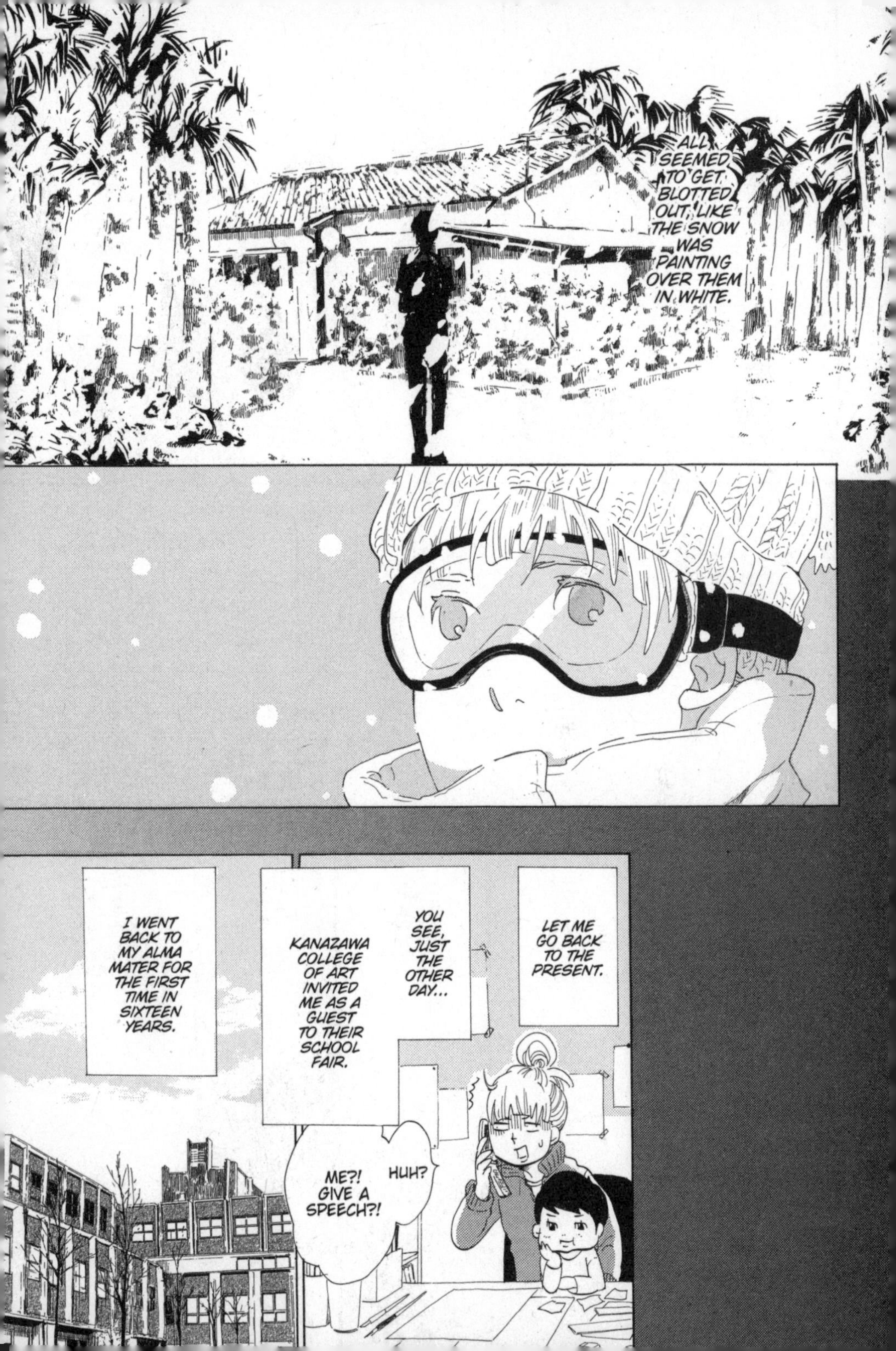
ALL SEEMED TO GET BLOTTED OUT, LIKE THE SNOW WAS PAINTING OVER THEM IN WHITE.
LET ME GO BACK TO THE PRESENT.
YOU SEE, JUST THE OTHER DAY...
KANAZAWA COLLEGE OF ART INVITED ME AS A GUEST TO THEIR SCHOOL FAIR.
HUH?
ME?! GIVE A SPEECH?!
I WENT BACK TO MY ALMA MATER FOR THE FIRST TIME IN SIXTEEN YEARS.

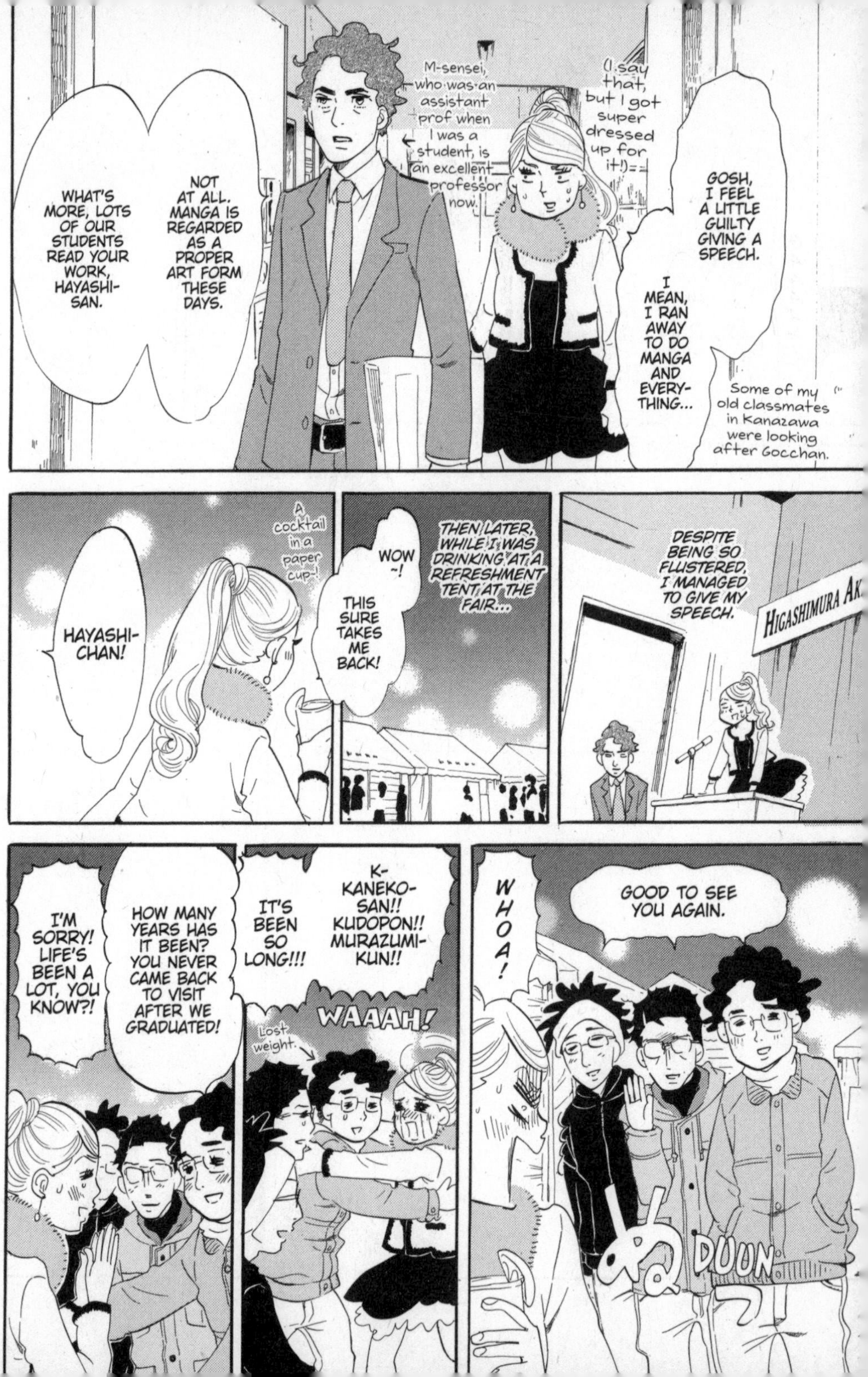
GOSH, I FEEL A LITTLE GUILTY GIVING A SPEECH.
I MEAN, I RAN AWAY TO DO MANGA AND EVERYTHING...
Some of my old classmates in Kanazawa were looking after Gocchan.
(I say that, but I got super dressed up for it!)
M-sensei, who was an assistant prof when I was a student, is an excellent professor now.
NOT AT ALL. MANGA IS REGARDED AS A PROPER ART FORM THESE DAYS.
WHAT'S MORE, LOTS OF OUR STUDENTS READ YOUR WORK, HAYASHI-SAN.
DESPITE BEING SO FLUSTERED, I MANAGED TO GIVE MY SPEECH.
HIGASHIMURA AK
THEN LATER, WHILE I WAS DRINKING AT A REFRESHMENT TENT AT THE FAIR...
WOW ~!
THIS SURE TAKES ME BACK!
A cocktail in a paper cup~!
HAYASHI-CHAN!
GOOD TO SEE YOU AGAIN.
WHOA!
DUUN
K-KANEKO-SAN!! KUDOPON!! MURAZUMI-KUN!!
IT'S BEEN SO LONG!!!
WAAAH!
Lost weight.
HOW MANY YEARS HAS IT BEEN? YOU NEVER CAME BACK TO VISIT AFTER WE GRADUATED!
I'M SORRY! LIFE'S BEEN A LOT, YOU KNOW?!

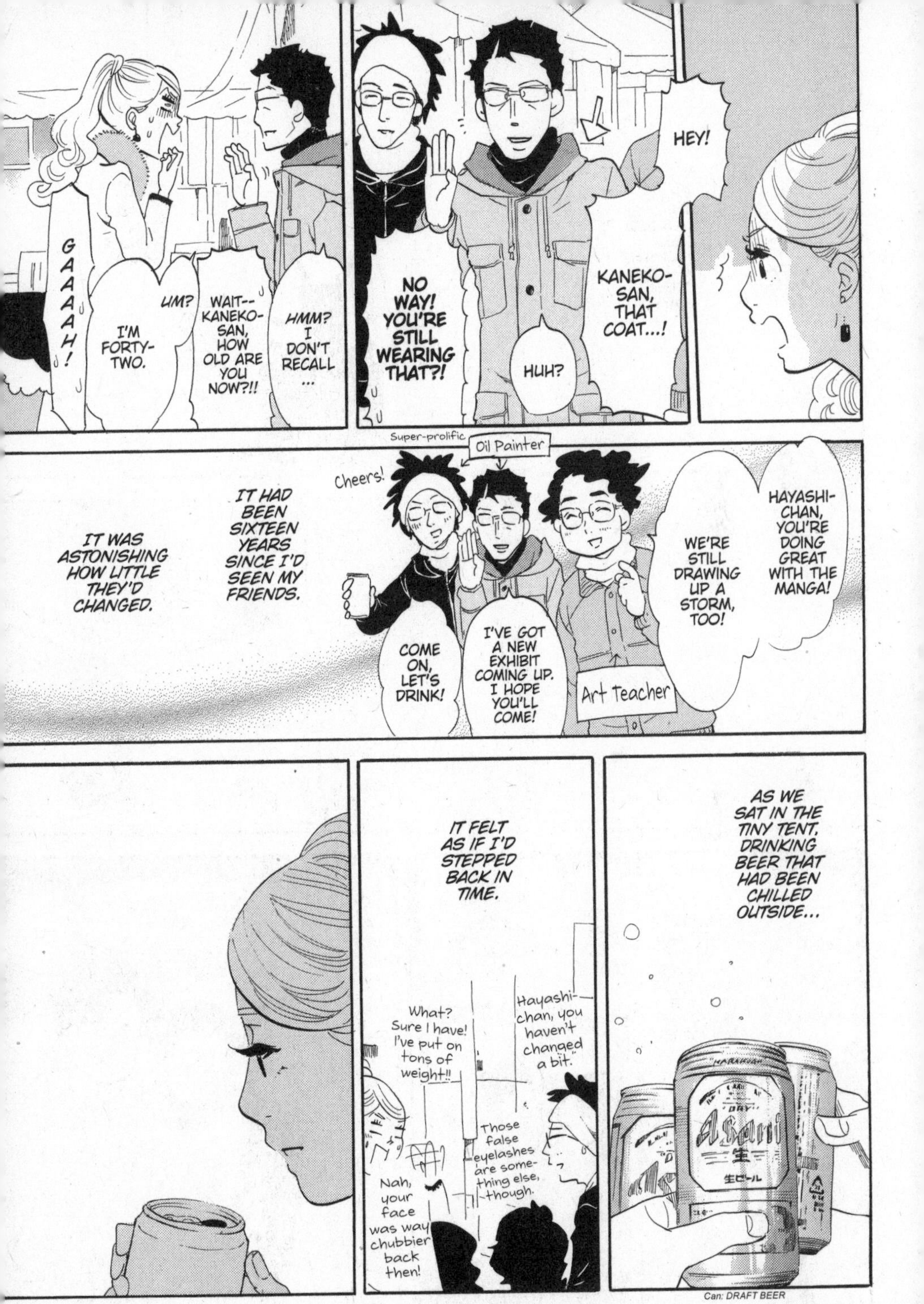
HEY!
KANEKO-SAN, THAT COAT...!
HUH?
NO WAY! YOU'RE STILL WEARING THAT?!
HMM? I DON'T RECALL...
WAIT-- KANEKO-SAN, HOW OLD ARE YOU NOW?!!
UM?
I'M FORTY-TWO.
GAAAAAH!
HAYASHI-CHAN, YOU'RE DOING GREAT WITH THE MANGA!
WE'RE STILL DRAWING UP A STORM, TOO!
Art Teacher
I'VE GOT A NEW EXHIBIT COMING UP. I HOPE YOU'LL COME!
Oil Painter
Super-prolific
COME ON, LET'S DRINK!
Cheers!
IT HAD BEEN SIXTEEN YEARS SINCE I'D SEEN MY FRIENDS.
IT WAS ASTONISHING HOW LITTLE THEY'D CHANGED.
AS WE SAT IN THE TINY TENT, DRINKING BEER THAT HAD BEEN CHILLED OUTSIDE...
IT FELT AS IF I'D STEPPED BACK IN TIME.
Hayashi-chan, you haven't changed a bit.
What? Sure I have! I've put on tons of weight!!
Those false eyelashes are something else, though.
Nah, your face was way chubbier back then!
Can: DRAFT BEER

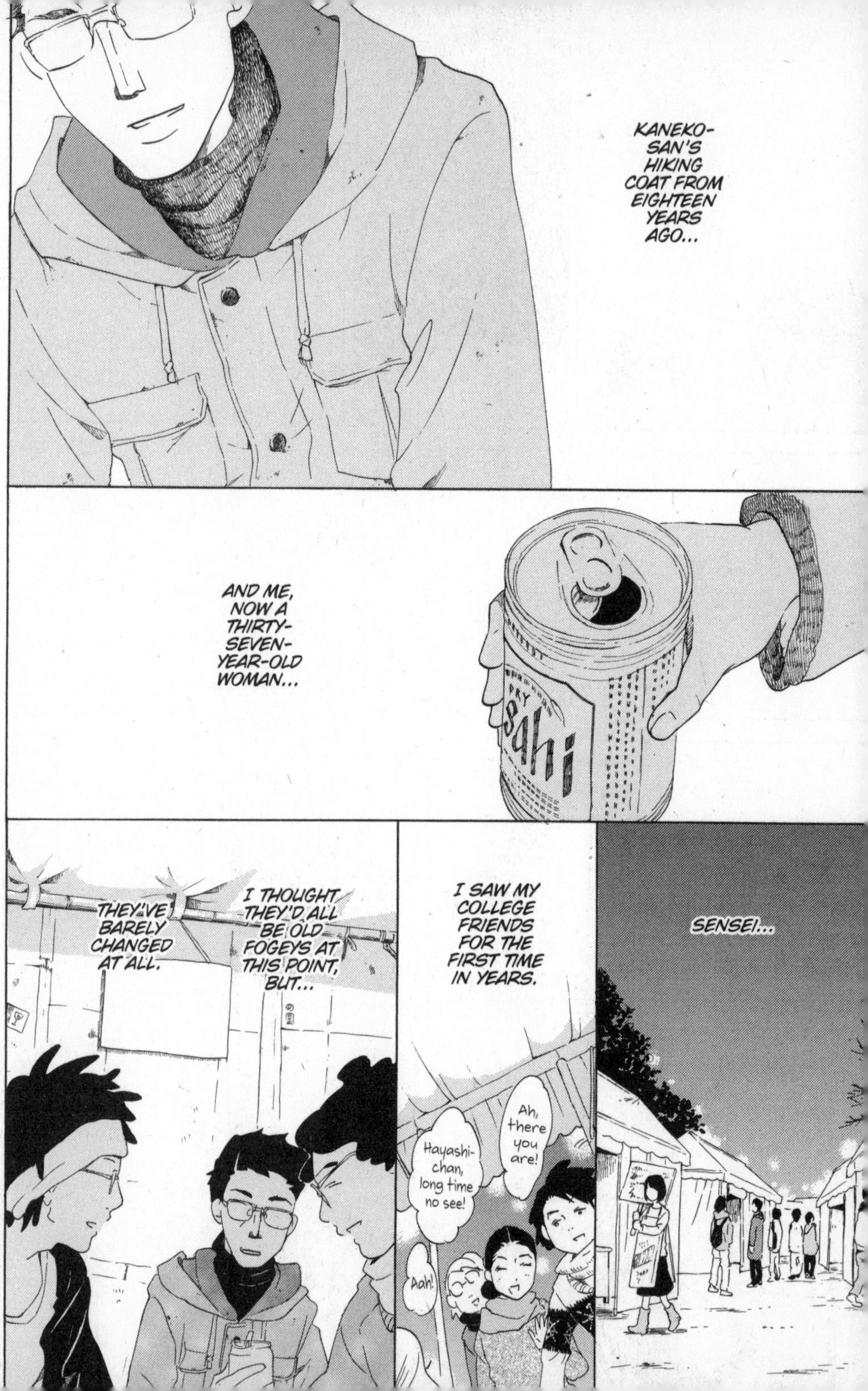
KANEKO-SAN'S HIKING COAT FROM EIGHTEEN YEARS AGO...
AND ME, NOW A THIRTY-SEVEN-YEAR-OLD WOMAN...
SENSEI...
I SAW MY COLLEGE FRIENDS FOR THE FIRST TIME IN YEARS.
Ah, there you are!
Hayashi-chan, long time no see!
Aah!
I THOUGHT THEY'D ALL BE OLD FOGEYS AT THIS POINT, BUT...
THEY'VE BARELY CHANGED AT ALL.

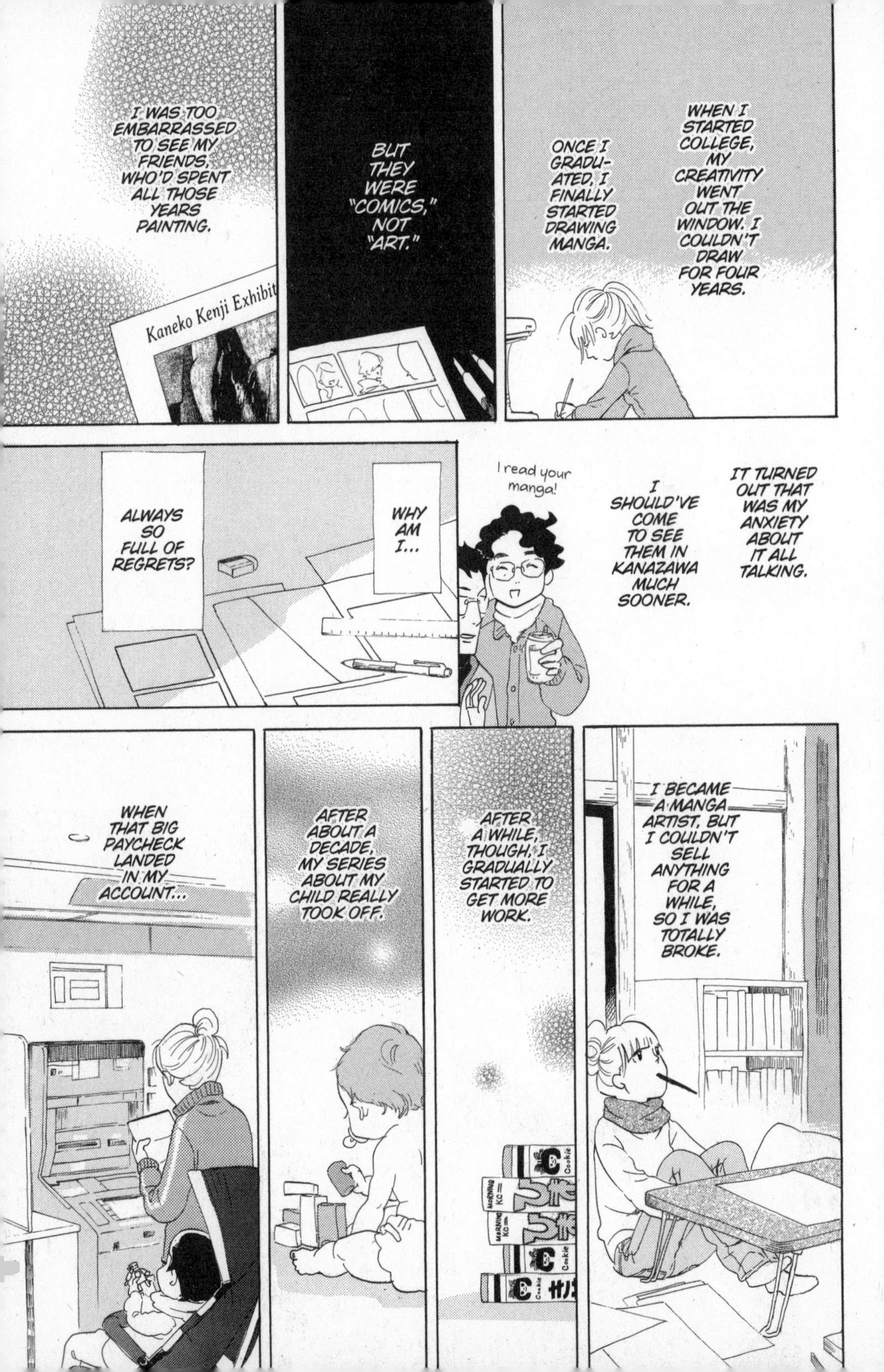

WHEN I STARTED COLLEGE, MY CREATIVITY WENT OUT THE WINDOW. I COULDN'T DRAW FOR FOUR YEARS.
ONCE I GRADUATED, I FINALLY STARTED DRAWING MANGA.
BUT THEY WERE "COMICS," NOT "ART."
I WAS TOO EMBARRASSED TO SEE MY FRIENDS, WHO'D SPENT ALL THOSE YEARS PAINTING.
Kaneko Kenji Exhibit
IT TURNED OUT THAT WAS MY ANXIETY ABOUT IT ALL TALKING.
I SHOULD'VE COME TO SEE THEM IN KANAZAWA MUCH SOONER.
I read your manga!
WHY AM I...
ALWAYS SO FULL OF REGRETS?
I BECAME A MANGA ARTIST, BUT I COULDN'T SELL ANYTHING FOR A WHILE, SO I WAS TOTALLY BROKE.
AFTER A WHILE, THOUGH, I GRADUALLY STARTED TO GET MORE WORK.
Cookie
MORNING KC
AFTER ABOUT A DECADE, MY SERIES ABOUT MY CHILD REALLY TOOK OFF.
WHEN THAT BIG PAYCHECK LANDED IN MY ACCOUNT...

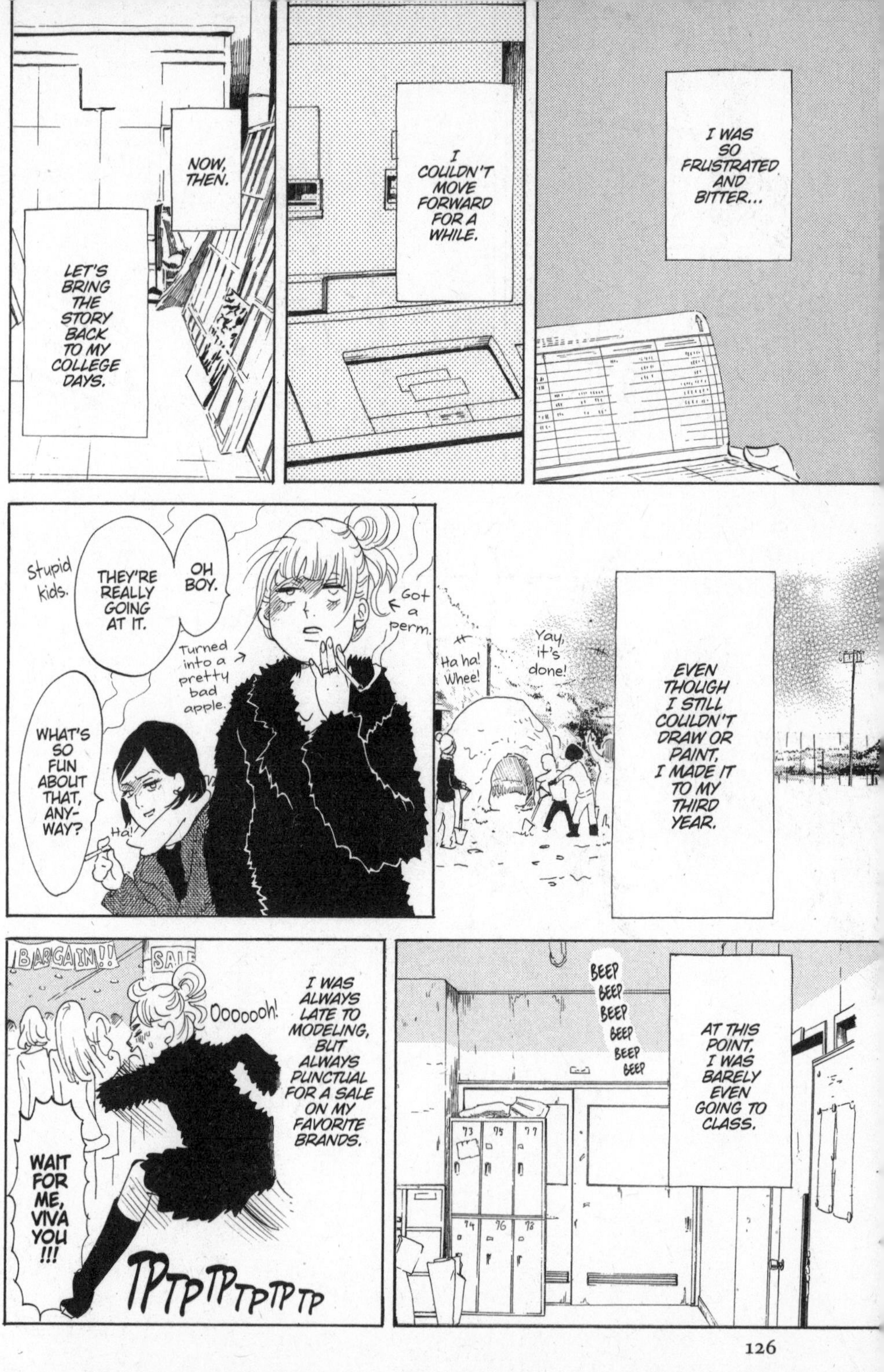
I WAS SO FRUSTRATED AND BITTER...
I COULDN'T MOVE FORWARD FOR A WHILE.
NOW, THEN.
LET'S BRING THE STORY BACK TO MY COLLEGE DAYS.
EVEN THOUGH I STILL COULDN'T DRAW OR PAINT, I MADE IT TO MY THIRD YEAR.
Yay, it's done!
Ha ha! Whee!
Got a perm.
OH BOY.
THEY'RE REALLY GOING AT IT.
Stupid kids.
Turned into a pretty bad apple.
WHAT'S SO FUN ABOUT THAT, ANY-WAY?
Ha!
AT THIS POINT, I WAS BARELY EVEN GOING TO CLASS.
BEEP BEEP BEEP BEEP BEEP BEEP
SALE
BARGAIN!!
I WAS ALWAYS LATE TO MODELING, BUT ALWAYS PUNCTUAL FOR A SALE ON MY FAVORITE BRANDS.
Oooooh!
WAIT FOR ME, VIVA YOU!!!
TPTPTPTPTPTPTP

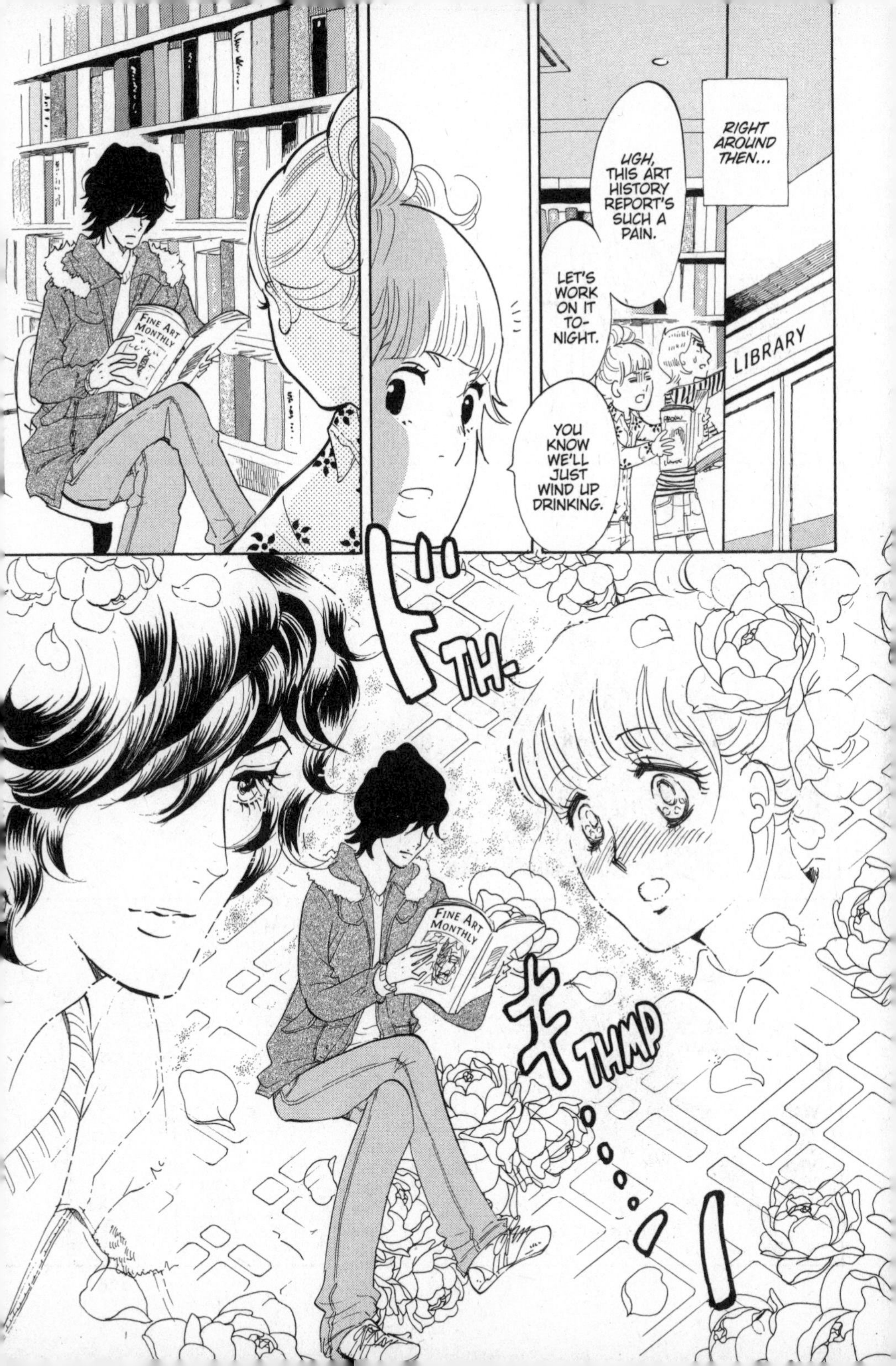

RIGHT AROUND THEN...
UGH, THIS ART HISTORY REPORT'S SUCH A PAIN.
LET'S WORK ON IT TO-NIGHT.
LIBRARY
YOU KNOW WE'LL JUST WIND UP DRINKING.
FINE ART MONTHLY
TH-
FINE ART MONTHLY
THMP

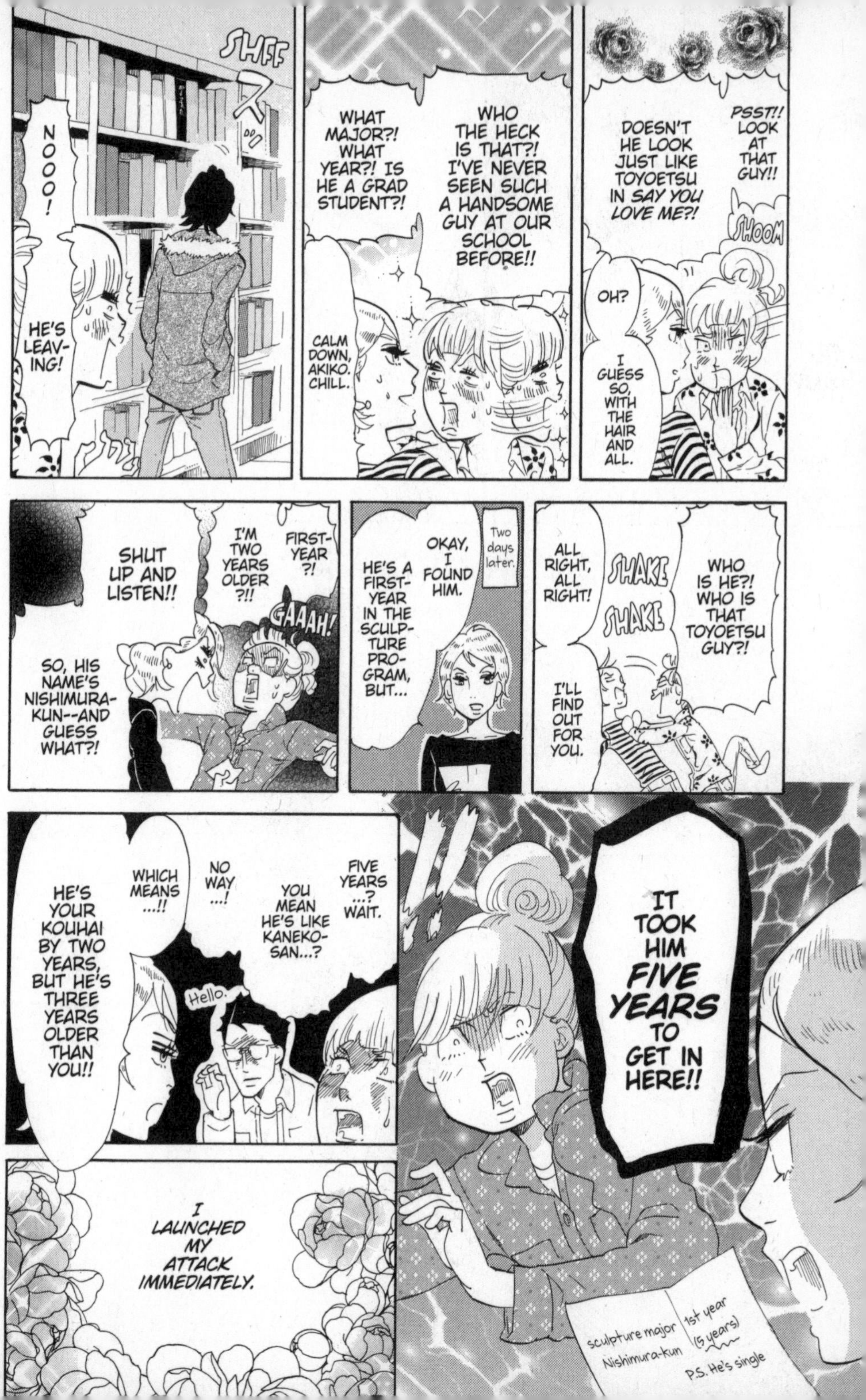
PSST!! LOOK AT THAT GUY!!
SHOOM
DOESN'T HE LOOK JUST LIKE TOYOETSU IN SAY YOU LOVE ME?!
OH?
I GUESS SO, WITH THE HAIR AND ALL.
WHO THE HECK IS THAT?! I'VE NEVER SEEN SUCH A HANDSOME GUY AT OUR SCHOOL BEFORE!!
WHAT MAJOR?! WHAT YEAR?! IS HE A GRAD STUDENT?!
CALM DOWN, AKIKO. CHILL.
SHFF
NOOOO!
HE'S LEAVING!
WHO IS HE?! WHO IS THAT TOYOETSU GUY?!
SHAKE
SHAKE
ALL RIGHT, ALL RIGHT!
I'LL FIND OUT FOR YOU.
Two days later.
OKAY, I FOUND HIM.
HE'S A FIRST-YEAR IN THE SCULPTURE PROGRAM, BUT...
FIRST-YEAR?!
I'M TWO YEARS OLDER?!!
GAAAH!
SHUT UP AND LISTEN!!
SO, HIS NAME'S NISHIMURA-KUN--AND GUESS WHAT?!
IT TOOK HIM FIVE YEARS TO GET IN HERE!!
sculpture major 1st year
Nishimura-kun (5 years)
P.S. He's single
FIVE YEARS ...? WAIT.
YOU MEAN HE'S LIKE KANEKO-SAN...?
NO WAY ...!
WHICH MEANS ...!!
HE'S YOUR KOUHAI BY TWO YEARS, BUT HE'S THREE YEARS OLDER THAN YOU!!
Hello.
I LAUNCHED MY ATTACK IMMEDIATELY.

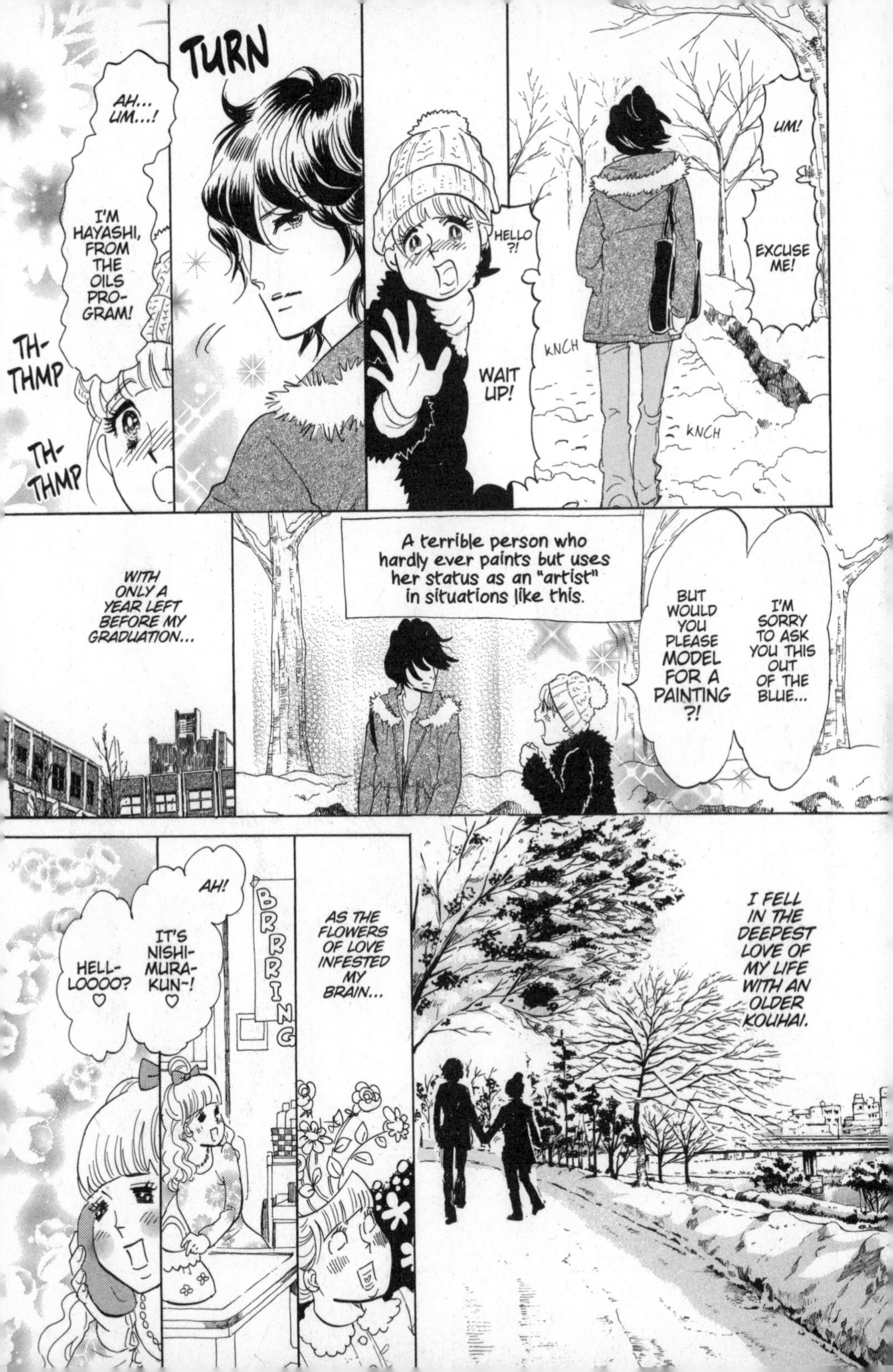
UM!
EXCUSE ME!
KNCH
KNCH
HELLO?!
WAIT UP!
TURN
AH... UM...!
I'M HAYASHI, FROM THE OILS PROGRAM!
TH-THMP
TH-THMP
I'M SORRY TO ASK YOU THIS OUT OF THE BLUE...
BUT WOULD YOU PLEASE MODEL FOR A PAINTING?!
A terrible person who hardly ever paints but uses her status as an "artist" in situations like this.
WITH ONLY A YEAR LEFT BEFORE MY GRADUATION...
I FELL IN THE DEEPEST LOVE OF MY LIFE WITH AN OLDER KOUHAI.
AS THE FLOWERS OF LOVE INFESTED MY BRAIN...
BRRRING
AH!
IT'S NISHIMURA-KUN~! ♡
HELL-LOOOO? ♡

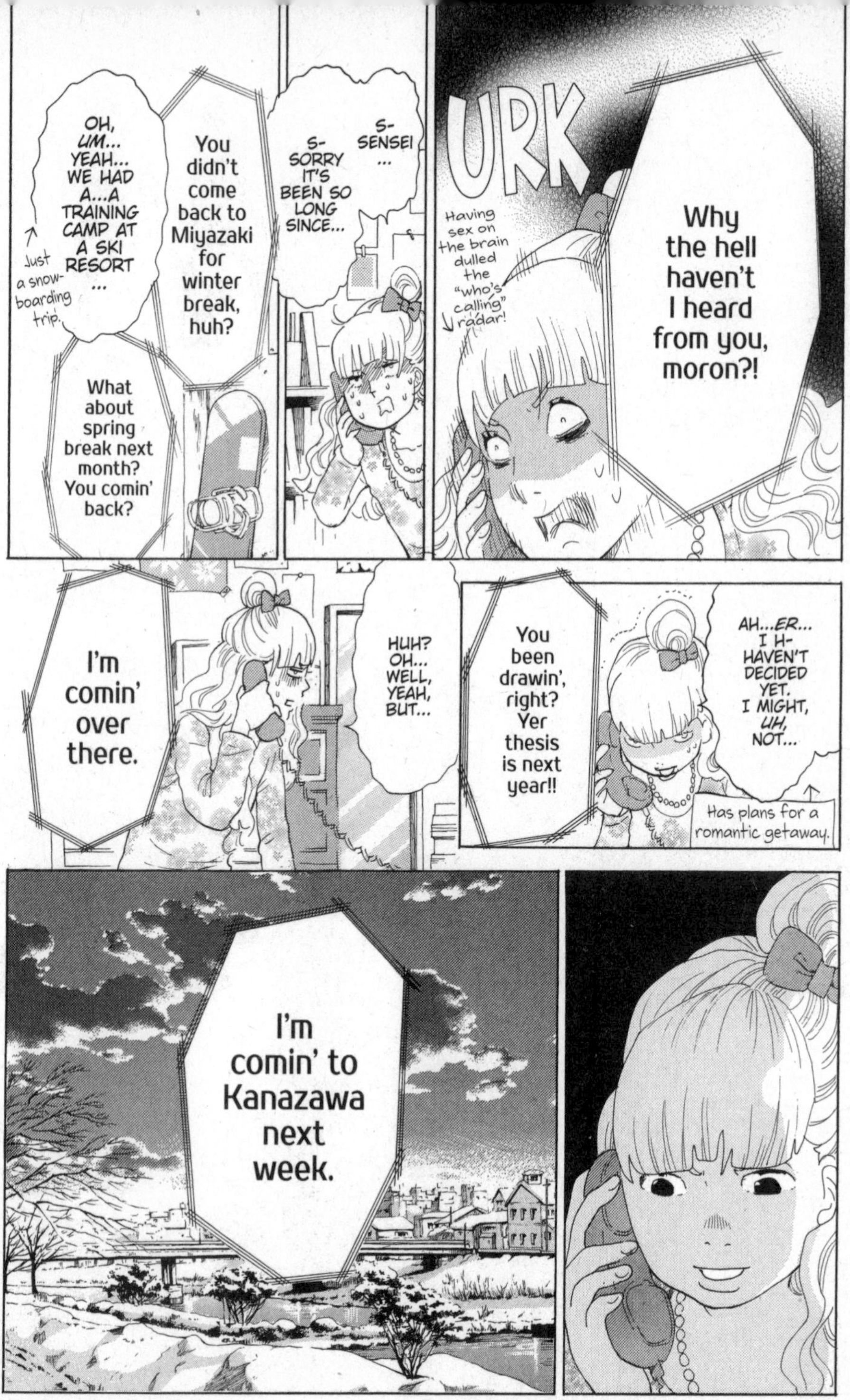
URK
Why the hell haven't I heard from you, moron?!
Having sex on the brain dulled the "who's calling" radar!
S-SENSEI...
S-SORRY IT'S BEEN SO LONG SINCE...
You didn't come back to Miyazaki for winter break, huh?
OH, UM... YEAH... WE HAD A...A TRAINING CAMP AT A SKI RESORT...
Just a snow-boarding trip.
What about spring break next month? You comin' back?
AH...ER... I H-HAVEN'T DECIDED YET. I MIGHT, UH, NOT...
Has plans for a romantic getaway.
You been drawin', right? Yer thesis is next year!!
HUH? OH... WELL, YEAH, BUT...
I'm comin' over there.
I'm comin' to Kanazawa next week.

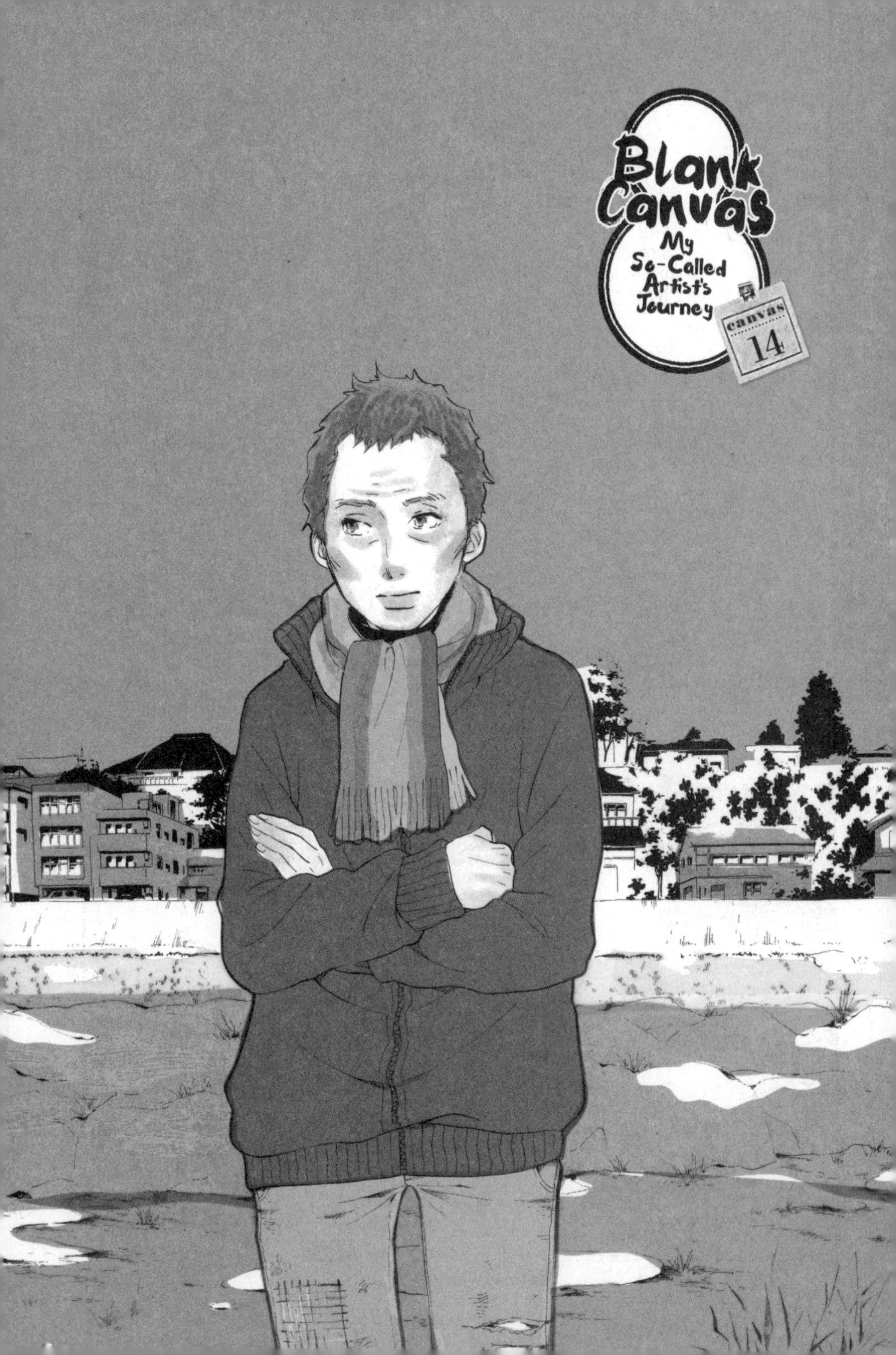
Blank Canvas
My So-Called Artist's Journey
canvas
14

Blank
Canvas
My So-Called
Artist's Journey

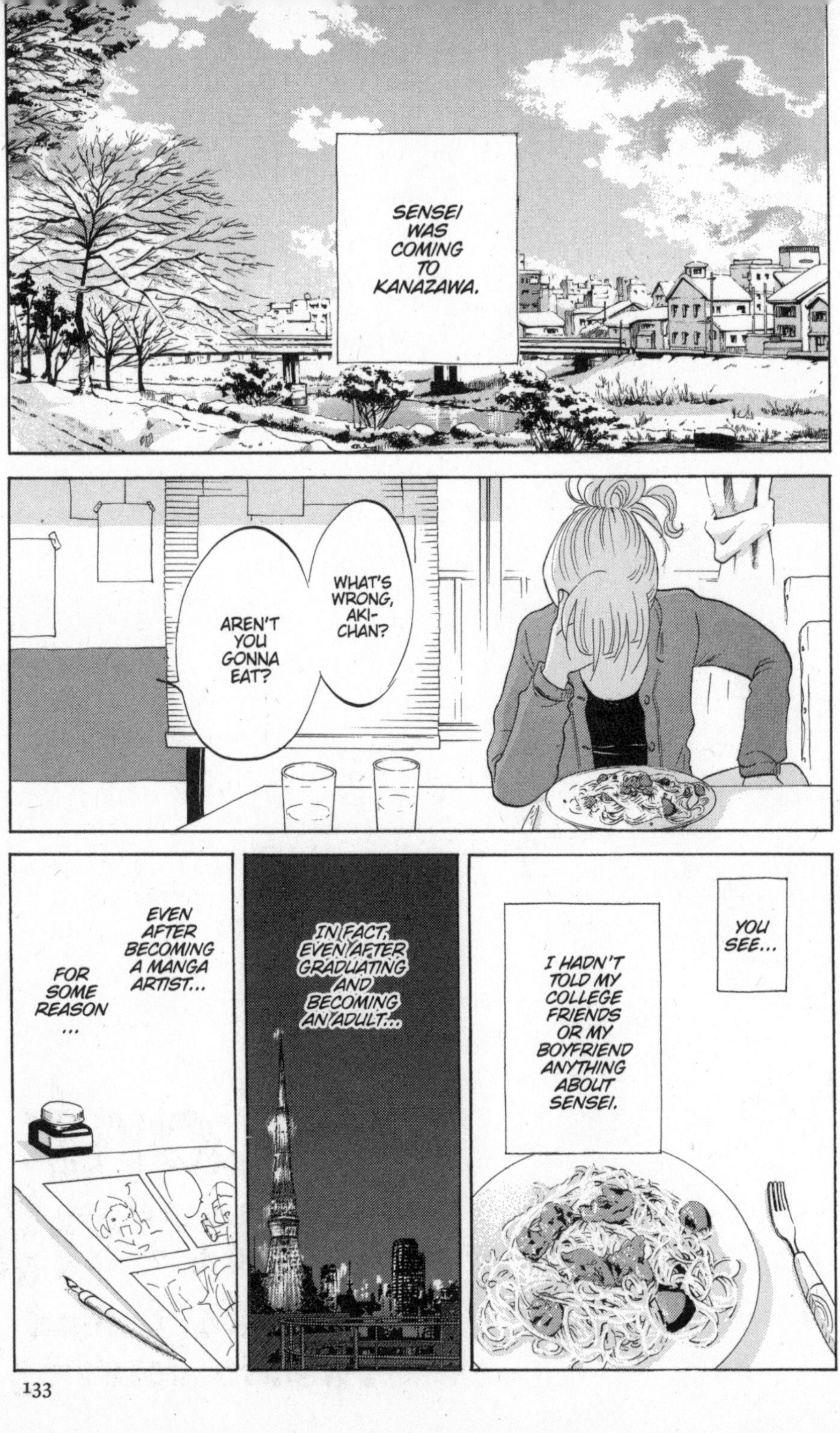
SENSEI WAS COMING TO KANAZAWA.
WHAT'S WRONG, AKI-CHAN?
AREN'T YOU GONNA EAT?
YOU SEE...
I HADN'T TOLD MY COLLEGE FRIENDS OR MY BOYFRIEND ANYTHING ABOUT SENSEI.
IN FACT, EVEN AFTER GRADUATING AND BECOMING AN ADULT...
EVEN AFTER BECOMING A MANGA ARTIST...
FOR SOME REASON...

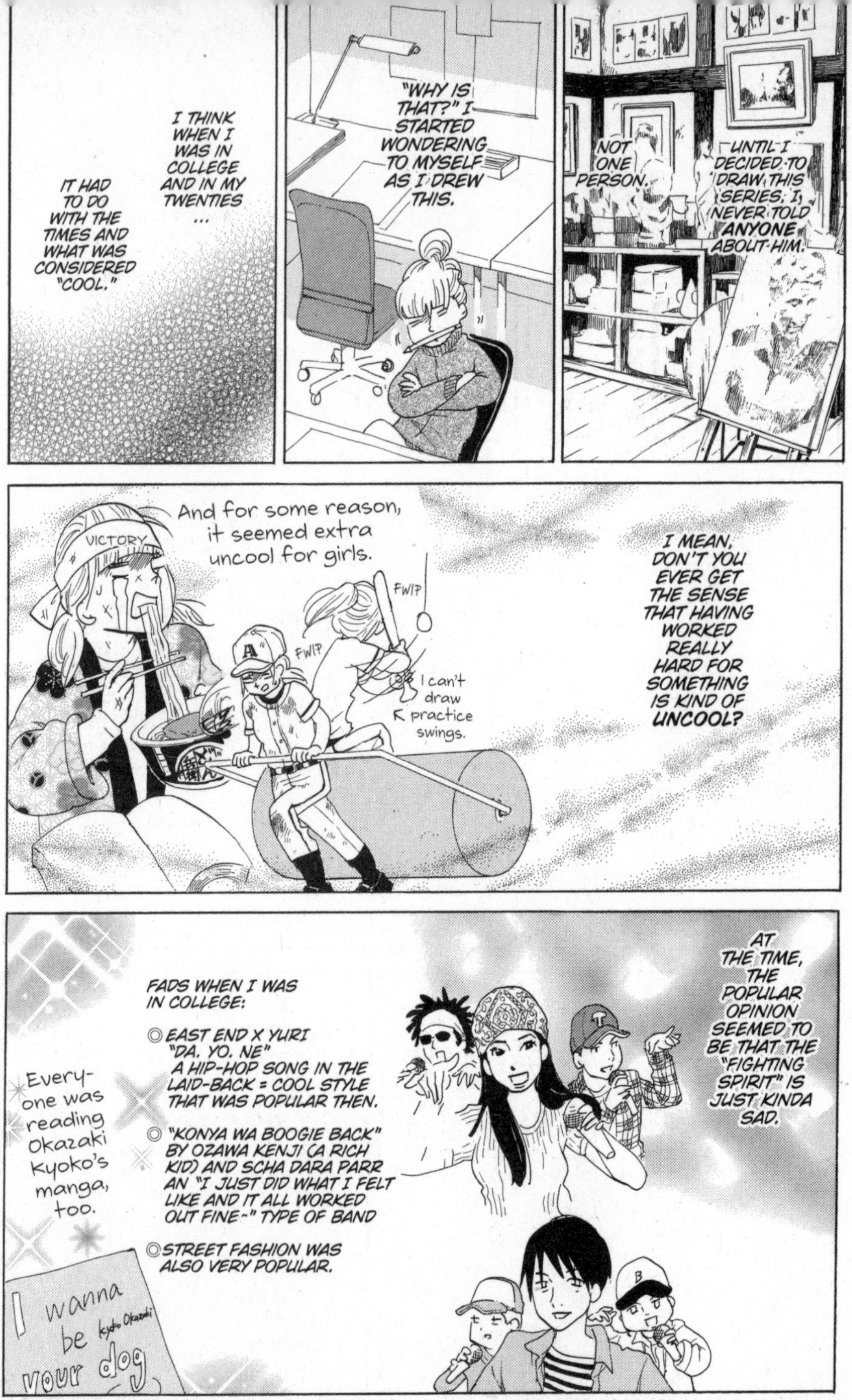
UNTIL I DECIDED TO DRAW THIS SERIES, I NEVER TOLD ANYONE ABOUT HIM.
NOT ONE PERSON.
"WHY IS THAT?" I STARTED WONDERING TO MYSELF AS I DREW THIS.
I THINK WHEN I WAS IN COLLEGE AND IN MY TWENTIES...
IT HAD TO DO WITH THE TIMES AND WHAT WAS CONSIDERED "COOL."
I MEAN, DON'T YOU EVER GET THE SENSE THAT HAVING WORKED REALLY HARD FOR SOMETHING IS KIND OF UNCOOL?
FWIP
I can't draw practice swings.
FWIP
A
And for some reason, it seemed extra uncool for girls.
VICTORY
AT THE TIME, THE POPULAR OPINION SEEMED TO BE THAT THE "FIGHTING SPIRIT" IS JUST KINDA SAD.
T
B
FADS WHEN I WAS IN COLLEGE:
◎ EAST END X YURI "DA. YO. NE" A HIP-HOP SONG IN THE LAID-BACK = COOL STYLE THAT WAS POPULAR THEN.
◎ "KONYA WA BOOGIE BACK" BY OZAWA KENJI (A RICH KID) AND SCHA DARA PARR AN "I JUST DID WHAT I FELT LIKE AND IT ALL WORKED OUT FINE~" TYPE OF BAND
◎ STREET FASHION WAS ALSO VERY POPULAR.
Everyone was reading Okazaki Kyoko's manga, too.
I wanna be your dog
Kyoko Okazaki

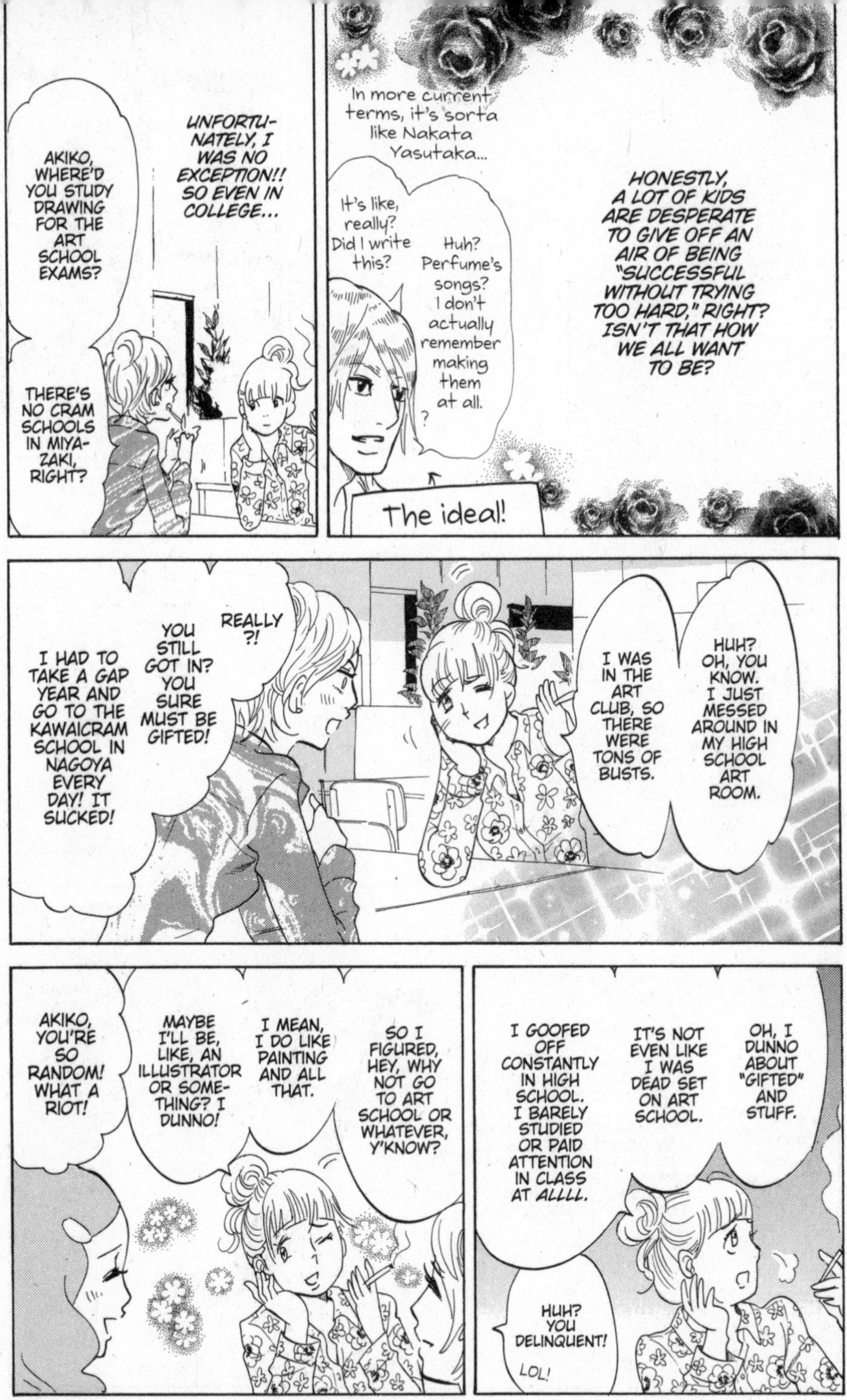
HONESTLY, A LOT OF KIDS ARE DESPERATE TO GIVE OFF AN AIR OF BEING "SUCCESSFUL WITHOUT TRYING TOO HARD," RIGHT? ISN'T THAT HOW WE ALL WANT TO BE?
In more current terms, it's sorta like Nakata Yasutaka...
Huh? Perfume's songs? I don't actually remember making them at all.
It's like, really? Did I write this?
?
The ideal!
UNFORTUNATELY, I WAS NO EXCEPTION!! SO EVEN IN COLLEGE...
AKIKO, WHERE'D YOU STUDY DRAWING FOR THE ART SCHOOL EXAMS?
THERE'S NO CRAM SCHOOLS IN MIYAZAKI, RIGHT?
HUH? OH, YOU KNOW. I JUST MESSED AROUND IN MY HIGH SCHOOL ART ROOM.
I WAS IN THE ART CLUB, SO THERE WERE TONS OF BUSTS.
REALLY?!
YOU STILL GOT IN? YOU SURE MUST BE GIFTED!
I HAD TO TAKE A GAP YEAR AND GO TO THE KAWAICRAM SCHOOL IN NAGOYA EVERY DAY! IT SUCKED!
OH, I DUNNO ABOUT "GIFTED" AND STUFF.
IT'S NOT EVEN LIKE I WAS DEAD SET ON ART SCHOOL.
I GOOFED OFF CONSTANTLY IN HIGH SCHOOL. I BARELY STUDIED OR PAID ATTENTION IN CLASS AT ALLLL.
HUH? YOU DELINQUENT!
LOL!
SO I FIGURED, HEY, WHY NOT GO TO ART SCHOOL OR WHATEVER, Y'KNOW?
I MEAN, I DO LIKE PAINTING AND ALL THAT.
MAYBE I'LL BE, LIKE, AN ILLUSTRATOR OR SOME-THING? I DUNNO!
AKIKO, YOU'RE SO RANDOM! WHAT A RIOT!

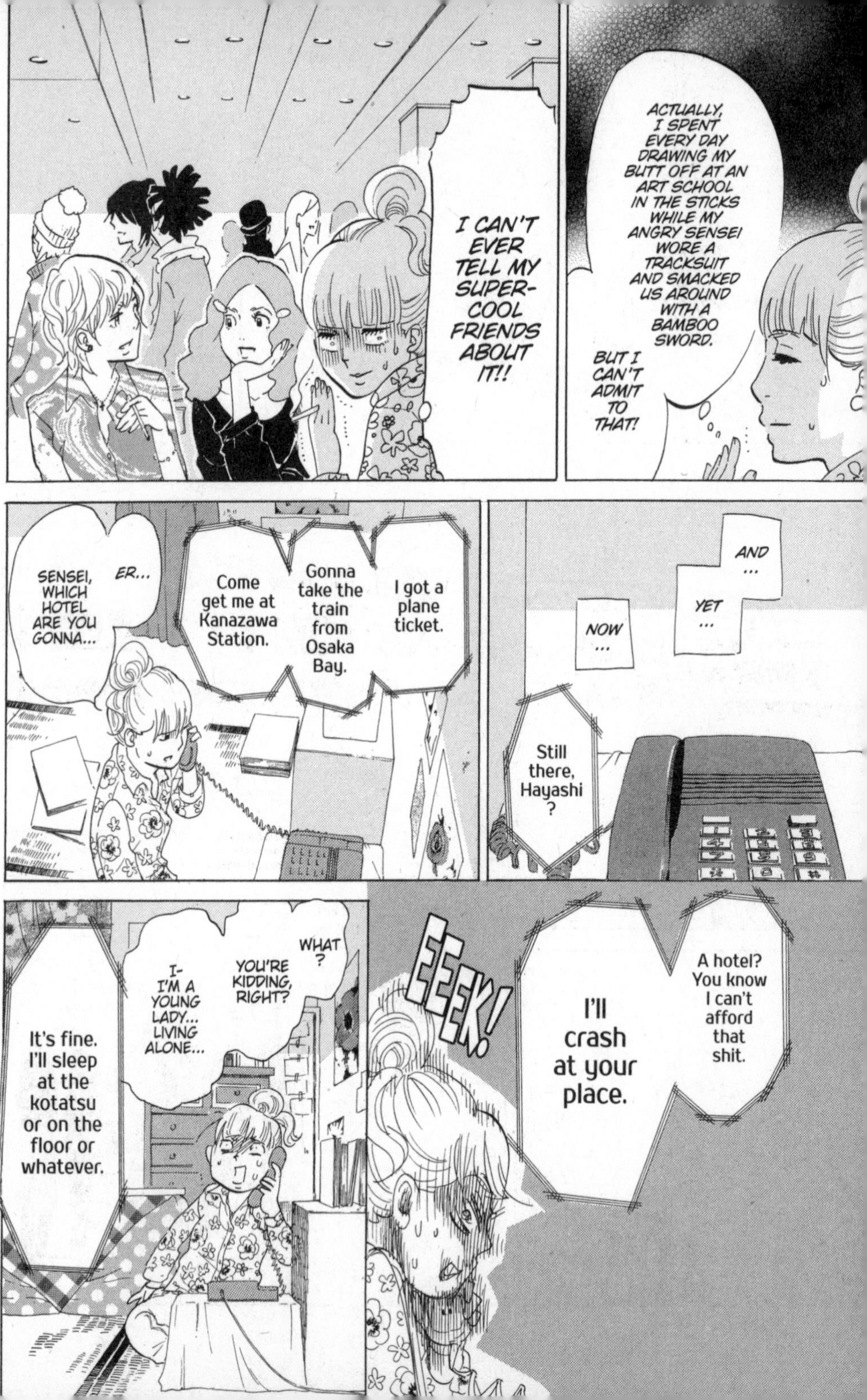
ACTUALLY, I SPENT EVERY DAY DRAWING MY BUTT OFF AT AN ART SCHOOL IN THE STICKS WHILE MY ANGRY SENSEI WORE A TRACKSUIT AND SMACKED US AROUND WITH A BAMBOO SWORD.
BUT I CAN'T ADMIT TO THAT!
I CAN'T EVER TELL MY SUPER-COOL FRIENDS ABOUT IT!!
AND ...
YET ...
NOW ...
Still there, Hayashi?
I got a plane ticket.
Gonna take the train from Osaka Bay.
Come get me at Kanazawa Station.
ER...
SENSEI, WHICH HOTEL ARE YOU GONNA...
A hotel? You know I can't afford that shit.
I'll crash at your place.
EEEK!
WHAT?
YOU'RE KIDDING, RIGHT?
I-I'M A YOUNG LADY... LIVING ALONE...
It's fine. I'll sleep at the kotatsu or on the floor or whatever.

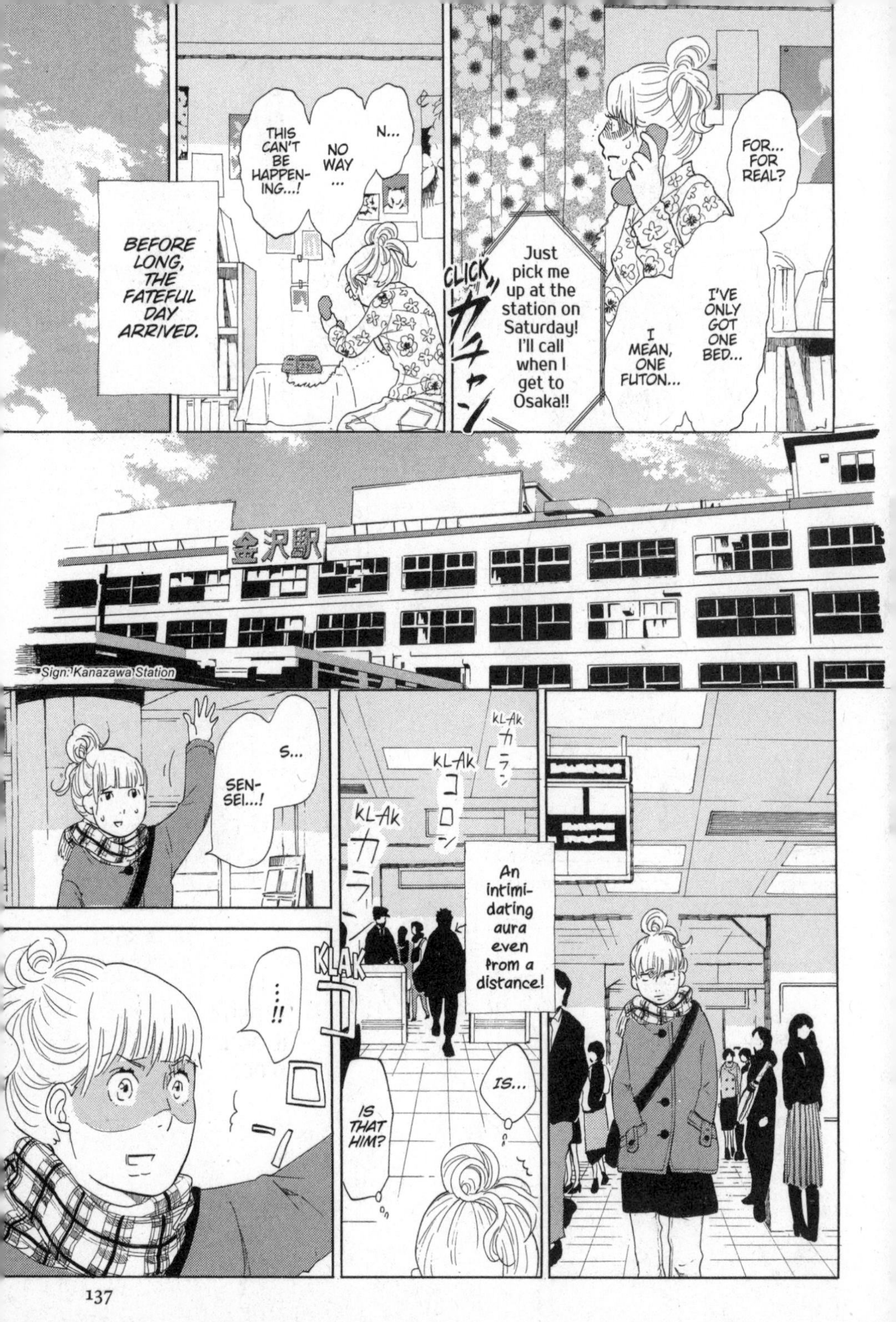
FOR... FOR REAL?
I'VE ONLY GOT ONE BED...
I MEAN, ONE FUTON...
Just pick me up at the station on Saturday! I'll call when I get to Osaka!!
CLICK
N...
NO WAY...
THIS CAN'T BE HAPPENING...!
BEFORE LONG, THE FATEFUL DAY ARRIVED.
金沢駅
Sign: Kanazawa Station
An intimidating aura even from a distance!
kLAk
kLAk
kLAk
KLAK
IS...
IS THAT HIM?
S...
SEN-SEI...!
...!!

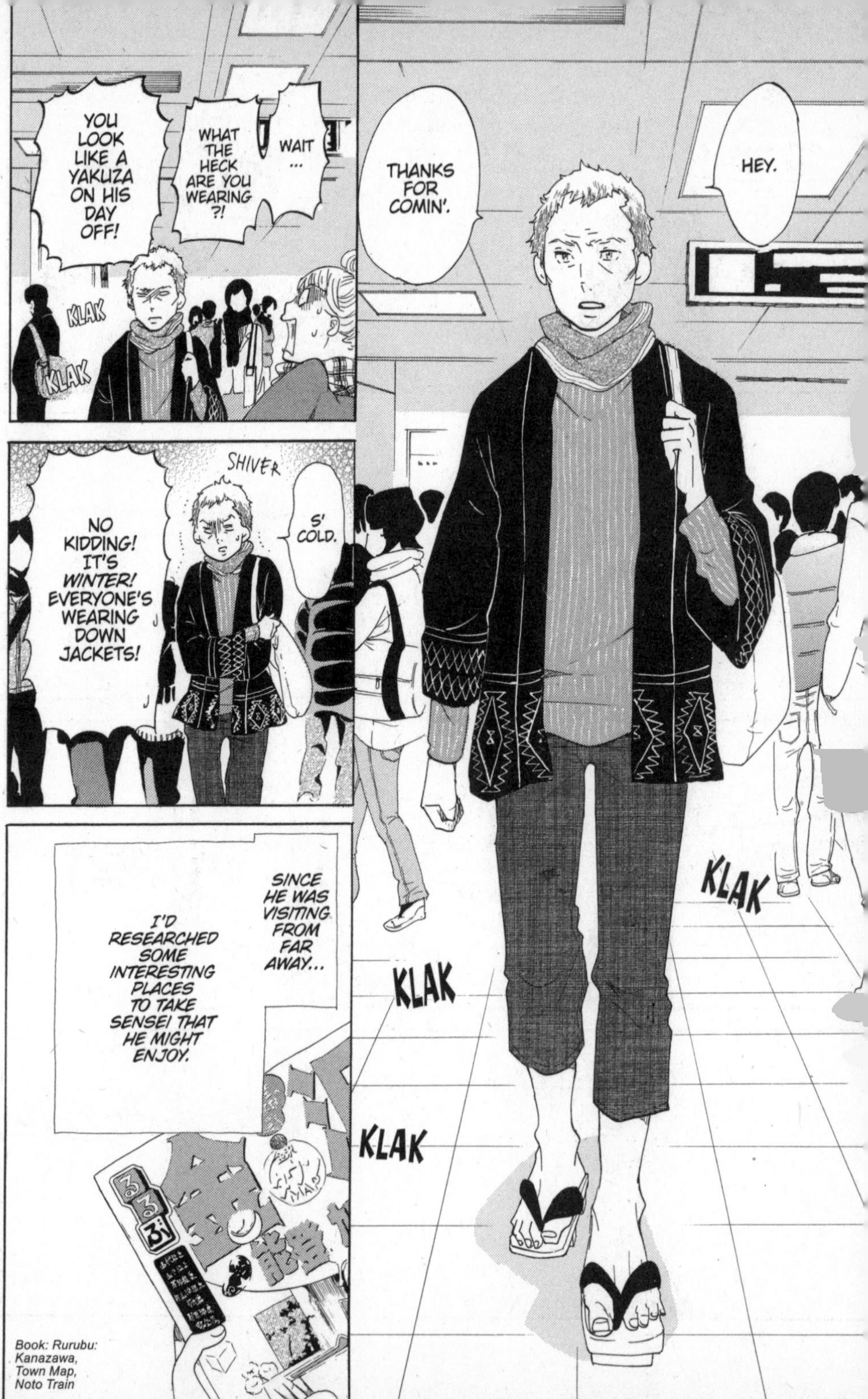
HEY.
THANKS FOR COMIN'.
KLAK
KLAK
KLAK
WAIT ...
WHAT THE HECK ARE YOU WEARING ?!
YOU LOOK LIKE A YAKUZA ON HIS DAY OFF!
KLAK
KLAK
S' COLD.
SHIVER
NO KIDDING! IT'S WINTER! EVERYONE'S WEARING DOWN JACKETS!
SINCE HE WAS VISITING FROM FAR AWAY...
I'D RESEARCHED SOME INTERESTING PLACES TO TAKE SENSEI THAT HE MIGHT ENJOY.
Book: Rurubu: Kanazawa, Town Map, Noto Train

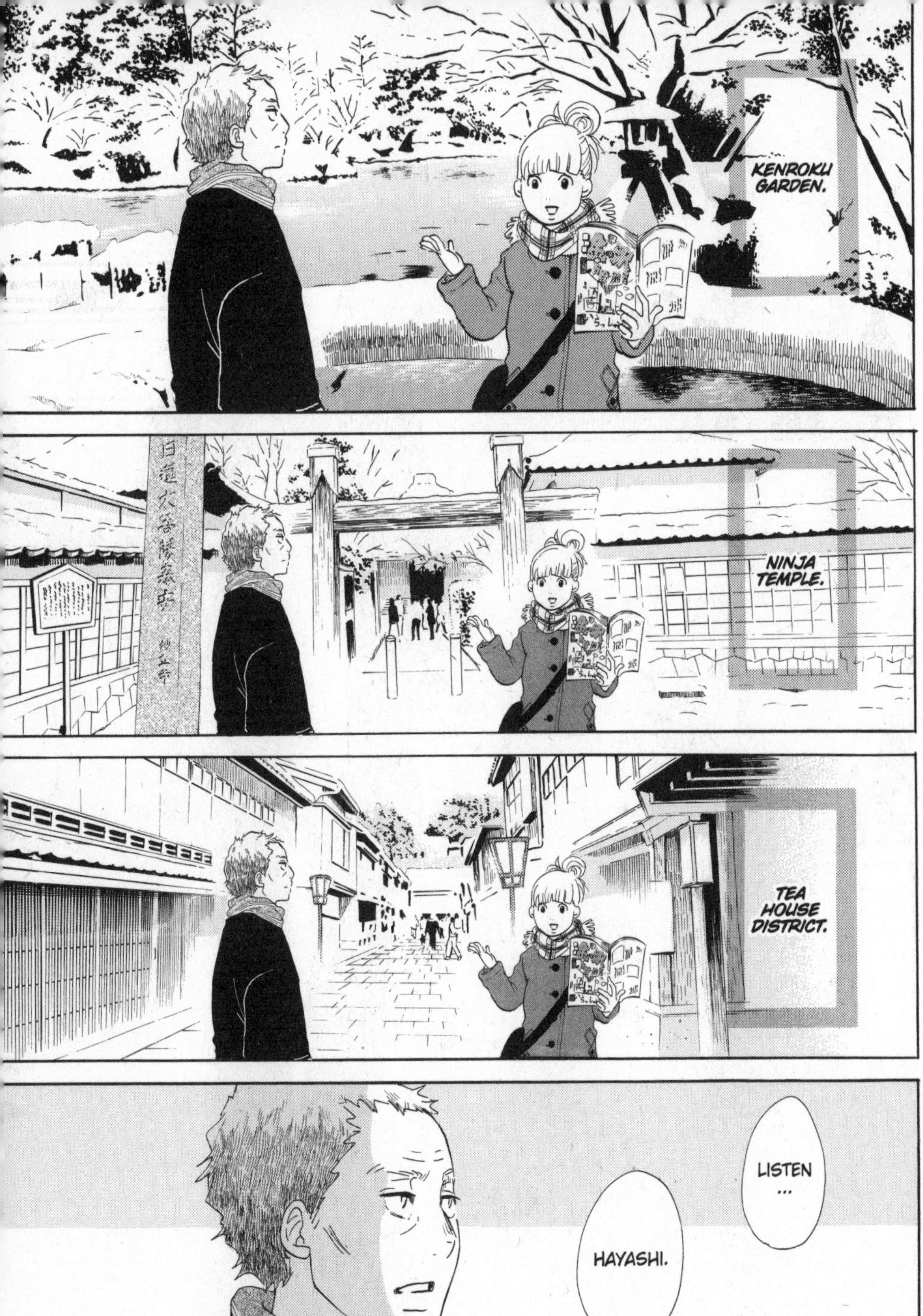
KENROKU GARDEN.
NINJA TEMPLE.
TEA HOUSE DISTRICT.
LISTEN ...
HAYASHI.

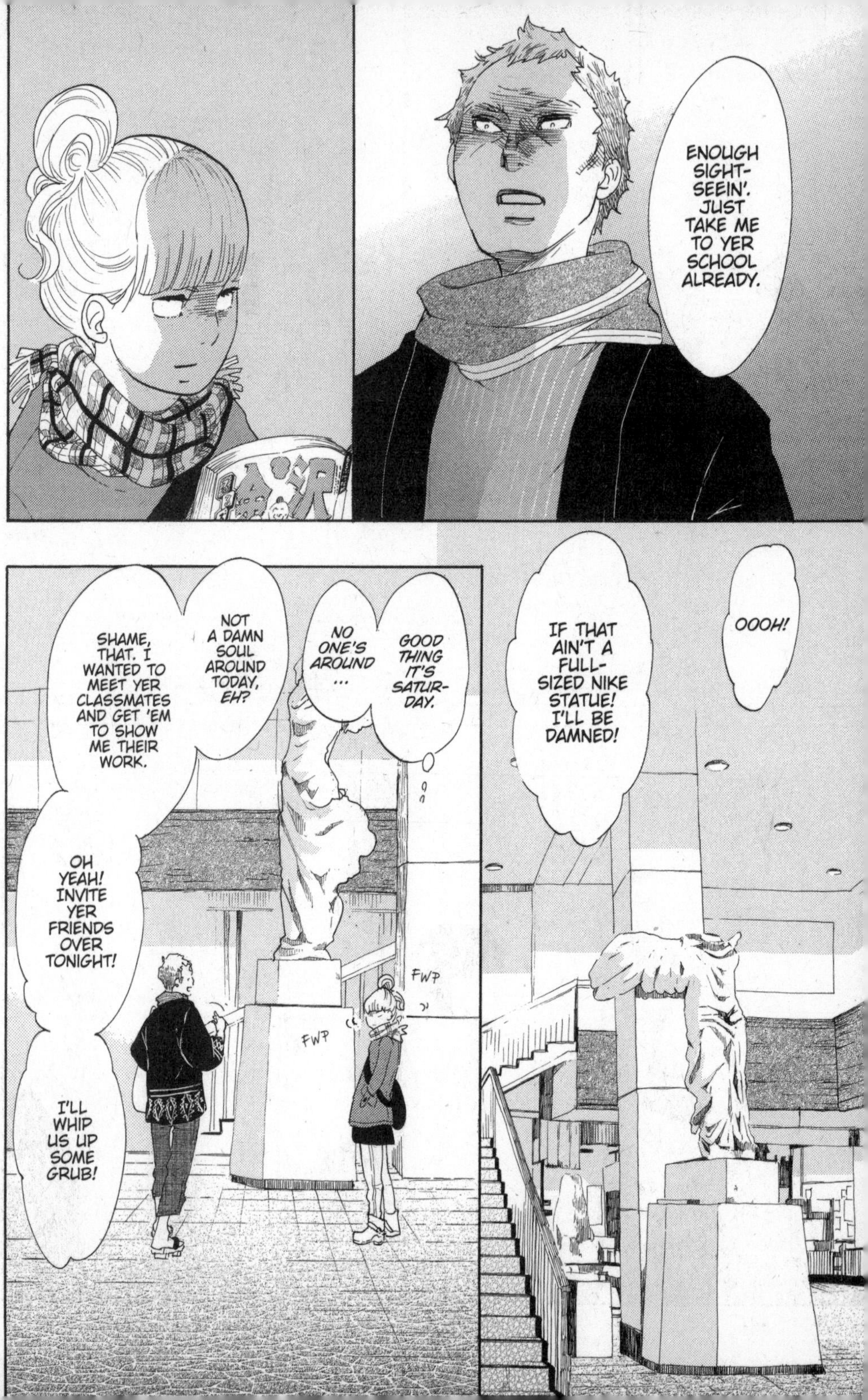
ENOUGH SIGHT-SEEIN'. JUST TAKE ME TO YER SCHOOL ALREADY.
OOOH!
IF THAT AIN'T A FULL-SIZED NIKE STATUE! I'LL BE DAMNED!
GOOD THING IT'S SATUR-DAY.
NO ONE'S AROUND...
NOT A DAMN SOUL AROUND TODAY, EH?
SHAME, THAT. I WANTED TO MEET YER CLASSMATES AND GET 'EM TO SHOW ME THEIR WORK.
FWP
FWP
OH YEAH! INVITE YER FRIENDS OVER TONIGHT!
I'LL WHIP US UP SOME GRUB!

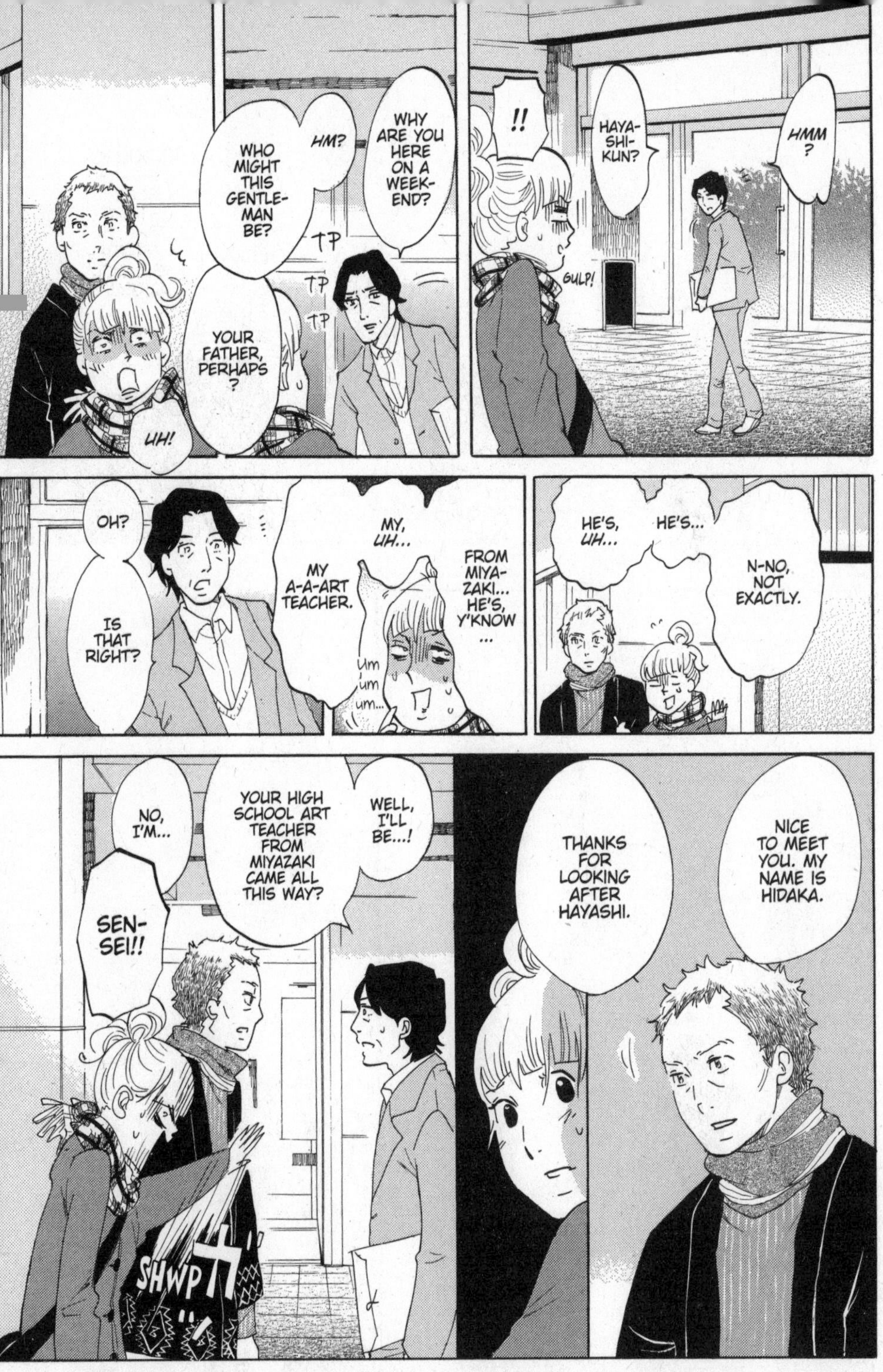
HMM?
HAYA-SHI-KUN?
!!
GULP!
WHY ARE YOU HERE ON A WEEK-END?
HM?
TP TP TP
WHO MIGHT THIS GENTLE-MAN BE?
YOUR FATHER, PERHAPS?
UH!
HE'S...
HE'S, UH...
N-NO, NOT EXACTLY.
FROM MIYA-ZAKI... HE'S, Y'KNOW...
MY, UH...
MY A-A-ART TEACHER.
Um um um...
OH?
IS THAT RIGHT?
NICE TO MEET YOU. MY NAME IS HIDAKA.
THANKS FOR LOOKING AFTER HAYASHI.
WELL, I'LL BE...!
YOUR HIGH SCHOOL ART TEACHER FROM MIYAZAKI CAME ALL THIS WAY?
NO, I'M...
SEN-SEI!!
SHWP

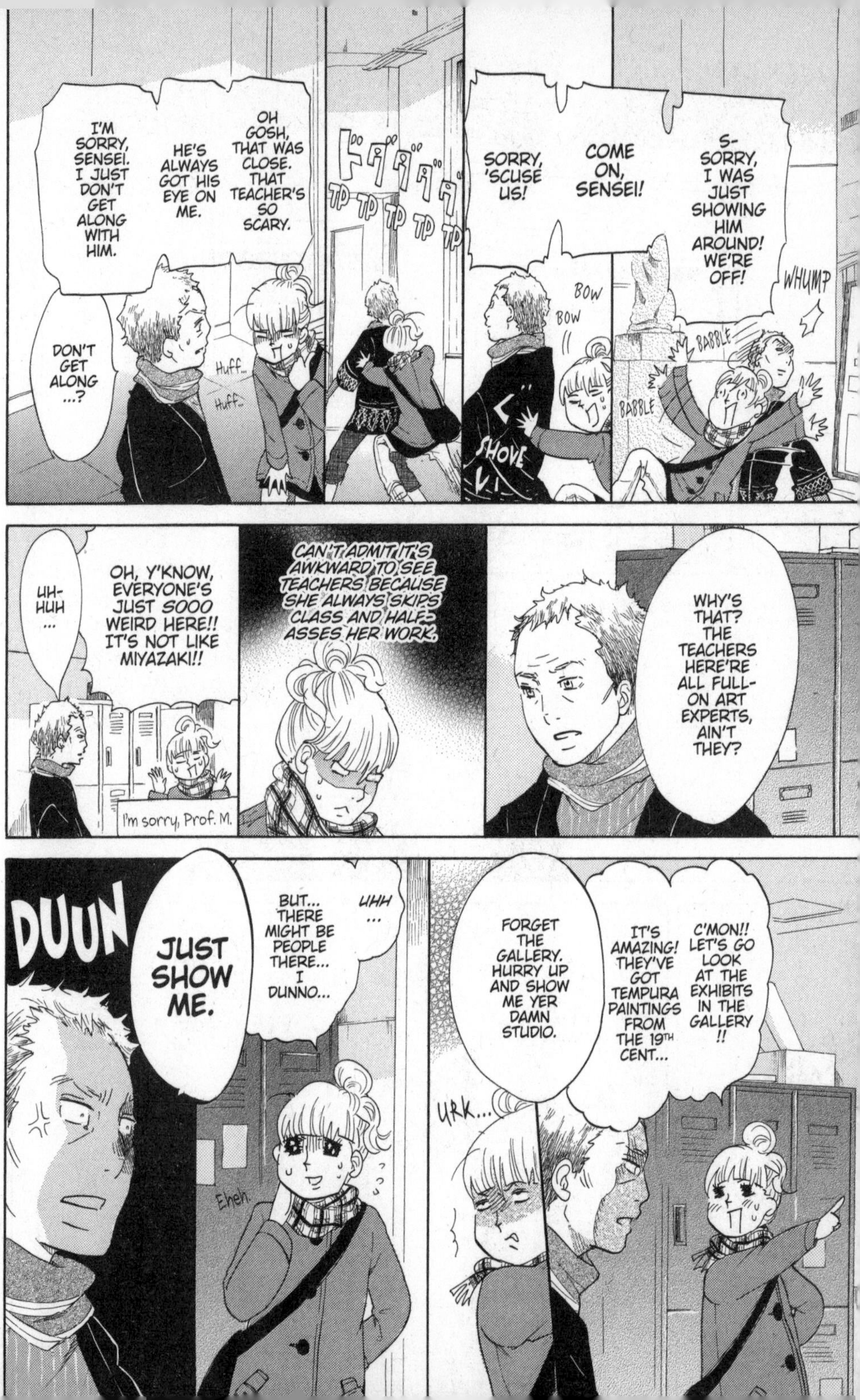
S-SORRY, I WAS JUST SHOWING HIM AROUND! WE'RE OFF!
WHUMP
BABBLE
BABBLE
COME ON, SENSEI!
SORRY, 'SCUSE US!
BOW
BOW
SHOVE
TP TP TP TP TP
OH GOSH, THAT WAS CLOSE. THAT TEACHER'S SO SCARY.
HE'S ALWAYS GOT HIS EYE ON ME.
I'M SORRY, SENSEI. I JUST DON'T GET ALONG WITH HIM.
Huff...
Huff...
DON'T GET ALONG ...?
WHY'S THAT? THE TEACHERS HERE'RE ALL FULL-ON ART EXPERTS, AIN'T THEY?
CAN'T ADMIT IT'S AWKWARD TO SEE TEACHERS BECAUSE SHE ALWAYS SKIPS CLASS AND HALF-ASSES HER WORK.
OH, Y'KNOW, EVERYONE'S JUST SOOO WEIRD HERE!! IT'S NOT LIKE MIYAZAKI!!
UH-HUH ...
I'm sorry, Prof. M.
C'MON!! LET'S GO LOOK AT THE EXHIBITS IN THE GALLERY !!
IT'S AMAZING! THEY'VE GOT TEMPURA PAINTINGS FROM THE 19TH CENT...
FORGET THE GALLERY. HURRY UP AND SHOW ME YER DAMN STUDIO.
URK...
UHH ...
BUT... THERE MIGHT BE PEOPLE THERE... I DUNNO...
Eheh.
JUST SHOW ME.
DUUN

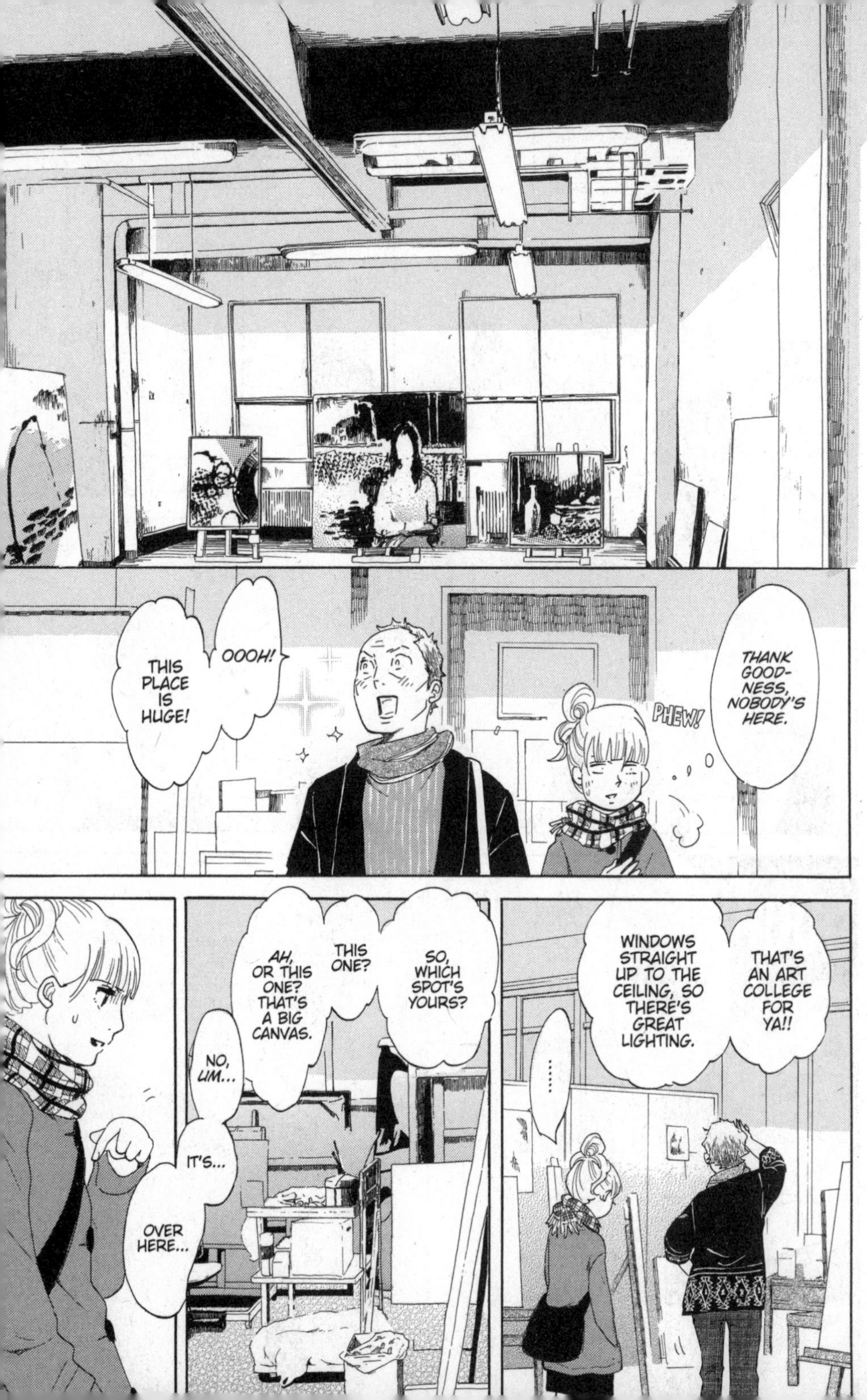
THANK GOODNESS, NOBODY'S HERE.
PHEW!
OOOH!
THIS PLACE IS HUGE!
THAT'S AN ART COLLEGE FOR YA!!
WINDOWS STRAIGHT UP TO THE CEILING, SO THERE'S GREAT LIGHTING.
......
SO, WHICH SPOT'S YOURS?
THIS ONE?
AH, OR THIS ONE? THAT'S A BIG CANVAS.
NO, UM...
IT'S...
OVER HERE...

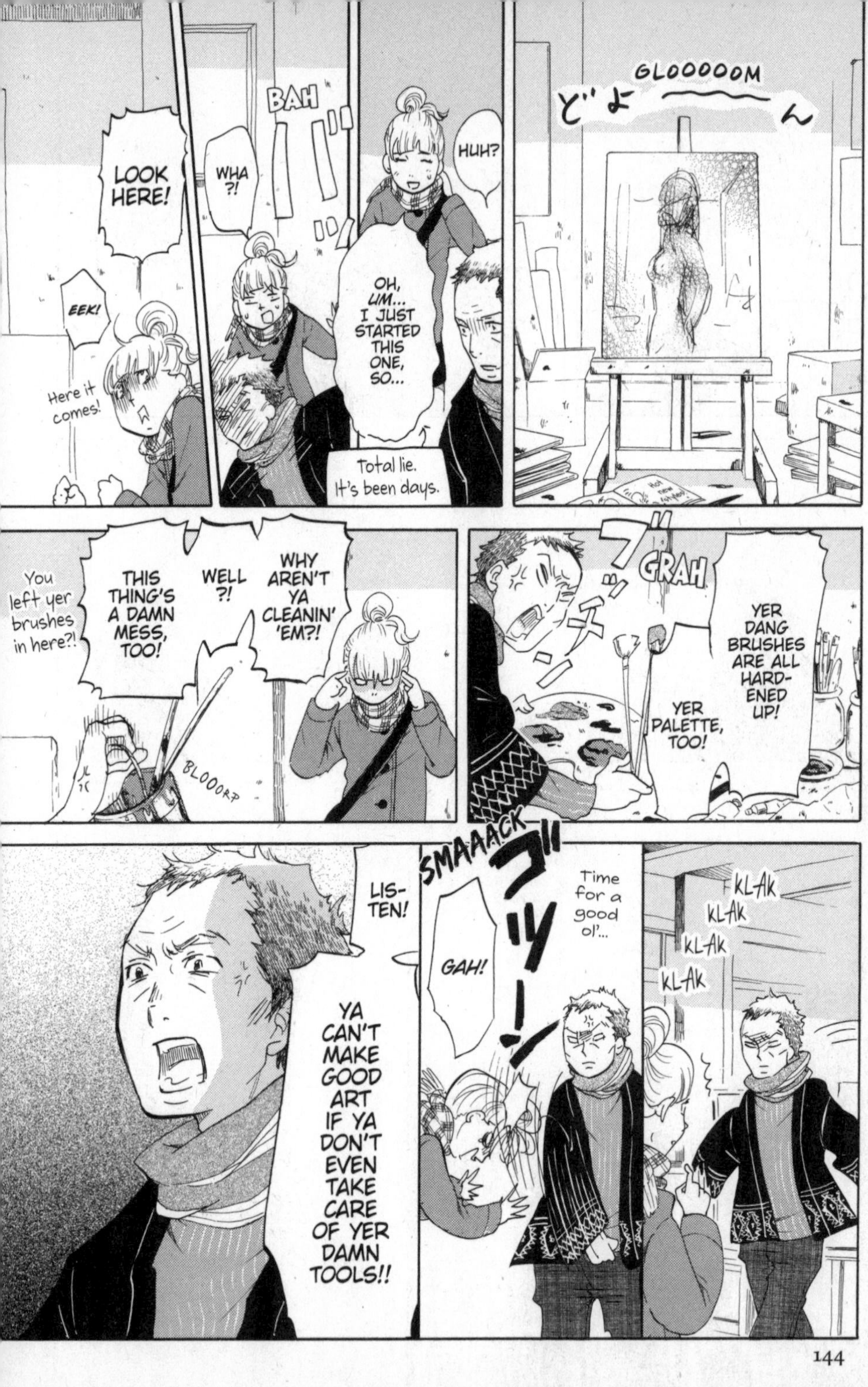
GLOOOOOM
どよ〜〜ん
HUH?
BAH
WHA ?!
OH, UM... I JUST STARTED THIS ONE, SO...
Total lie. It's been days.
LOOK HERE!
EEK!
Here it comes!
GRAH
YER DANG BRUSHES ARE ALL HARD-ENED UP!
YER PALETTE, TOO!
WHY AREN'T YA CLEANIN' 'EM?!
WELL ?!
THIS THING'S A DAMN MESS, TOO!
You left yer brushes in here?!
BLOOORP
KLAK
KLAK
KLAK
KLAK
Time for a good ol'...
SMAAACK
GAH!
LIS-TEN!
YA CAN'T MAKE GOOD ART IF YA DON'T EVEN TAKE CARE OF YER DAMN TOOLS!!

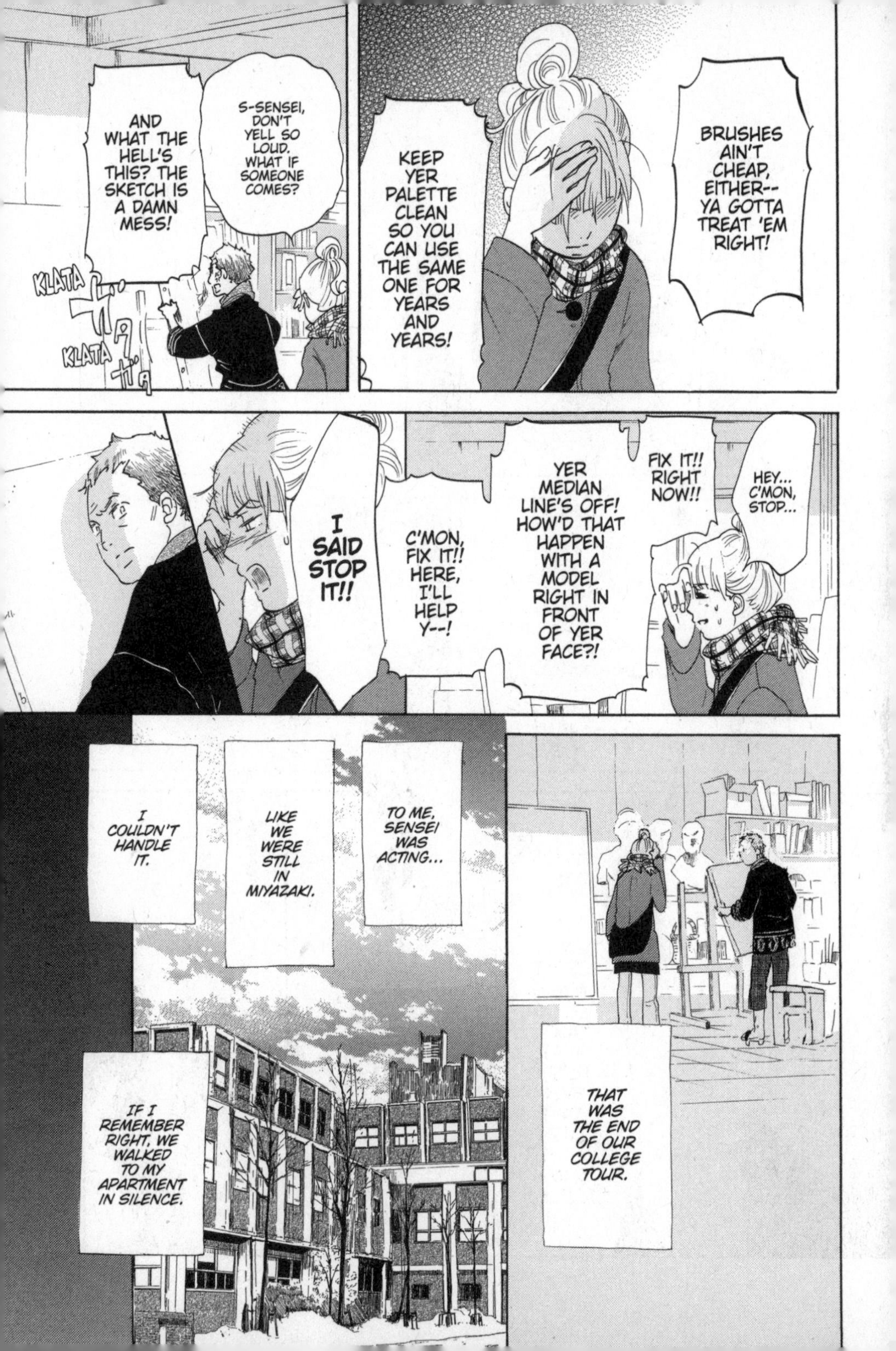
BRUSHES AIN'T CHEAP, EITHER-- YA GOTTA TREAT 'EM RIGHT!
KEEP YER PALETTE CLEAN SO YOU CAN USE THE SAME ONE FOR YEARS AND YEARS!
S-SENSEI, DON'T YELL SO LOUD. WHAT IF SOMEONE COMES?
AND WHAT THE HELL'S THIS? THE SKETCH IS A DAMN MESS!
KLATA
KLATA
HEY... C'MON, STOP...
FIX IT!! RIGHT NOW!!
YER MEDIAN LINE'S OFF! HOW'D THAT HAPPEN WITH A MODEL RIGHT IN FRONT OF YER FACE?!
C'MON, FIX IT!! HERE, I'LL HELP Y--!
I SAID STOP IT!!
THAT WAS THE END OF OUR COLLEGE TOUR.
TO ME, SENSEI WAS ACTING...
LIKE WE WERE STILL IN MIYAZAKI.
I COULDN'T HANDLE IT.
IF I REMEMBER RIGHT, WE WALKED TO MY APARTMENT IN SILENCE.

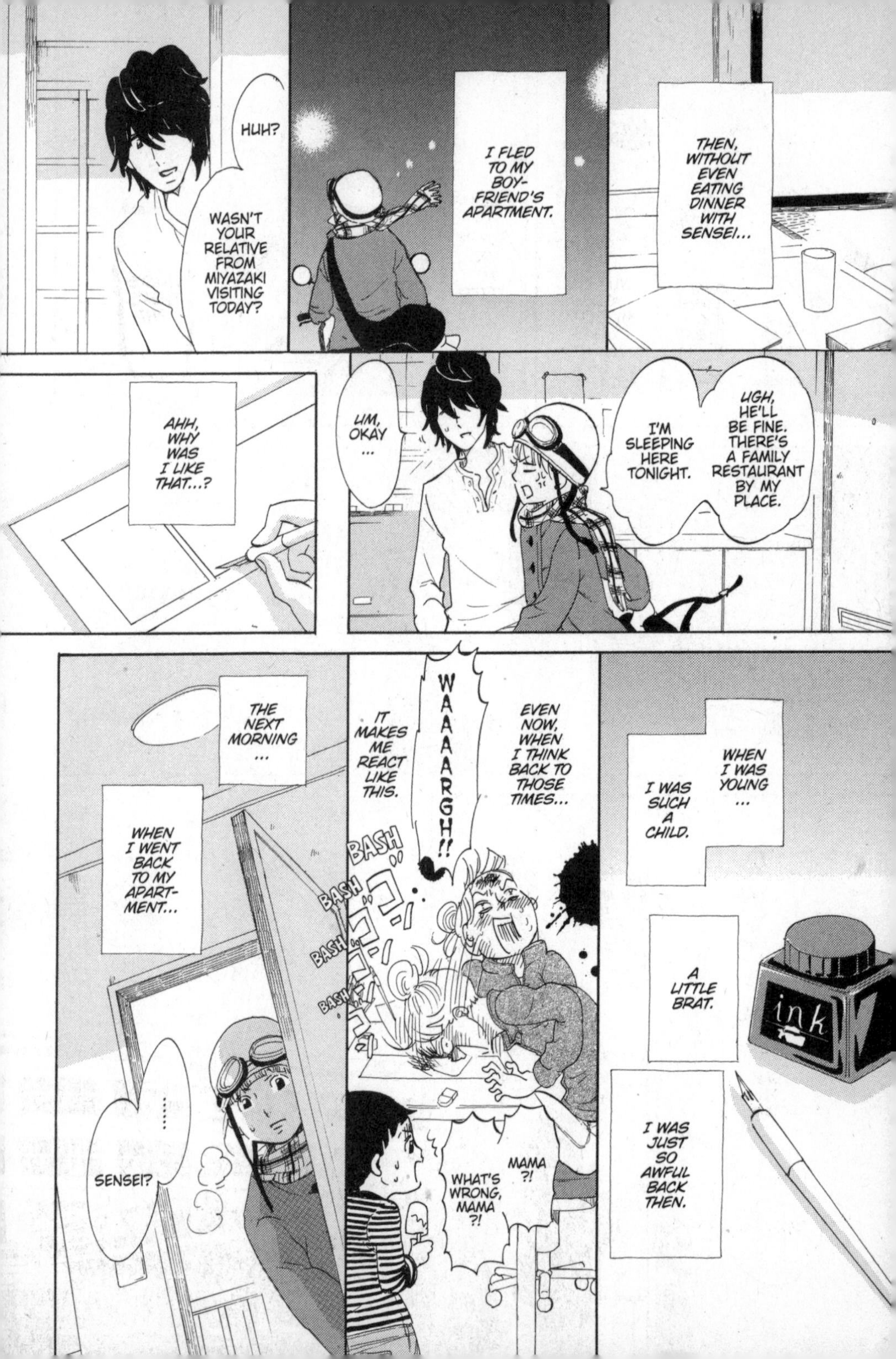
THEN, WITHOUT EVEN EATING DINNER WITH SENSEI...
I FLED TO MY BOY-FRIEND'S APARTMENT.
HUH?
WASN'T YOUR RELATIVE FROM MIYAZAKI VISITING TODAY?
UGH, HE'LL BE FINE. THERE'S A FAMILY RESTAURANT BY MY PLACE.
I'M SLEEPING HERE TONIGHT.
UM, OKAY...
AHH, WHY WAS I LIKE THAT...?
WHEN I WAS YOUNG...
I WAS SUCH A CHILD.
A LITTLE BRAT.
ink
I WAS JUST SO AWFUL BACK THEN.
EVEN NOW, WHEN I THINK BACK TO THOSE TIMES...
WAAAAARGH!!
IT MAKES ME REACT LIKE THIS.
BASH
BASH
BASH
BASH
MAMA?!
WHAT'S WRONG, MAMA?!
THE NEXT MORNING...
WHEN I WENT BACK TO MY APARTMENT...
......
SENSEI?

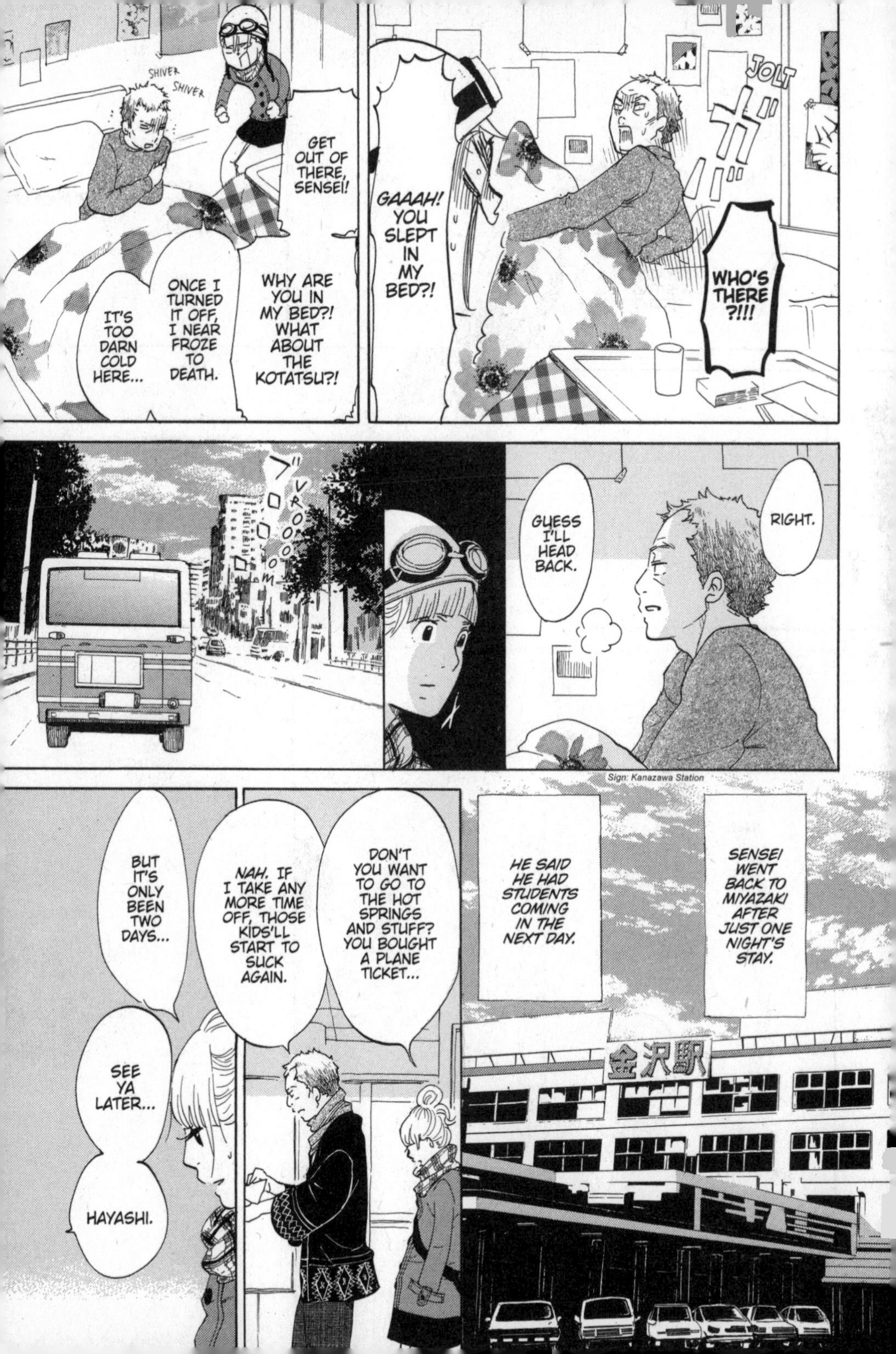
JOLT
WHO'S THERE ?!!!
GAAAH! YOU SLEPT IN MY BED?!
GET OUT OF THERE, SENSEI!
WHY ARE YOU IN MY BED?! WHAT ABOUT THE KOTATSU?!
SHIVER SHIVER
ONCE I TURNED IT OFF, I NEAR FROZE TO DEATH.
IT'S TOO DARN COLD HERE...
RIGHT.
GUESS I'LL HEAD BACK.
VROOOOM
Sign: Kanazawa Station
SENSEI WENT BACK TO MIYAZAKI AFTER JUST ONE NIGHT'S STAY.
HE SAID HE HAD STUDENTS COMING IN THE NEXT DAY.
金沢駅
DON'T YOU WANT TO GO TO THE HOT SPRINGS AND STUFF? YOU BOUGHT A PLANE TICKET...
NAH. IF I TAKE ANY MORE TIME OFF, THOSE KIDS'LL START TO SUCK AGAIN.
BUT IT'S ONLY BEEN TWO DAYS...
SEE YA LATER...
HAYASHI.

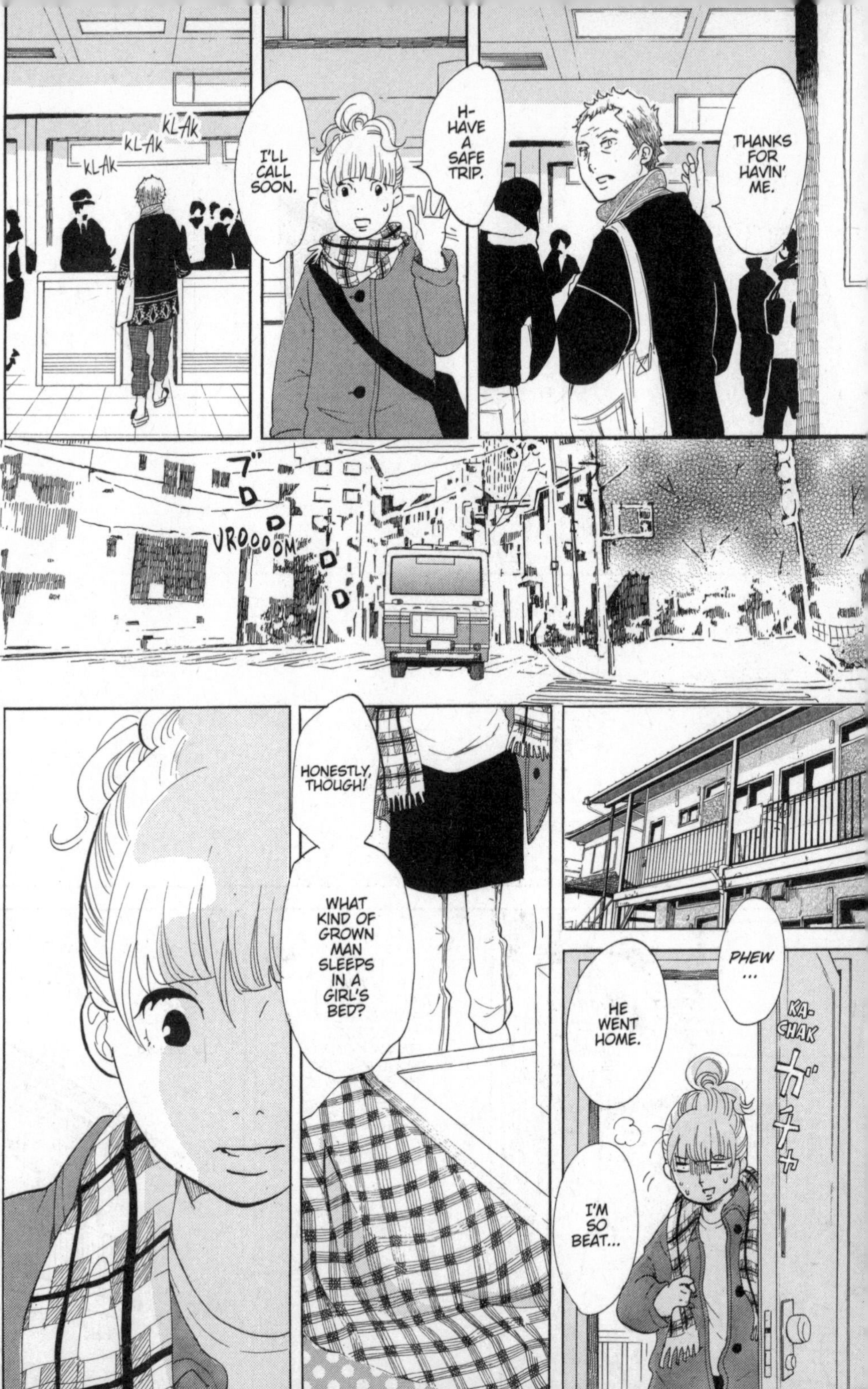
THANKS FOR HAVIN' ME.
H-HAVE A SAFE TRIP.
I'LL CALL SOON.
KLAK
KLAK
KLAK
VROOOOM
PHEW...
KA-CHAK
HE WENT HOME.
I'M SO BEAT...
HONESTLY, THOUGH!
WHAT KIND OF GROWN MAN SLEEPS IN A GIRL'S BED?

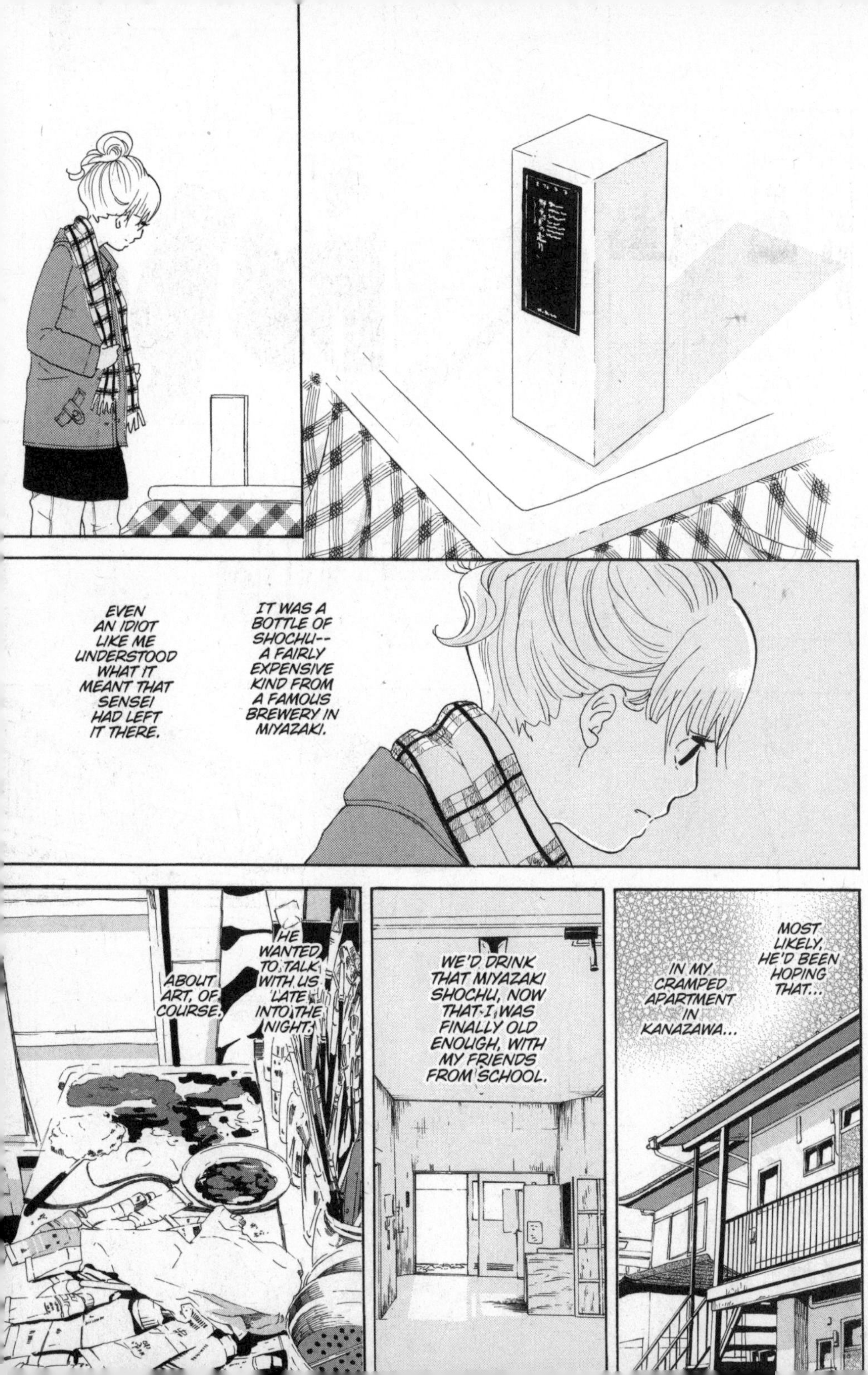
IT WAS A BOTTLE OF SHOCHU-- A FAIRLY EXPENSIVE KIND FROM A FAMOUS BREWERY IN MIYAZAKI.
EVEN AN IDIOT LIKE ME UNDERSTOOD WHAT IT MEANT THAT SENSEI HAD LEFT IT THERE.
MOST LIKELY, HE'D BEEN HOPING THAT...
IN MY CRAMPED APARTMENT IN KANAZAWA...
WE'D DRINK THAT MIYAZAKI SHOCHU, NOW THAT I WAS FINALLY OLD ENOUGH, WITH MY FRIENDS FROM SCHOOL.
HE WANTED TO TALK WITH US LATE INTO THE NIGHT.
ABOUT ART, OF COURSE.

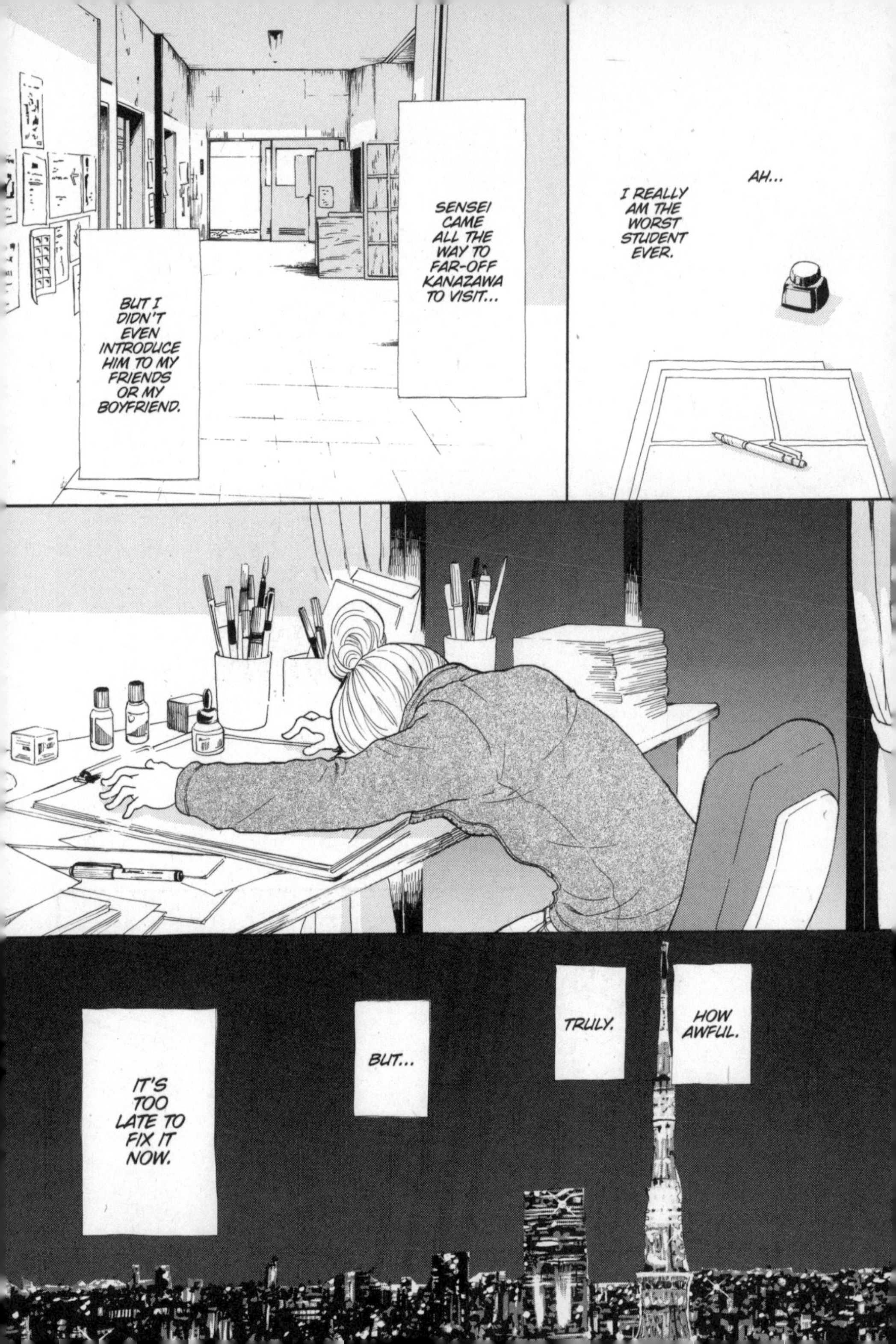
AH...
I REALLY AM THE WORST STUDENT EVER.
SENSEI CAME ALL THE WAY TO FAR-OFF KANAZAWA TO VISIT...
BUT I DIDN'T EVEN INTRODUCE HIM TO MY FRIENDS OR MY BOYFRIEND.
HOW AWFUL.
TRULY.
BUT...
IT'S TOO LATE TO FIX IT NOW.

SEVEN SEAS ENTERTAINMENT PRESENTS

Blank Canvas

My So-Called Artist's Journey

story and art by AKIKO HIGASHIMURA VOLUME 2

TRANSLATION
Jenny McKeon

ADAPTATION
Ysabet MacFarlane

LETTERING AND LAYOUT
Lys Blakeslee

COVER DESIGN
KC Fabellon

PROOFREADER
Kurestin Armada
Danielle King

EDITOR
Jenn Grunigen

PRODUCTION MANAGER
Lissa Pattillo

MANAGING EDITOR
Julie Davis

EDITOR-IN-CHIEF
Adam Arnold

PUBLISHER
Jason DeAngelis

First published in Japan in 2011 by SHUEISHA Inc., Tokyo.
English translation rights arranged by SHUEISHA Inc.
through TOHAN CORPORATION, Tokyo.

Seven Seas press and purchase enquiries can be sent to Marketing Manager Lianne Sentar at press@gomanga.com. Information regarding the distribution and purchase of digital editions is available from Digital Manager CK Russell at digital@gomanga.com.

ISBN: 978-1-64275-070-6

Printed in Canada

First Printing: August 2019

10 9 8 7 6 5 4 3 2 1

FOLLOW US ONLINE: ***www.sevenseasentertainment.com***

READING DIRECTIONS

This book reads from ***right to left***, Japanese style. If this is your first time reading manga, you start reading from the top right panel on each page and take it from there. If you get lost, just follow the numbered diagram here. It may seem backwards at first, but you'll get the hang of it! Have fun!!

1
2
3
4
5
6
7
8
9

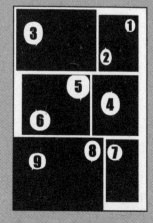

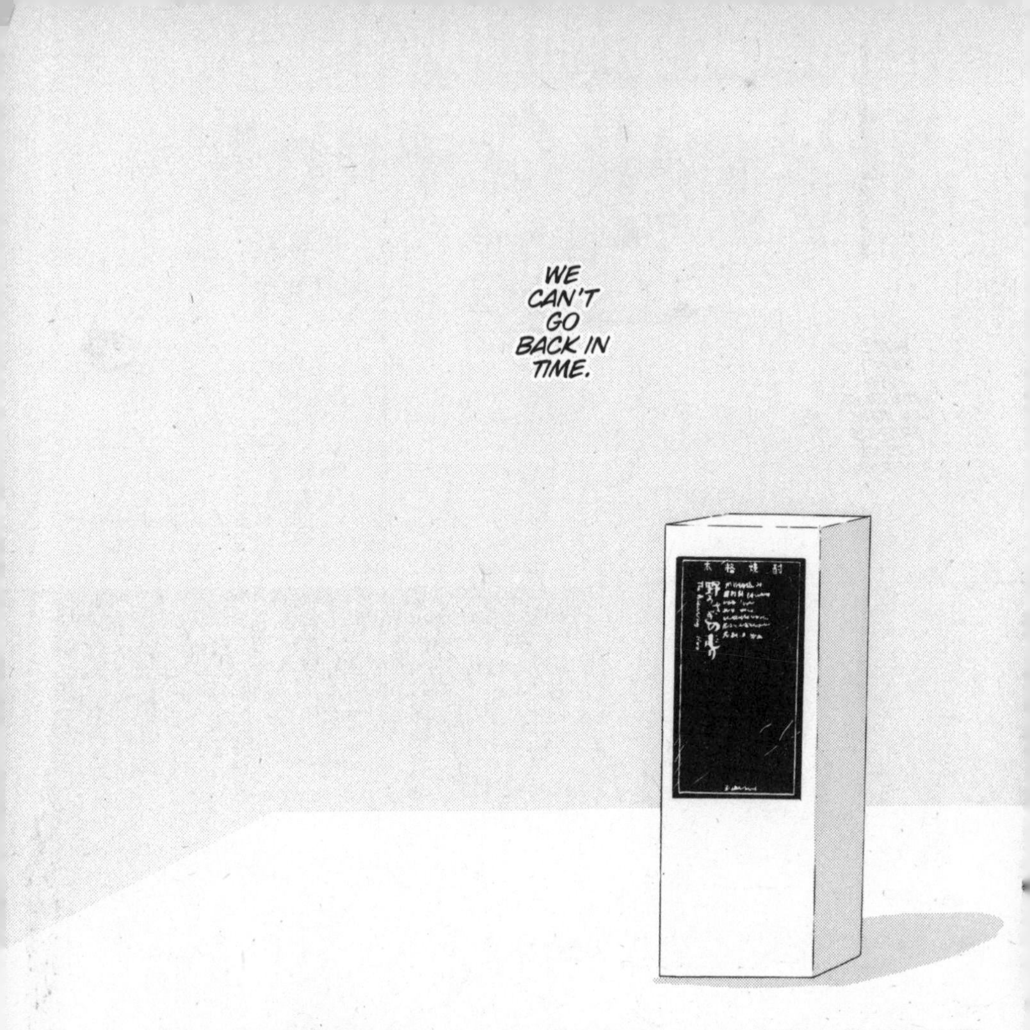
WE CAN'T GO BACK IN TIME.

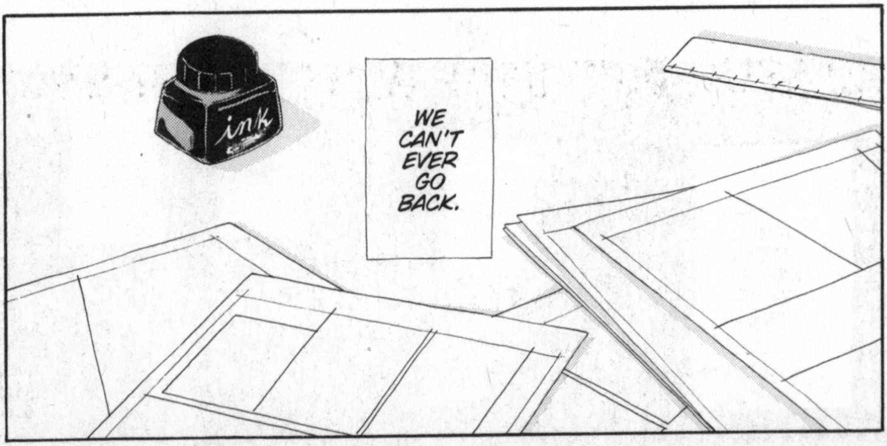
ink
WE CAN'T EVER GO BACK.

Blank Canvas: My So-Called Artist's Journey ② —END—